Further Praise for
To Walk About in Freedom

"In this timely and evocative narrative, Carole Emberton follows Priscilla Joyner and the first generation of formerly enslaved Americans on a search for something more than legal emancipation alone. In their long pursuit of happiness, home, education, belonging, a comfortable old age, and love, they defined what freedom meant in the face of new dangers and continuing traumas. Emberton's 'small book about big things' is equally a big book about the small, intimate things that make every life valuable and unique."

—W. Caleb McDaniel, author of *Sweet Taste of Liberty*

"Carole Emberton gives us a powerful new history of emancipation, one anchored in the inner life of an ordinary woman. Beautifully written using overlooked archival sources, *To Walk About in Freedom* is essential reading, reminding us that freedom was and is a lived experience with deep emotional resonance."

—Megan Kate Nelson, author of *Saving Yellowstone*

TO WALK
ABOUT IN
FREEDOM

TO WALK ABOUT IN FREEDOM

. —— .

The Long Emancipation
of Priscilla Joyner

. —— .

CAROLE EMBERTON

W. W. NORTON & COMPANY
Independent Publishers Since 1923

For information about permission to reproduce selections from this book, write to
Permissions, W. W. Norton & Company, Inc., 500 Fifth Avenue, New York, NY 10110

For information about special discounts for bulk purchases, please contact
W. W. Norton Special Sales at specialsales@wwnorton.com or 800-233-4830

Manufacturing by Lake Book Manufacturing
Book design by Marysarah Quinn
Production manager: Lauren Abbate

Library of Congress Cataloging-in-Publication Data

Names: Emberton, Carole, author.
Title: To walk about in freedom : the long emancipation of Priscilla Joyner / Carole Emberton.
Description: First edition. | New York : W. W. Norton & Company, [2022] |
Includes bibliographical references and index.
Identifiers: LCCN 2021050570 | ISBN 9781324001829 (hardcover) |
ISBN 9781324001836 (epub)
Subjects: LCSH: Joyner, Priscilla, 1858–1944. | African American women—Virginia—
Suffolk—Biography. | African American women—North Carolina—Biography. | Racially
mixed women—North Carolina—Biography. | Joyner family. | Freedmen—North Carolina—
Biography. | Freedmen—Social conditions—Southern States. | Slaves—Emancipation—Social
aspects—Southern States. | Federal Writers' Project. | Nash County (N.C.)—Biography. |
Suffolk (Va.)—Biography.
Classification: LCC F234.S9 E43 2022 | DDC 306.3/62092 [B]—dc23/eng/20211105
LC record available at https://lccn.loc.gov/2021050570

W. W. Norton & Company, Inc., 500 Fifth Avenue, New York, N.Y. 10110
www.wwnorton.com

W. W. Norton & Company Ltd., 15 Carlisle Street, London W1D 3BS

1 2 3 4 5 6 7 8 9 0

FOR AMELIA,

you are my sunshine

. —— .

How did you first learn you were free?
What did you do when you learned you were free?
Were the slaves glad to be free?
Where did you go after freedom?

—Sample questions for interviewing ex-slaves,
Federal Writers' Project

I will walk about in freedom, for I have sought out
your precepts.

—Psalms 119:45

CONTENTS

LIST OF ILLUSTRATIONS

PROLOGUE

The Interview

THE CAR STOPPED in front of her small wood-framed house on Second Avenue in Williamstown, a Black neighborhood in Suffolk, Virginia. Three people got out. One was the school principal, a man well known in the community. The other two were strangers.

Priscilla Joyner stood up slowly. She was nearly eighty years old. She did everything slowly these days. As her guests exited their car, she held up her hand in a half-hearted hello from the yard. Like the principal, who always wore a jacket and tie, the other two, a man and a woman, were smartly dressed. Priscilla had made sure her dress was pressed before she put it on that morning. Over it she tied a faded checked apron, also clean and pressed, just in case she brushed up against something or maybe to hide a stain or worn spot on the garment underneath. She hated it that she couldn't get on any decent shoes. Her feet swelled terribly, and the only thing that fit was a pair of her husband Lewis's old boots, if she took the laces out. They were run over at the heels, but it was the best she could do. Maybe her visitors wouldn't notice.[1]

The visitors made their way toward Priscilla, who stood near the porch waiting for them. The principal made the introductions. The other man was named Roscoe Lewis, and he was a Black professor from Hampton University. That fact was meant to impress her, but if it did, she didn't let on. Founded as a school for freed slaves right after the war, Hampton was a jewel in the crown of Black America and a source of local pride, but none of Priscilla Joyner's children had been able to attend college. The woman was Thelma Dunston, a young Black teacher from nearby Portsmouth, who acted as Lewis's assistant helping him collect life stories of ex-slaves.[2]

Lewis and Dunston wanted to interview Priscilla and use her story in a book they were writing about the history of Black people in Virginia. It would be the first book of its kind, Lewis said, a retelling of the history of the state from the Black point of view. His face beamed as he explained how important this project was, and how he had been selected to supervise Miss Dunston and other Black workers who were collecting stories all over the state. The book would highlight their people's many achievements and chart their determined rise from servitude to freedom.

"That's nice," Priscilla said. "Would you like to see my garden?"[3]

Lewis and Dunston shared a knowing glance. Yes, they would love to see her famous flower garden. The principal had told them about it on the ride over. They followed Mrs. Joyner around the side of the house and into the backyard, listening patiently as she pointed out her favorite plants. Rose bushes climbed the side of the house and some hardy petunias still blossomed before the first hard frost settled. Pink petals, delicate reminders of another summer nearly gone, carpeted the ground. Mrs. Joyner apologized for all the weeds and explained how she wasn't able to keep up with the garden like she used to. She just didn't have the breath anymore. Her daughter, Liza, helped when she could, but she had her own family to tend to.[4]

Lewis and Dunston oohed and aahed periodically, allowing her to talk about a topic she enjoyed in the hope she would eventually open up to them about things she might find less enjoyable to recall. They were used to such polite disinterest in their work and adept at overcoming it. Patience was the key. And besides, the garden was impressive.

"During the spring the biggest white ladies in town send out here to buy my flowers," Priscilla told them with just a hint of pride in her voice.[5]

As any dedicated gardener will tell you, gardening can be a therapeutic activity that provides you with a respite from worries big and small. The feel of the soil between your fingers cools your mind just as it does your palms. The sight of seedlings breaking through the earth each spring reminds you that life always finds a way. As it does for gardeners everywhere, the acts of tilling, planting, and tending fed Priscilla Joyner's desires to create and nurture, providing her with a sense of accomplishment. She was a painter, and the ground was her canvas, never finished and always changing. It must have made her feel good to know that she could coax beauty from a world that contained so much ugliness. It likely gave her satisfaction to pocket that cash, too, when those white ladies picked up their corsages and centerpieces.[6]

It's not surprising that when the interviewers came to ask questions about her past that Priscilla retreated to her garden, her place of refuge. Because the questions were unsettling. *What did she remember about slavery? Who was her master? What was he like? Did he whip her? Did she get enough to eat? What happened during the war? What was she doing when she learned she was free?* She could talk about flowers all day, but slavery?[7]

Priscilla's hesitation suggests that she had spent many years trying to forget that time, the time before she was with Lewis. Before the children, before her garden, before she managed to grasp hold of some happiness. Before it all began to slip away, a little at a time. Any person who had lived as long as she had was bound to have experienced great loss—children, a husband, the ability to rely on your own body. But the time before existed for her as a terrible void she had never been able to completely fill. Questions swirled in that void, questions that now could never be answered. So, what was the point of going back over it all again? What little she had told her children upset them, especially Frank, her oldest. He got so worked up about it the last time he came down from New York to visit her.[8]

It was best that the letter from her half-brother, the one about her inheritance, had been lost. Frank tore up the house looking for it, swearing he would get a lawyer, but she told him it didn't matter. She didn't want anything Jolly Joyner had. She only wanted a good visit with the son she saw so rarely, and now that he was here, all he could talk about was North Carolina, her mother's farm, and how she had been swindled out of what she was owed. The past kept intruding on her life. And here it came again.[9]

Sensing that she might be uneasy talking to men, Dunston convinced Lewis and the principal to leave her alone to talk with Priscilla. Lewis excused himself to run an errand he had forgotten about and took the principal with him. Without an audience, Dunston gave her a more personalized version of the "sales talk," explaining how important it was to record the experiences of former slaves, to tell history through their eyes. Sensing Priscilla's reluctance, Dunston said she would come back later, another day perhaps, when she felt more like talking. And then she waited. Soon Priscilla closed her eyes and took a deep breath. "No, this is as good a time as any. I'll tell you all about my history," she relented.[10]

Something in Dunston's manner had eased Priscilla Joyner's reluctance to talk. Perhaps it was the gentleness of her approach, or the simple way she explained what she was there to do and its importance. Maybe deep down, Priscilla Joyner wanted to talk. Maybe she wanted someone to understand what she had been through and the way it shaped her life. Maybe she wanted to understand it herself. Whatever the reason she overcame her reluctance that day, for a moment Priscilla Joyner glimpsed a much larger history that gave some meaning to her personal pain.

Priscilla Joyner. COURTESY OF HAMPTON UNIVERSITY ARCHIVES

"I don't like to talk about it to folks," she admitted, "but don't mind telling it for the work you are doing. If it will do any good to have my life in a book, you can use it."[11]

.———.

You will not find the details of Priscilla Joyner's life inscribed in any American history textbook. Except for a few historical documents—census schedules, a marriage license, a death certificate—her life, like the vast majority of human lives, passed without much notice outside her immediate family. Were it not for the life history she narrated to Thelma Dunston, she undoubtedly would have slipped into the quiet oblivion that most of us do because we lead ordinary, unremarkable lives. Historians, and perhaps more importantly, their readers, are drawn to stories about exceptional people who did extraordinary things. Glance at the shelves of your nearest bookstore if you think I am wrong.

Priscilla Joyner's story reveals a woman unlikely to become the focus of a historical biography, at least if we believe historian Laurel Thatcher Ulrich's mantra that "well-behaved women seldom make history." Priscilla Joyner was just that—a well-behaved woman who got on and got by without any fuss. She spent her life caring for others, including a husband and thirteen children, and later grandchildren and others who lived with her periodically. Although she attended school for a while, the census records all list her as being unable to read or write, which may say more about the presumptions of the white census takers than her literacy. There is no evidence she ever traveled any farther than the one hundred miles or so from her birthplace near Rocky Mount, North Carolina, to her home in Suffolk, Virginia, where she lived from the late 1880s until her death in 1944. She did not marry a powerful man. Her husband, Lewis, worked odd jobs that over the years included farm laborer, drayman, and fisherman. Priscilla herself never held any occupation other than wife and mother, a signal achievement for a Black woman born in the age of slavery and testament to Lewis's determination to do whatever job came his way in order to keep his wife in her own home raising her own children instead of someone else's.[12]

As the transcript to her interview with Dunston reveals, she was a reluctant witness to history. And yet her story is central to American history as it unfolded from the Civil War to the Great Depression. Priscilla's life spanned eight decades and several different Souths—the slave South, the wartime South, the Reconstruction South, and the Jim Crow South. Violent transformations ripped each new South from the subsequent ones. But for all the change that was wrought on the land and its people, many things remained the same. A brutal racial caste system continued to shape Black southerners' political, social, and cultural lives. Exploitation, poverty, and degradation still defined much of their day-to-day existence.

Priscilla's story brings to light the inner lives of the charter generation of freedom, the men and women born into slavery who experienced firsthand what historians now call the long emancipation: an extended struggle in which slavery died over many decades after 1863.[13] Today's legacy of that protracted death—police brutality, mass incarceration, the retrenchment of voting rights, and racial disparities in access to education, health care, and employment—suggests that slavery's long shadow continues to hang over the American political and cultural landscape. Full emancipation remains an unfulfilled promise.[14]

The narrative Priscilla dictated to Thelma Dunston shows us this truth, that the charter generation did not experience emancipation as a single event. Nor was it only a political struggle. For those who lived through it, the long emancipation was also an emotional struggle. For Priscilla, that struggle involved an extended search for belonging. She never knew the identity of her father, a painful absence she shared with many former slaves. She also wondered about the woman she knew as her mother but whose mothering left her in doubt. Slavery stole Priscilla's people, as it did for so many of the charter generation. The legal abolition of slavery often failed to rectify these wrongs, and freedpeople carried the collective trauma of these absences with them into the future.[15]

But Priscilla's story is not just a woeful story of racist oppression. While her life narrative charted what at times must have seemed like insurmountable obstacles to achieving full and meaningful freedom, it also exposes the many ways, big and small, that the charter generation found joy; how they created families and communities in the most inhospitable places; how they lovingly tended magnificent gardens in their yards and in their hearts with the few precious materials they had at hand.

Priscilla Joyner's emancipation story became part of the first government-sponsored history project in the United States. In an effort to stem the tide of massive unemployment during the Great Depression, the Federal Writers' Project (FWP) hired out-of-work writers, editors, and teachers, like Thelma Dunston, to collect the life histories of everyday Americans, including former slaves. Between 1935 and 1943, the FWP collected more than 10,000 first-person narratives. FWP workers interviewed maids and midwives, Pullman porters and prostitutes, farmers and factory hands, the "resourceful, unembittered men and women coping with social disaster," as one historian described them. The interviews aimed to capture the simple dignity of unremarkable people and to document the "details of survival" that made the Great Depression just one hardship in a long history of hardships marked by migration, war, poverty, natural catastrophes, and personal tragedies. The project's directors in Washington believed these life stories offered important lessons for the American public facing hard times and envisioned multiple publications showcasing them.[16]

"We must give back to the people what we have taken from them and what rightfully belongs to them in a form they can understand and use," wrote B. A. Botkin, a renowned folklorist who advocated for the inclusion of more than 2,000 ex-slaves in the project. Fieldworkers like Lewis and Dunston scoured the southern countryside and city streets looking for subjects to interview, armed with a long list of potential questions about a variety of topics of interest to the other project architects. Folklorists like Botkin were particularly interested in superstitions and spirituals, but there were also questions about everyday life. Harlem Renaissance poet Sterling Brown, who would become the director of the Ex-Slave Narratives project within the FWP, wanted fieldworkers to probe the minutiae of enslaved people's daily existence: what they wore, what they ate, what kinds of work they performed, who they interacted with, what those interactions were like, and how they felt during those moments. Brown was a student of Black vernacular expression. The language southern Blacks used to describe the world and their lives had inspired the poet's most acclaimed work. He wanted the interviews to capture the vibrancy of that language and the depth of ex-slaves' feelings about what they had experienced.[17]

Although the FWP endeavored to create a truly usable past, not everyone believed that ex-slaves could contribute to such a project. Eudora Ramsay Richardson, the white director of the Virginia Writers' Project (VWP), the state-level iteration of the FWP that employed Lewis and Dunston, worked to ensure that only stories she deemed acceptable and accurate were included in the project. A former suffragist and self-styled liberal when it came to racial issues, Richardson saw herself as the guardian of Virginia's noble heritage and bristled at anything that might cast her native state in a bad light. As state director, she supervised the dozen or so Black fieldworkers who collected interviews in Virginia—one of the few states to employ a sizable number of Black interviewers. Richardson also edited, with a heavy hand, manuscript drafts of *The Negro in Virginia*, the book Lewis mentioned to Priscilla when he met her that day in her front yard.[18]

Priscilla Joyner appears only briefly in *The Negro in Virginia*. Richardson whittled down her lengthy testimony to a few curious lines about how her mistress refused to let her live in the slave quarters and instead raised Priscilla as her own child. For Richardson, this was yet another example of a slaveholder's benevolence and the close, loving ties that bound masters to the people they enslaved. But Priscilla's full testimony survived, unnoticed for many years in Lewis's personal papers until published in a collection of Virginia ex-slave interviews in the late 1970s. Until now, however, it has been largely ignored. What it reveals is a family drama that upended Eudora Ramsay Richardson's genteel white vision of American history.

Like Richardson, historians have often been skeptical of these interviews and question their utility. Of all the formerly enslaved people alive in the 1930s, the FWP interviewed only a fraction of them, leading many to question the representativeness of the narratives. Perhaps more troubling were the racial dynamics of the interview situations. Most of the FWP fieldworkers were white southerners raised on stories of happy slaves and their benevolent masters. Their questioning often veered toward this moonlight-and-magnolias view of the Old South, and elderly former slaves, adept at reading the expectations of white people and all too familiar with the consequences of not fulfilling them, answered accordingly. Thus the narratives sometimes seem to confirm the white southern viewpoints that the fieldworkers telegraphed to their subjects. *Yes, my master was a kind man who never whipped us. We were sorry when slavery was over.*[19] But closer readings often reveal subtle (and sometimes not so subtle) indictments of these kinds of questions, and recently historians have begun to reassess the importance of these interviews as one of the few sources of firsthand testimony of formerly enslaved people in existence.[20] Flawed as they might be—and as all historical sources are—these interviews reveal aspects of the charter generation's lived experience of freedom that no other source can, lifting them from the depths of the "enforced anonymity" that slavery relegated them to. In these interviews, we meet men and women with names, addresses, families, and stories. Those stories open a space to consider the interior lives of formerly enslaved people—their thoughts, feelings, dreams, desires, fears, and sorrows—as they walked their individual paths toward freedom.[21]

To the best of my ability, I have tried to verify key details of Priscilla Joyner's story. I have scoured the census, public records, and historical archives in North Carolina and Virginia. I have traveled to the locations where she lived in a feeble yet necessary attempt to retrace her steps, to feel the ground she walked under my feet, in the hope of knowing something of her that the scant documentation cannot tell me.

Try as I might, I am unable to know with certainty many of the things I wish to know about her. That goes for most, if not all, of the charter generation. When faced with such fragmented archives, historians must make a choice. Either we find a subject with more but no less problematic material to work with, or we dig deeply, read *very* closely, and think more creatively about how to write history. To accomplish this, the writer must develop what historian Paula Fass terms a "disciplined imagination" that is unafraid to speculate about what might have been said or thought or felt or seen or heard.[22]

So, from time to time, when I am not sure, I use words like "probably" and "maybe" and "possibly." I also call upon my own understanding of human behavior, drawn from personal observations as well as the observations and work of others—psychologists, philosophers, poets, writers, and artists—to consider questions about the contours of personal lives and intimate relationships that historians who cling too tightly to the illusion of empirical certainty dismiss as unknowable.[23]

In the chapters that follow, I have endeavored to provide an account of Priscilla Joyner's life and her long emancipation. It is not the entire story; there are simply too many gaps in the documentary records, too many silences in her interview to write a traditional biography. What follows is more of a microhistory, a small book about big things.

When Priscilla's voice cannot be heard, either because she did not speak on a particular topic or because the interviewer may have neglected to record her full response to a question, I rely on other members of the charter generation to provide additional insight. So, while this book bears her name in the title, it is not her story alone.

For men and women like Priscilla Joyner, emancipation did not come on the winds of civil war or presidential proclamation. Instead, it was a meandering journey that took months, years, or even whole lifetimes to complete. These journeys were not defined by protest or the kinds of militant resistance that historians are trained to analyze and celebrate. Instead, Priscilla's life and the lives of those thousands of nearly forgotten ex-slaves whose stories make up the FWP archive allow us to see the grandest sweep of history through the intimate, personal stories of everyday people whose search for freedom focused on achievements that rarely make the history books. They contain, in the words of Zora Neale Hurston, one of the FWP's most acclaimed interviewers, "the boiled down juice of living." In them, we find people searching for connection, belonging, and love.[24]

Priscilla Joyner's search for these things began, as it does for so many people, at birth.

A NOTE ON LANGUAGE

When I quote from the FWP narratives, I have chosen to standardize the written dialect used in many of the interview transcripts. Sterling Brown advised the mostly white fieldworkers to avoid using dialect to portray Black speech. Many of them did so anyway, relying upon cultural conventions they had grown accustomed to and found amusing or more "authentic." Their unwillingness to follow Brown's instructions have diminished the interviews' usability for many scholars, teachers, and readers, who find the rendering of Black speech antiquated and racist.

But in his own work, Brown displayed an ear for Black language, especially the language of the rural Black South, and preserved the community's idiomatic expressions with respect, tenderness, and a realness that most of the interviewers who worked for him could not. So, I have followed Brown's original instructions for rendering Black speech. I have preserved idioms, turns of phrase, and unique vocabulary when they appear, but I have used standard English spellings when interviewers attempted a caricatured version (replacing like for *lak*, was for *wuz*, etc.). I did this in the hope that the words of the charter generation will engage and inspire readers rather than distract or repel them.

TO WALK
ABOUT IN
FREEDOM

ONE

2/F/M

·——·

WHEN JOHN BRYANT became an assistant United States marshal tasked with collecting data for the Eighth Census sometime in the spring of 1860, he probably counted himself lucky. It was a highly sought-after job for which dozens of men in each enumeration district applied but only a few were selected. Each assistant marshal earned two cents per person counted, as well as ten cents for every farm and fifteen cents for each industrial establishment, such as a mill or ironworks. For the first time in the census's eighty-year history, enumerators were paid for counting people who had died in the previous year—two cents each, the same as for those who still walked above ground. This supplemental income would increase a man's yearly earnings by at least $250, the minimum an enumerator in even the smallest district might receive. Perhaps Bryant was one of the "judicious, temperate, reliable, intelligent, and active men" the Census Bureau required for the job. Or maybe he was just someone's brother-in-law or nephew. Despite the stated qualifications, securing such a plum position was typically more a question of who you knew rather than what kind of man you were.[1]

Still, it was not a job for the disorganized, the dishonest, or the disabled. Not only did enumerators face stiff fines and jail time for falsifying or failing to complete their returns, the job itself required considerable physical stamina. Each dwelling, business, and person in the district had to be visited personally, either on horseback or on foot. One of Bryant's exhausted counterparts in Virginia reported that he had opened no fewer than 2,000 garden gates and gotten on and off his horse at least fifty to sixty times a day. The enumeration commenced in June 1860 and proceeded for two of the hottest months of the year. In their saddlebags, Bryant and the other assistant marshals stuffed their leather portfolios containing a portable inkwell and pen, blank copies of the awkwardly sized and cumbersome enumeration pages, which they were forbidden to fold, and the thirty-six-page instruction manual that they were required to keep with them at all times. When poor roads or rough terrain did not permit a horse to go any farther, the enumerator would have to lug his pack to the next dwelling, however far it might be.[2]

Bryant's district, Nash County in northeastern North Carolina, like most of the state, was overwhelmingly rural. An unimproved, uncultivated, uncultured backwater, according to famed landscape architect Frederick Law Olmsted, who lamented its sad accommodations, transportation, food, and general living conditions in his 1853 travel narrative. After leaving the comparatively civilized capital of Raleigh, where hogs rooted in the pasture adjacent to the statehouse, Olmsted penned his observations on the housing he saw there. If he expected grand estates with gardens and lawns, or even tidy little farms with fields filled with crops, he was sorely disappointed:

"I do not think I passed in ten miles, more than half a dozen homesteads, and of these but one was above the character of a cabin."[3]

At thirty-eight years old, Bryant was relatively young and used to the physical labor of running a farm. He worked on his own, although he may have rented enslaved help from a slave owner occasionally if he could afford it. June and July were hot, but it was laying-by time, when his crops needed only weeding, something his wife, Jane, and ten-year-old daughter, Susan, could do while he was out on his rounds. Even his son John's five-year-old hands could carry a bucket to slop the livestock. By the time he had counted one thousand three hundred and twenty-one families, it was July 28, and the instructions weighing down his horse reminded him that he needed to get the count completed and his tabulations to Washington in the next few weeks. He had no time to tarry. But family number 1322 surely gave him pause.[4]

It belonged to Rix Joyner, a thirty-year-old farmer, and his twenty-three-year-old wife Ann Eliza. Rix and Ann Eliza had four children: Mourning, who was five; Margaret, four; Priscilla, two; and Robert, eight months. Bryant recorded these basic statistics in the first two columns of the census schedule. Bryant made no mark for Rix, Ann Eliza, Mourning, Margaret, and Robert in the third column, the one reserved for the race of the household members. (A blank space served as the default signifier for whiteness for all census enumerators at the time.) But in the space next to Priscilla's name, the one for race, he wrote "M" for mulatto, one of two possible designations for people who appeared non-white to the census taker. The other designation, "B" for Black, noted someone with dark skin who appeared to have no white lineage. Both of these categories were wildly subjective, depending on the enumerator's judgment about a person's physical presentation. Nineteenth-century Americans believed a person's race could be

1860 census entry for the household of Rix Joyner. COURTESY ANCESTRY.COM determined visually, and they worked hard to maintain that myth even when evidence to the contrary confounded their sense of racial order.

In Priscilla's case, there was little doubt that she was not white. Bryant noticed that her skin color was darker than the other Joyner children. It was not unusual for white families to have a Black child living in their household. Apprenticeship was common throughout the period, and impoverished free Black families were often forced to bind out their children when the state deemed them incapable of caring for them. And of course, slavery brought Black children into white homes. Both Rix and Ann Eliza came from slaveholding families, and at one time, according to Priscilla, had owned two enslaved laborers themselves. But the fact that Bryant listed Priscilla's last name as Joyner suggests that Rix and Ann Eliza claimed her as one of their own. Apprenticed children retained their own surnames. Enslaved people were counted on a special census, the slave schedule, where they were listed only as numbers under the names of their enslavers. Their individual names were not recorded.

This document raises far more questions than answers. *Who were Priscilla's parents? If they were not the Joyners, then where did Priscilla come from? Where were her people? Was she enslaved or free . . . or something else?* As much as these questions might intrigue us, readers and students of history in the twenty-first century, they haunted Priscilla for most of her life and created within her a great emptiness. The only answers she had came from Ann Eliza, and they settled little if anything about who she really was.

Nearly eighty years later when Thelma Dunston, an enumerator of a different sort, entered her home to take account of her life, Priscilla Joyner explained the situation as Ann Eliza had related it to her: "I never saw my real father. He left, I learned later, on the day I was born."[5]

TWO

CHILD OF NO ONE

.⸺

O N A COLD NIGHT in January 1858, Ann Eliza Joyner gave birth to a mixed-race daughter. The child's father was a Black man, possibly a slave, but just as likely a member of the sizable free Black community living in Nash County. The extent of his relationship with Ann Eliza is unclear. She told Priscilla hardly anything about him, not how they came to know each other or what feelings she held for him. The man knew of Ann Eliza's pregnancy and that the baby's skin color would reveal his and Ann Eliza's secret, putting him in serious danger. Rix had left her and their children months before. If he returned, he would know the child was not his. The rural world of Nash County was small and close-knit. Rix would probably know about Priscilla before he even made it to the farm.

Priscilla's father could do little to protect his child. He would have to leave that to Ann Eliza. But first he had to know if the baby and its mother had made it through the delivery. "Whoever my father was," Priscilla told Thelma Dunston, "he waited to find if I and my mother were alright. Then he left the place, never to come back no more."[1]

This was the story of Priscilla's birth as Ann Eliza told it. Over the years, Priscilla asked for more details, but Ann Eliza refused to provide them. She was particularly tight-lipped with regards to the identity of Priscilla's father. Priscilla assumed that was because making his identity known might have put him or his relatives in danger even years after the event. Such information was bound to stir up trouble, and Ann Eliza seemed committed to taking the secret of her daughter's paternity to her grave.

Countless members of the charter generation knew little or nothing about their fathers. It was "almost impossible for slaves to give a correct account of their male parentages," wrote the self-liberated Henry Bibb in his autobiography. Bibb knew his father's name, the white slaveholder who had raped his mother, but nothing more. His mother found the subject too painful and deflected his questions. So did Patsy Mitchner's mother and other members of her family. "They would not talk to me about who my father was nor where he was at," Mitchner told the FWP interviewer at her home in Raleigh, North Carolina. "Mother would laugh sometime when I asked her about him." That laughter may have masked a deep wound. It was likely that Mitchner's father was also a white man—the owner, one of his sons, or his overseer—who assaulted her mother.[2]

Priscilla also had questions about her mother's identity. Although Ann Eliza claimed to be her mother, Priscilla had her doubts. "You understand, of course," she told Dunston, "that I'm only telling you what was told to me. I really don't know who my parents were. But Miss Ann Liza claimed me and made me call her 'mother.'" Priscilla admitted that all her knowledge of the events that happened came from Ann Eliza, who was anything but forthcoming about the details of Priscilla's origins.[3]

Because Priscilla's emancipation story hinges on Ann Eliza's story of a forbidden affair, a troubled marriage, and a white mother's determination to love her mixed-race child, it's necessary to interrogate Ann Eliza's version of events. Historians today have tools that allow us to probe Ann Eliza's story in ways that Priscilla could not. And while we too may come up short in the search for who Priscilla's parents actually were, we can better understand why her father's absence meant so much to her and for other members of the charter generation, as well as how the questionable actions of the woman who claimed to be her mother shaped her life and her search for freedom.

It is possible that the story Ann Eliza told was true. It is just as likely that it was not, or only partially true. Whether she was Priscilla's biological mother, or whether she took a Black child into her household to raise as her own—a common practice many white slaveholding women employed to instill unquestioning loyalty in enslaved children—Ann Eliza's choice to bring up a Black child in a white, slaveholding household had a lasting impact on Priscilla's life.

. —— .

ANN ELIZA'S STORY of a white woman's illicit sexual relationship with a Black man churns up the muddy history of race and sexual intimacy in the slave South. Obvious to anyone with eyesight keen enough to detect the varying gradations of skin color present in the region's people, both free and enslaved, interracial sex happened frequently in the South, far more frequently than most white people cared to admit. White slaveholding men's sexual relationships with enslaved women were an open secret within planter society, one that might be snickered about in other people's families but denied in one's own. "Any lady is ready to tell you who is the father of all the mulatto children in everybody's household except her own. Those, she seems to think, drop from the clouds," plantation mistress Mary Chesnut confided in her diary.[4]

Sex between white women and Black men, although less common, did occur in the early South. And while white women who crossed the sexual color line did not enjoy the almost permissive acceptance that white men did—some were banished, others whipped or imprisoned in the colonial era—southern society often tolerated their behavior. This was particularly true if the woman came from a family with wealth and status. While these liaisons did not incite the kind of hysteria that often led to the lynchings of the later Jim Crow era, by the time Priscilla was born, that earlier ambivalence had evaporated.[5]

With chattel slavery firmly embedded in the South's social and economic systems, the birth of a Black child to a white woman threatened to upend the delicate balance of power that supported racial slavery. Southern lawmakers focused on ensuring the system's perpetual existence long before Priscilla's birth. "[A]ll children borne in this country shall be held bond or free only according to the condition of the mother," stated Virginia's law of primogeniture, passed in 1662. Other slaveholding colonies followed suit. Written to prevent the increasing number of mixed-race children born to enslaved mothers from suing for freedom because their fathers were free, these colonial laws ensured the heritability of slavery and created a racial caste system whereby Blackness and servitude were more or less equated. This caste system became the foundation of the slave society that emerged in North Carolina and throughout the South in the eighteenth and nineteenth centuries.[6]

A white woman who became pregnant with a mixed-race child complicated matters of racial caste. By giving birth to a Black child, she contributed to the growth of a population of "slaves without masters," individuals who were legally free but lived on the margins of slavery, marked as outsiders by their skin color. If Ann Eliza *was* her biological mother, Priscilla may have been technically free because she was born to a white woman. But that doesn't mean Priscilla lived the life of a free child.[7]

Priscilla was raised in a slaveholding household by a woman accustomed to the power and everyday brutality involved in "slave management." Ann Eliza was the eldest child of Wright Batchelor, who owned a smaller but still substantial $1,000 farm in Nash County. A typical small slaveholder, Batchelor claimed ownership of five people ranging in age from eleven to thirty-three. There were three males aged thirty-three, twenty-five, and twenty-one, who would have been considered prime field hands. In addition, there were two young girls aged eighteen and eleven. The older girl may have worked in the field, or she and the younger girl may have helped Mary, Ann Eliza's mother, with household duties. Batchelor would have expected both girls to bear children and increase his wealth.[8]

Batchelor's property, both his real estate and his enslaved laborers, helped secure his family's social standing in Nash County. Slavery enabled him to educate Ann Eliza and her two sisters. While the two enslaved girls were forced to cook, sew, clean, and reproduce, Ann Eliza learned to read and write.[9]

Wright Batchelor probably had high hopes for his eldest daughter. He would have considered Rix Joyner, the eldest son of a more prominent planter, a good match. Jonathan Joyner owned a sizable farm valued at $3,000 according to the 1850 census. In addition to Rix and his sixteen-year-old brother, Robert, who was also listed as a farmer, at least twenty enslaved people also worked on Jonathan Joyner's farm. They ranged in ages from one to eighty-four; eight were female and twelve were male. The census enumerator did not record their names.[10]

Both fathers would have valued the opportunity to bind their two families together. Rural life grew out of kinship networks that extended their many benefits to members by blood and by marriage. These benefits might include, from time to time, material support in the form of shelter, food, land, and other supplies, including access to enslaved labor. Also included were nonmaterial elements like social connections, fellowship, and trust. This connectedness, cooperation, and companionship between extended kin could, in fact, offset lack of property or financial capital that various members may have experienced.

In the antebellum South, the single greatest source of social capital was slavery, which meant the Batchelors and Joyners had strong shared interests as slaveholders. Marriages such as Rix's union with Ann Eliza tightened the bonds between the family groups and strengthened the wider community of small slaveholding families in Nash and surrounding counties. In contrast, enslavers like Wright Batchelor and Jonathan Joyner used the system of chattel bondage to minimize, if not entirely eliminate, enslaved people's ability to draw upon the kind of social benefits that he and his family relied upon. Networks of connection, mutual help, and sympathy existed among enslaved people, and in some cases between enslaved people, free Blacks, and poor, non-slaveholding whites, but enslavers took great pains to limit them because they threatened to undo slaveholder dominance and might bolster enslaved people's independence.[11]

Slaveholders, through laws and customs, clamped down on enslaved people's ability to gather together, worship, read, and create friendships. Because they could sell family members at any time, these relationships were always threatened, if not broken. After moments of rebellion, such as Gabriel Prosser's in 1800 or Nat Turner's in 1831, enslavers moved to crush the seeds of discontent by restricting the movement of enslaved people and free Blacks as well as their interactions with each other, outlawing Black preachers, and limiting the size of groups who could meet outside the supervision of whites. At no time were slave marriages recognized as legal. Masters approved any unions enslaved people wished to solemnize with a marriage ceremony, but the shadow of the auction block darkened any hope newlywed couples might hold for the future. Other times, enslavers forced unwanted sexual unions with other slaves or with themselves.[12]

Yet enslaved people achieved the kind of social connectedness that slaveholders sought to prohibit. In slavery, southern Blacks laid the foundations for religious and civic institutions that blossomed after emancipation and continue to this day. Churches, mutual aid societies, fraternal societies, women's clubs—not to mention schools, colleges, and universities—spoke to the deep roots of Black networks nurtured in slavery. One of the ways the resiliency of Black culture and the connectedness of Black people were conveyed was in the love and determination of enslaved families whose physical bodies may have been parted but whose emotional ties stretched unimaginable distances. Despite the threat of sale and separation, the enslaved made great emotional investments in *their people*—blood as well as fictive kin, people so close they considered them family. Their peopleness saw them through slavery's trials, the long and bloody Civil War, and the dawning (and subsequent disappointments) of freedom. That sense of love and connection defined freedom, or its absence, for so many in the charter generation.[13]

Despite what their parents may have thought was a solid union, Rix and Ann Eliza's marriage was troubled almost from the start. When they married in 1854, Rix was twenty-three and Ann Eliza was seventeen. Although she was six years younger than her husband, Ann Eliza may have wielded considerable power in the marriage. According to Ann Eliza, their problems stemmed from Rix's resentment of her ownership of the family farm, which she may have received from her father when she married, as well as her independent ownership of two enslaved laborers her father had given her. As historian Stephanie Jones-Rogers points out, such arrangements often bred hostilities within slaveholding marriages as husbands often expected to take control over the management of farms and slaves, even if they didn't hold legal title to them. To twenty-first-century readers, the story of a woman owning land and slaves in the antebellum South may seem far-fetched. In fact, it was common for white women to be both landholders and slaveholders. The 1860 census listed no fewer than sixty female slaveholders in Nash County, six of them in Ann Eliza's neighborhood, Dortches.[14]

Rix showed little interest in working the land. He "wasn't much of a farmer, it seemed," Priscilla explained to Dunston. "He wouldn't plant in time, nor supervise the slaves, nor even stay on the place. He used to go away for months at a time and come back in rags, without a cent in his pocket." If he liked to gamble and drink, Rix's irresolute habits did nothing to help his relationship with Ann Eliza. The final straw came when Rix took the two enslaved people to town and sold them. With Rix unwilling to do any work, these enslaved laborers likely kept the farm running. And they were worth a considerable sum of money to the cash-strapped couple, money that Rix may have intended to keep for himself.

Ann Eliza had had enough. Her husband had no right to sell her property. When she found out what Rix had done, she kicked him out and told him "not to come back until he brought the slaves back with him." The census records bear out this part of Ann Eliza's story to a degree. In 1860, she was not listed among those eight female slave-holders in her district. However, if the slaves Rix sold sometime in 1857, the year before Priscilla's birth, were the only ones she owned, then this is not surprising.[15]

When he deeded the slaves to Ann Eliza, her father may have stipulated that they were exclusively her property. It was common for slaveholding fathers to protect their daughters' interests this way. A greedy husband might dispose of his wife's property against her will; an irresolute one might lose them at the card table. To help ensure that their daughters did not become destitute, slaveholding fathers like Batchelor explicitly stated in their deeds of gift that their daughters were the sole owners of the enslaved property and that their current or future husbands would have no rights over them.[16]

Just as Batchelor likely feared when he gave his daughter exclusive control of the two slaves, their unauthorized sale threatened Ann Eliza's financial security. In 1860, the couple had no slaves, only $600 in real estate, and $100 in personal property, which included all the farm implements and household items. This meant that, by 1860, the social distance between the Joyners and their poorer neighbors, including free Blacks, narrowed.

Unlike counties in the western part of the state, where the Appalachian Mountains guarded against the encroachment of cash crops and by extension slavery, nearly half of the population of Nash County was non-white. Out of 11,687 people residing there in 1860, 4,684 were enslaved and 687 were free people of color. Although subjected to extensive legal and economic disabilities that made them in many cases "slaves without masters," some free people of color attained social status and financial stability comparable with Ann Eliza and Rix Joyner. Among their neighbors was Menga Spears, a twenty-three-year-old butcher who owned $200 in real estate. Fifty-five-year-old Violet Jones, a housekeeper, accumulated $450 in real estate and $150 in personal property. William Wilkins, a twenty-eight-year-old carpenter, supported his mother and younger brother, with a home and business worth a total of $370. In addition, Wilkins employed an eight-year-old apprentice named Azariah Locus, a member of a less-fortunate free Black family living throughout Nash County. A number of Locus children were bound out to both Black and white employers.[17]

These were some of the free Black men, women, and children among whom the Joyners lived and worked. Menga Spears may have butchered their livestock. William Wilkins may have made fence rails or repaired a roof for Ann Eliza when Rix was not to be found. And in some lonely moment, one of them may have had a relationship with Ann Eliza. If Ann Eliza blamed her downward mobility on her husband's laziness, then might another man who embodied the skill and motivation Rix lacked not stir her desire? Or, if she was in need of household help, might the now slaveless Ann Eliza take on a Black child whose parents had willingly or unwillingly bound out? Either scenario was possible. But if Ann Eliza's story is true, and she found herself pregnant with the child of a Black man she had been with while Rix was gone, then she faced quite a dilemma. The choices she made shaped not only her life but the lives of her husband, her baby's father, and most importantly, her unborn daughter.

· —— ·

As FAR BACK as the seventeenth century, evidence of liaisons between white women and Black men appears in colonial court records. Not only did white women and Black men sometimes marry in early colonial North Carolina, they did so without raising much ire among their neighbors. By 1830, state law prohibited intermarriage, but some couples cohabited without the benefit of matrimony. Griffin Stewart and Penny Anderson had lived together "as man and wife for many years," testified a neighbor when Stewart was charged and ultimately convicted for Anderson's murder in 1849. Anderson wore a gold ring, and the free Black community in Nash County accepted them as a couple despite the racial difference. In Rutherford County, Alfred Hooper and Elizabeth Suttles "lived together and cohabited as man and wife" for ten years before they were brought before the court for fornication and adultery in 1842. The previous year, Joel Fore and Susan Chestnut, the parents of a small child, faced similar charges in Lenoir County. Like Hooper and Suttles, Fore and Chestnut had "bedded and cohabited together as man and wife" for some time before charges were brought. Not only had the county clerk issued their marriage license, the 1840 census taker had listed Fore as a free man of color living with Chestnut, a white woman. Perhaps it was a disgruntled neighbor who reported these couples to the authorities in revenge for some dispute or squabble. This was often how such cases became the focus of court proceedings. Each one demonstrates how easy it was to skirt the law in rural communities where the state's watchful eye was all but nonexistent. Unless someone decided to turn them in and force a magistrate to prosecute, some interracial couples lived openly without much fear of state interference.[18]

The free Black community may have accepted Penny Anderson, but white women who entered into sexual relationships with Black men risked alienating the white community. This was especially true for poor white women who lacked the respectability afforded those who came from more elite backgrounds. Assumptions about poor women's promiscuity compromised their social standing as well as that of their family and neighbors. Long after the Civil War, a white North Carolinian related how "low white women who married or cohabited with free negroes" were ostracized by his community. One such woman became a source of childhood fascination and ridicule:

"I can recollect that many times I hurriedly climbed the front gatepost to get a good look at the shriveled old white woman trudging down the lane, who, when young, I was told, had had her free-negro lover bled, and drank some of his blood, so that she might swear she had negro blood in her, and thus marry him without penalty."[19]

When Ann Eliza "took up with a colored man," as Priscilla put it, she most likely would have been the subject of stinging gossip in the neighborhood. With her economic standing already diminished, some of her former friends and even family members may have turned their backs on her once a dark-skinned baby made an appearance. With little if any support from her family, the pregnant Ann Eliza and the baby's father faced some hard choices. On the night Ann Eliza gave birth, the father waited to find out if mother and baby survived. He wanted to see his new daughter, but Ann Eliza refused his request. Perhaps she was worried that the sight of the newborn might change his mind about leaving. If he stayed, it would only make a bad situation worse. She knew that someday Rix would probably return. In the meantime, Ann Eliza might claim abandonment, a well-worn route to divorce for antebellum women, but Rix might sue her for adultery in return, with the evidence of a child that most definitely did not belong to him. If he won, as he most likely would, she would lose her property and her children—Mourning and Margaret would stay with their father.[20]

She would lose Priscilla, too, even though Priscilla didn't belong to Rix. State law mandated that "all free base born [illegitimate] children of color" were to be bound out, raised by anyone in the county who could post the $500 bond to feed, house, and train them in a trade or occupation until they were of age. For boys, that meant until they were eighteen, girls until they were twenty-one. Eager to avoid paying for the care of such children, counties apprenticed them to someone who would fulfill the role of parent. The fact that many of these children, like the mixed-race Locus children who were bound out to families across Nash County, had parents and families to care for and love them did not matter. The Latin term used by the statute to describe children such as Priscilla was *filius nullius*, child of no one.[21]

Nancy Midgett probably loved her two mixed-race sons, and she was capable of caring for them, but in 1855, just three years before Priscilla was born, the Currituck County court bound them out anyway. Midgett's father had taken them in, building a house for her and his grandsons. He "kept them diligently and industriously employed" and was himself, in the words of the court, "an honest, respectable, and industrious man" who was willing to care for his daughter even though a Black man had fathered her children. While any single woman was at risk of losing her children to apprenticeship, normally a woman like Nancy Midgett who had the financial and moral support of her father, might avoid it.[22] Knowing this, Midgett appealed the county's decision to the state supreme court, and despite proving that she and her father could care for the children, the justices ruled against her, declaring that "the county court . . . has power to bind out children of color, without reference to the occupation or condition of the mother." While acknowledging that the legitimate free Black children whose parents were "honest" and "industrious" were excepted from the apprenticeship law, "[t]hese considerations do not arise where the child is a bastard."[23]

Ann Eliza might lose her daughter if she could not persuade Rix to stay with her when he returned. After 1830, when the population of free Blacks began to expand, apprenticeship in North Carolina became almost an exclusively racial institution as laws like the one that claimed Midgett's sons made every free Black or biracial child eligible to be bound out. By 1860, the state of North Carolina apprenticed nearly 2,000 free Black children almost exclusively to whites. Seventy of those were in Nash County, the second-highest number in the state.[24]

If she were bound out, Priscilla's experience would depend a lot on her master. Because she was biracial, her master would not be required to teach her to read. A revision to the apprenticeship law in 1838 removed that mandate for Black children. The training options for girls were limited. She would have pursued one of two career paths: servant or seamstress. In either case, she would have performed a variety of domestic labor much like the enslaved girls who worked in Ann Eliza's childhood home. Unlike those girls, Priscilla, because she was free, could ask the courts to intervene if her master mistreated her, but that would depend on her knowledge of the law and her ability to pay for legal representation. She would also need white witnesses to testify on her behalf since people of color could not testify against whites in court. Evidence of apprentices suing their masters is exceedingly rare, as might be expected from the financial constraint and the unwillingness of a white person to testify on her behalf.[25]

Knowledge of how the apprenticeship system worked would have played in Ann Eliza's mind as she faced the future, pregnant and alone. For some women in her position, panic might set in. Ann Eliza could have claimed that the baby's father raped her, as other white women did, but she could rely on neither the courts nor public opinion to support her unequivocally. Decades later, a white woman's cry of rape meant that someone, usually a Black man, would die. Poor white women's accusations of rape against Black men in the antebellum era typically faced much higher levels of scrutiny than those made in the post-emancipation years. Without any certainty that they would be believed, some women chose to press charges anyway. Whether out of fear of their families' reaction, or in a feeble attempt to salvage their reputations, or because they had, in fact, been assaulted, women like Ann Eliza made rape allegations against Black men knowing that people who already suspected them of immorality due to their low social status would stand in judgment of them.[26]

There was another way out. She could give the baby away.

"The colored people knew all about it," Priscilla explained, meaning they knew about Ann Eliza's pregnancy and who the father was, and they "wanted to take care of me in the quarters." It was not an unreasonable offer. Fearful of the treatment she might receive from the white community, including members of her own family, the "colored people," whether slaves belonging to the extended Joyner or Batchelor families, or free people living in the neighborhood, may have believed that Priscilla would be better off living with them. Ann Eliza's secret would remain hidden, and Priscilla would grow up among people who looked like her, who accepted her, and who loved her for who she was. Could the same be said of a white mother who might come to resent the sacrifices she had to make for her mixed-race daughter? How could anyone expect Rix to truly care for her? Even Priscilla had to admit it was a lot to ask of a man. "His wife asking him to accept a little brown baby must have been enough to try anybody. From what I heard later those must have been troublous days," she said.[27]

Ann Eliza must have had many hard questions as she contemplated her best course of action. What if Rix divorced her? What if Priscilla was bound out to someone who was neglectful or cruel? Might it be better for her to live with free Blacks or even as a slave than to be nobody's child?

But Ann Eliza flatly refused to give her daughter up. She told the people in the quarters that she was Priscilla's mother and no one else would raise her.

.———.

WHEN RIX FINALLY RETURNED HOME, he found "a new baby with a brown face." He may have demanded that his wife get rid of her. He may have threatened to do it himself. But according to Ann Eliza, she proposed a deal. In exchange for forgiving him the debt he owed for the two enslaved laborers he had sold and not brought back, Rix would agree to not divorce her and allow her to keep the baby. By doing so, he would effectively claim Priscilla as his own child despite the obvious fact that she was of mixed race.[28]

Surely no one believed such a charade? The fact was that it didn't really matter. No one had to believe that Priscilla belonged to Rix as long as he, the white man who headed the Joyner household, said it was so. That was the power white men, even white men like Rix Joyner, who was on a downward economic track, possessed in ante-bellum southern society. In 1860, a former professor at the University of North Carolina reported a similar case of racial make-believe when the daughter of a prominent planter gave birth to a child fathered by one of the family slaves. Before word could get out, the family enlisted not one but two justices of the peace to take the mother's sworn statement that the father was white. Although Ann Eliza did not possess these kinds of resources—who knows how much the justices were paid to turn a Black child white—if her husband did not charge her with adultery, then the outcome was essentially the same: a child fathered by a Black man became, in the eyes of the law if not the rest of the community, white.[29]

According to the story, Rix accepted Ann Eliza's offer. His family members probably thought he was crazy, but he may have loved his wife. Or maybe he couldn't make the public admission that his wife was unfaithful, that she had taken a Black man to her bed, which a divorce proceeding would require. The thought of standing up in court, in front of all his family, friends, and neighbors, while they listened to the sordid details of Ann Eliza's betrayal maybe was too much to bear. News travels fast through rural communities, though, so if his wife had given birth to a Black child, everyone knew about it. John Bryant would have known long before he arrived at the Joyner farm to collect the census data. It would have galled Rix to have to stand before another white man to be counted, to be judged. A raised eyebrow, a smirk, the almost imperceptible click of Bryant's tongue on the back of his teeth—Rix Joyner would have bristled at the slightest acknowledgment of his unusual family situation from the census taker.

But what if Priscilla was not, in fact, Ann Eliza's biological daughter, but Rix's? As Mary Chesnut pointed out, this was a far more common explanation for the light-skinned Black children one saw on almost every plantation and farm in the South. These open secrets created "a cage of obscene birds" that set husbands against wives and children against parents. In retaliation for their husbands' behavior, wives often harassed and abused the mothers of those children whom they saw as rivals for their husbands' affections despite the rape that had produced the children. One way slaveholding women could reassert their authority within the plantation household was to take the Black child to raise.[30]

In her memoir *Proud Shoes*, Pauli Murray recalls the effects such an arrangement had on her maternal grandmother, the child of a North Carolina planter's son who had raped an enslaved woman, Murray's great-grandmother. When the planter's spinster daughter realized that her brother had fathered a Black child, she believed the only way to remedy her family's disgrace was to take the child (her niece) away from her mother and raise her within the white household. Seeing herself as the child's savior, the aunt made sure Murray's grandmother had little contact with the other slaves on the plantation, including her own mother. The girl knew who her mother was, but her loyalty lay with the white family. Her aunt saw to that. Murray's grandmother "looked up to [the aunt] for everything." The aunt chose what she wore, who she talked to, and what duties she performed. All the while, the child's mother "hovered anxiously in the background, completely overshadowed by the superior authority of her mistress." Long after slavery had ended and the aunt had died, Murray's grandmother still "looked upon her as one looks upon a parent." But for her own mother she "seemed to have more pity than daughterly affection."[31]

Sarah Debro recounted a similar experience with her owner, Miss Polly, to the FWP interviewer who visited her home in Durham, North Carolina. "Whenever she [Miss Polly] saw a child down in the quarters that she wanted to raise by hand, she took them up to the big house and trained them," Debro explained. Miss Polly intended the little girl to be her personal maid. Debro was small, though, and at first all she could do was "tote [Miss Polly's] basket of keys" and pick up her handkerchief if she dropped it. Debro's mother had no say in this arrangement and was heartbroken to lose her daughter: "The day she took me my mammy cried because she knew I would never be allowed to live at the cabin with her no more."[32]

Debro was so young. She missed her mother, but Miss Polly plied her with clean, starched dresses, a soft bed, and extra food. Miss Polly knew that the girl especially loved riding next to her in the carriage and took her out often. Soon, just as Miss Polly had hoped, Debro began to love her mistress. That was part of her training. Miss Polly knew if she could make the child love her and the starched sheets and plentiful food and clean aprons and carriage rides, then she had something that gave her more power than any deed of ownership ever could. In fact, when freedom came and Debro's mother came to the house to reclaim her, she refused to go. Her mother had to physically carry her ten-year-old daughter away. For months, the girl pined for Miss Polly and the soft bedding and the clean dresses, wishing she could go back to live with her mistress once more. Even decades later, as she recounted the story to the FWP, she spoke kindly of Miss Polly and enjoyed recalling the special favors she received from her.[33]

After years of living among freedpeople, Priscilla probably had heard many stories of how white slaveholding women like Miss Polly manipulated Black children for their own benefit. But the doubts she harbored about Ann Eliza had set in long before Priscilla left the Joyner farm to find her own people. Priscilla likely knew some of the Black people who lived and worked nearby, maybe the same "colored people" who supposedly knew all about Ann Eliza's affair with a Black man and had wanted to take care of the baby. Ann Eliza also employed a Black carriage driver who continued to work for her once freedom came—Priscilla even wondered if he might be her father. But like Miss Polly, Ann Eliza must have kept Priscilla close, making sure she formed no meaningful connections with anyone who might reveal the truth about her identity. Although Ann Eliza could read and write, she did not teach her daughter those skills. Of course, the war may have intervened in any plans Ann Eliza had for her daughter's education, but the fact remains that as the years passed, Priscilla grew increasingly isolated and lonely within the Joyner household. She was a child of no one.

Whether Ann Eliza was Priscilla's biological mother or not, one thing becomes clear as we learn more about Priscilla's upbringing in the Joyner household. By attempting to raise her with the other white children and keep her father's identity a secret, Ann Eliza acted the part of the slaveholding woman who bought and sold enslaved children, who twisted and manipulated their loyalties and affection, and robbed them of the love and support of their own people.[34]

Ann Eliza believed she could give Priscilla everything she needed, and for a while, it may have looked to her as if everything would be all right. Rix was home, and it appears that he and Ann Eliza more or less reconciled. Ann Eliza quickly gave birth to two more children: Robert in late 1859, and Jolly two years later. Ann Eliza and Rix may have called a truce, but the war within the Joyner household was far from over.

THREE

THE EBB AND FLOW OF FREEDOM

· —— ·

R IX DID NOT WANT to go to war. When the calls for volunteers began in the days after North Carolina seceded from the Union on May 20, 1861, he ignored them. At thirty-one, he was considerably older than most of the young men, many barely more than teenagers, who sprang to action in anticipation of what they thought would be a great adventure. Like most men who joined the Confederate and the Union armies, Rix had no military experience, but he had enough life experience to know that things rarely turned out the way you expected.

In reality, Rix was a man already at war. Although he and Ann Eliza had struck an accord that produced two sons, Rix did not embrace this new arrangement. "I was still a small tot when he died," Priscilla told Dunston, "but I don't think Rix Joyner ever spoke to me." Whether she was his child or Ann Eliza's, or had been bought by Ann Eliza, Rix simply could not bear Priscilla's presence and waged a proxy war against the child.[1]

He enlisted the other children, especially the older girls, Margaret and Mourning, to fight his battles. The girls were big enough to notice that Priscilla received special treatment. She had her own room, while they had to share. It's clear from Priscilla's narrative that Ann Eliza doted on her, showering her with affection and attention that the other children did not receive. Maybe she sensed Rix's resentment and tried to make up for it, but she only succeeded in alienating the other children from Priscilla. Rix manipulated the older girls' jealousy to his own advantage. And like other white fathers, he undoubtedly instilled in his daughters and sons the importance of their skin color and their superiority over those who did not share it, including the little Black girl who lived in their house, sister or not.

It did not take long for Rix to claim victory. Priscilla recalled the day it happened. She believed she was about four or five—old enough to remember the details of what transpired. It was memorable because it was the day she realized she was different from the others. The children were playing house out in the yard. "We marked out the house in the dirt," she explained, "and Mornin' [Mourning] was the father and Jolly, the little baby." This game proceeded cheerfully until Margaret suddenly announced a change in the rules. "Prissy, you can't stay in here with us," she said. The imaginary house they had sketched out in the dirt was now off-limits to Priscilla. "You have to stay in the slave quarters. Papa says that's where you belong, anyway," Margaret declared. "I didn't understand what they meant, but when they wouldn't let me play, I cried and ran to my mother," Priscilla recalled. The memory of this encounter is so vivid that we can almost feel the sting of Margaret's meanness and hear the wails of a young child whose playmates have cast her out.[2]

It's unclear whether Rix witnessed Margaret's assault on Priscilla. He may have been drafted into the Confederate army by that time. His attempts to evade the war ended in the spring of 1862 when the Confederate Congress passed the Conscription Act. The first of its kind in American history, the Conscription Act required all able-bodied white men between eighteen and thirty-five to serve in the Confederate forces for three years. Men holding specified valuable occupations were exempt: railroad workers, shoemakers, telegraph operators, millwrights, apothecaries, cotton and wool factory managers, superintendents of lunatic asylums. But Rix did not have an essential job and lacked the cash necessary to hire a substitute, a price that could run into the thousands of dollars in certain locations. He also didn't qualify for an exemption under the "Twenty Negro Law," the section of the Conscription Act that enabled larger planters to keep their sons and overseers at home. By June of that year, Rix was just another poor man fighting a rich man's war.[3]

Back home in Nash County, Priscilla was left to wonder about what he said to Margaret, that she did not belong in the house with the white children, that she belonged in the quarters with the slaves. The dismissal surely wounded Priscilla, and the fact that she remembered the event so clearly nearly eighty years later suggests the wound never fully healed. But what if Rix was right? What if she did belong with other unfree or marginally free Black folks? What if her people were out there waiting for her?

Slavery was an enterprising thief. It stole people's time, their labor, and their physical strength. But of all the things it stole, family proved to be the most painful thing to lose, and sometimes the hardest thing to regain.

When Rix mustered into the 1st North Carolina Infantry in the summer of 1862, he joined a unit of about 1,000 men. They set off to become a part of the Army of Northern Virginia under the command of Robert E. Lee and would see action at places with now-iconic names: Antietam, Chancellorsville, Gettysburg. Three years later, on April 26, 1865, there were only sixty men in his unit left to surrender outside Petersburg, Virginia. Rix Joyner was not among them. His war was over.

For Rix, the Civil War was yet another burden he had to bear. However, for Priscilla, an unfree girl living in a slaveholding household, and for the more than 330,000 enslaved North Carolinians—as well as the nearly 31,000 free Blacks in the state who lived on slavery's periphery and were vulnerable to its gravitational pull—the war meant something else entirely. It was an opportunity to find their people and make a place where they truly belonged. But slavery would not die quickly or easily. A wild animal can be the most dangerous when it is in its death throes.

. —— .

THE WAR ARRIVED in earnest in North Carolina on February 7, 1862, when a ragtag Union flotilla defeated the small Confederate fleet guarding the Outer Banks and landed an amphibious force of 15,000 troops on Roanoke Island. The man who planned and led the expedition possessed limited military experience. A West Point graduate, Ambrose Burnside arrived in Vera Cruz just as the guns of the Mexican-American War fell silent. While he was stationed in New Mexico Territory, an Apache arrow grazed his neck. This was as close as he'd come to battle. Bored with long stretches of lonely frontier duty, he retired from the army in 1852. His close friendship with the commander of the Army of the Potomac, General George McClellan, ensured his commission when war broke out. Once again in the service, he quickly became known not for his martial prowess but for his striking appearance. His head was bald, but a banner of hair festooned his face, a fuzzy half-moon draping each cheek bridged by a mustache that lay like a garland over his top lip, his chin shaved clean. Widely considered to be one of the handsomest men in the Union Army, one newspaper correspondent declared Burnside to be "the very beau ideal of a soldier."[4]

Burnside was more than just a pretty face. Despite his lackluster performance during the Confederate rout of Union forces at the First Battle of Bull Run, he devised an ingenious plan to take possession of valuable rebel ports on the North Carolina coast. In the

fall of 1861, he began amassing a collection of "unseaworthy old tubs"—
retired passenger steamboats, coal
scows, and makeshift gunboats. Upon
seeing the dilapidated state of their
transportation to go into the "Grave-
yard of the Atlantic," as the Outer
Banks had been known among sailors
for centuries, the men assigned to the
expedition protested so vehemently
that Burnside was forced to move his
headquarters to the most ramshackle
vessel of the lot just to prove his commitment to the mission and his men.
Strong gales off the coast nearly cap-
sized several of the boats, but they
had little trouble defeating the poorly
defended Confederate forts guarding

Major General Ambrose Burnside.
COURTESY LIBRARY OF CONGRESS

Albemarle and Pamlico Sounds. As the expeditionary force moved
southward from Roanoke Island, it captured North Carolina's most
important ports: Elizabeth City, New Bern, and Beaufort.[5]

Yet, without the help of enslaved watermen, Burnside's plan
would have failed. One waterman, referred to as "Uncle Ben" or "Old
Ben" in newspaper accounts, possessed crucial information Burnside
needed in order to succeed in his risky mission. A "skillful inland
sailor" who knew "all about the inlets and outlets, the winds and the
currents, the moon and tides," Ben Tillett showed Burnside the best
location to land his force. He also informed the general of details
regarding the rebel battery defending the island since he had helped
build it. According to eyewitness reports, Tillett "was one of, if not
the very first, to fire into it."[6]

Black boatmen had sailed, ferried, and fished the coastal waterways for generations. They had also conducted countless runaways to the Atlantic shore where northbound vessels waited to carry them to freedom. Newspaper ads routinely warned captains to be on the lookout for men and women seeking passage on their ships. One of the most famous escapees, Harriet Jacobs, who would later pen her harrowing tale of escape, found her way to Edenton, North Carolina, and then aboard a ship to Philadelphia with the aid of a free Black boatman named Peter. In antebellum North Carolina, freedom ran eastward toward the sea.[7]

Thanks to the help of such men, the Union's coastal victories stunned Confederates, who had underestimated Union naval capabilities and the impact Black boatmen would have on the invasion. They were also unprepared for the tidal wave of self-emancipation that Burnside's victory would set off. Almost as soon as the first Union soldiers waded ashore, enslaved people began making their way to the coast. Vincent Colyer, an abolitionist missionary who traveled with the expedition, reported that the first group of about twenty individuals arrived within hours of the landing at Roanoke. They had rowed a small dinghy down the Chowan River. Like the scores of others Colyer witnessed arriving at New Bern in the coming weeks, they traveled the coastal region's myriad rivers, streams, and inlets by night, dodging Confederate patrols. They brought only what items they could carry, whether a few necessary household items or some bedding. They wheeled old people on carts and wagons, while mothers carried babies and led small children barefoot through the boggy wilderness, to arrive at Union lines and take possession of their freedom.

Such scenes became a hallmark of wartime emancipation. From the North Carolina coast to the back roads and trails of the inland South, enslaved people quit plantations by the thousands and made their way toward the Union Army wherever it was located. Photographers cap-

Contrabands crossing the Rappahannock River (Virginia) into Union territory.
COURTESY LIBRARY OF CONGRESS

tured wagons bulging with household items and people—old people, children, entire families. Refugees risked everything to make it to a Union army camp, but they did not receive a warm reception upon arrival. Union soldiers often resented the destitute refugees and, animated by racial prejudice, treated them with indifference, at best, and outright violence, in the worst cases. In the war's first two years, officers who harbored southern sympathies might refuse them admittance and turn them over to their masters when they appeared to collect their wayward property. Until the federal government adopted a clear policy with regards to emancipation, there were no guarantees that the Union lines would be the safe haven refugees hoped they would be.[8]

And still the refugees came. Like their counterparts in northern

Virginia and all along the Eastern Seaboard, the North Carolina refugees who headed toward Burnside's coastal strongholds must have been apprehensive about the reception they might receive. Throwing yourself on the mercy of unknown armed white men took a considerable leap of faith. But the men under Burnside's command, New Englanders mostly, welcomed the refugees with food, hot coffee, and eight dollars a month plus clothing for those able to work. And there was much work to be done.[9]

The "contrabands," as they were officially known, quickly set about building what would become a freedmen's colony on Roanoke Island. Under the direction of Horace James, a Massachusetts chaplain with the invading force, the freedpeople who fled to Roanoke began planning their city, complete with streets, cottages, and a sawmill. They also fed Burnside's men the fish and oysters they caught, ferried supplies to and from shore, escorted raiding parties up and down the rivers, and scouted for rebel soldiers who were an ever-present threat to the small occupying force. Eventually, James City, named in honor of the original director, would replace the government-funded colony after it folded in 1867. In all, 3,000 contrabands flocked to Roanoke Island during the war, making it far more successful than the first colony established—and lost—there in 1587.[10]

Thousands more flocked to Union lines all along the coast. By the summer of 1862, an estimated 10,000 formerly enslaved people lived in refugee camps that dotted the Outer Banks. They came from as far inland as Fayetteville, over ninety miles down the Cape Fear River, seeking freedom. Some came individually, but most came in groups, some as large as a hundred or more. Kate Edmonson, the wife of a Roanoke River planter, witnessed a group of that size leaving her neighborhood, and although she was as outraged as other Confederates to see their slaves take flight, she was impressed at how orderly they traveled. It was almost as if they had been waiting for the right moment to come. "[S]o much method they seem to observe and so well are they piloted that the idea of its being a panic seems to lose ground," she wrote in her diary.[11]

While enslaved people made their way to the coast, Burnside's forces pushed their way inland. Throughout the summer and fall of 1862, Union troops conducted raids up and down the coastal riverways. They foraged for supplies and targeted any

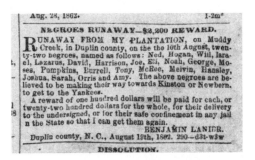

Twenty-two enslaved people from Duplin County made their way to Yankee lines at New Bern in August 1862. Wilmington Journal, *August 20, 1862.*
COURTESY UNIVERSITY OF
NORTH CAROLINA–GREENSBORO

rebel fortifications they might come upon. Their biggest success, however, came in the continued "liberation" of enslaved people, many of whom were living on plantations already abandoned by owners who had fled westward in advance of the approaching Union Army.

The growing numbers of refugees pushed the federal government toward a broader emancipation policy. By the end of the summer of 1862, Lincoln was ready to issue a blanket emancipation, if only an elusive battlefield victory could be attained. Burnside's North Carolina Expedition aside, the first year and a half of the war held few unequivocal Union successes. McClellan's half-hearted attempt to capture Richmond in the Peninsula Campaign failed to provide the swift end to the war that summer as Lincoln had hoped. Resigned to the need for military emancipation, Lincoln now waited for the right moment: a victory on the field so his proclamation would not seem like an act of desperation. As McClellan's army regrouped outside of Washington, Burnside and most of his men pulled out of North Carolina to join his troops. Rix Joyner, too, headed north to join his regiment. Soon they would converge on a cornfield in northeast Maryland just a few miles from the Pennsylvania border where Lincoln hoped federal troops finally would prove their strength.

. —— .

ON THE MORNING of September 15, 1862, the men of the 1st North Carolina arrived at the small town of Sharpsburg, Maryland. Over the next two days, 39,000 other Confederate troops would join them. Fewer than a thousand people lived in Sharpsburg. Its main street was little more than a horse track dotted with white clapboard buildings on either side. The Chesapeake & Ohio Canal kept the little town humming with business and goods, but Sharpsburg's residents mostly enjoyed quiet lives. That changed in the middle of September as the armies began to congregate in the fields and woods surrounding the town. Sensing the danger, farmers set loose their livestock, driving the animals north away from town and the troops massing from the south and east. Some families began packing their wagons to leave. Those who stayed looked for shelter in cellars in anticipation of the coming onslaught. As he marched down Main Street, Rix Joyner would have seen Sharpsburg's remaining residents in furious preparation, shuttering windows, latching doors, gathering supplies to keep them going for the days or weeks ahead. The tension in the air was palpable as he and his fellow soldiers walked through the village and out the other side, taking up position in a cornfield on the ridge north of town. They settled in to wait, helping themselves to the corn and pumpkins in a nearby field.

The battle of Antietam left nearly 23,000 Union and Confederate soldiers dead, missing, or wounded. Rix survived, but he was severely wounded and would spend the next year trying to heal. After being transported to a Confederate general hospital, possibly Chimborazo in Richmond, he returned home to Ann Eliza to recuperate and hoping to wait out the rest of the war. It was during this convalescence that he and Ann Eliza conceived their fourth child, a boy they named Jolly, who was born in 1863. It also may have been at this point that he taught his daughters, Margaret and Mourning, to taunt Priscilla. But if Rix thought the war could not touch him on his remote North Carolina farm, he was wrong. He may have escaped relatively intact from Antietam, but slavery, the reason that Rix found himself on the battlefield that warm September day, would not emerge from that battle unscathed. While it may not have been the unequivocal victory Lincoln had waited for, it was enough. Lee's invasion of Maryland had been thwarted even if his army had not been destroyed. Five days after the battle, the president issued a preliminary Emancipation Proclamation giving the rebels ninety days to lay down their arms or lose their slaves.

The community Rix Joyner found upon his return from Antietam sometime in late 1862 had grown gaunt and grim during his absence. The enthusiasm for war that he had witnessed in the conflict's early days was nowhere to be seen.

"The white folks went off to the war; they said they could whip [the Yankees], but the Lord said, 'No,' and they didn't whip [them]. They went off laughing, and many were soon crying, and many did not come back," was how Clara Jones, a formerly enslaved woman from Raleigh, recalled the swift change in attitude.[12]

North Carolina gave more men to the Confederate cause than any other rebel state. In the aftermath of Gettysburg in early July 1863, North Carolinians suffered one-quarter of *all* the casualties, over 6,000 men, lost in that three-day battle. In all, over 40,000 men from the Old North State are believed to have died in the war, although new research suggests that the figure was probably higher.[13]

But with the war at their doorsteps, white civilians had little time to mourn their dead. Eastern North Carolina became a center for low-level guerrilla warfare, as Confederates attempted to dislodge Union forces from the coast and stop Yankee raiding parties from moving farther inland, confiscating civilian property, including enslaved people, as they went. In the spring of 1863, Union raiding parties made it to Rocky Mount, nearly one hundred miles from the coast and the seat of Nash County, to attack the rail depot there and seize 800 bales of cotton stored in its warehouses. Unable to transport such a large quantity, they burned the cotton and destroyed 1,000 barrels of flour and "immense quantities of hardtack" meant for Lee's army in Virginia. After cutting the telegraph lines, the raiding party receded back down the Tar River toward the sea, taking with them several hundred horses and mules, around a hundred Confederate prisoners of war, and as many as three hundred enslaved people. No longer merely contrabands of war, these Black men and women were now "forever free" after the final Emancipation Proclamation went into effect on January 1, 1863. Some of them may well have been enslaved by extended Joyner or Batchelor families on farms spread throughout Nash County.[14]

While enslaved people fled toward the coast, white refugees fled further inland, away from the Union Army, away from the mounting tide of freedom. The roads in and out of the eastern half of state, from New Bern to Raleigh, and beyond to the remote peaks of the Blue Ridge Mountains in the western part of the state—the same higgledy-piggledy system of rough dirt tracks that Frederick Law Olmsted had bounced to and fro on a decade earlier—became choked with traffic. Among those footsore travelers was William Sykes, an enslaved man from the Outer Banks. Sykes's owner, who feared that the "damn Yankees" near the coast were going to "take my niggers from me," uprooted all his able-bodied property and marched them across the state to Buncombe County near Asheville. Sykes was imprisoned in the North Carolina state penitentiary for manslaughter when he spoke to the FWP interviewer. At the time, he had served ten months of a three-to-five-year sentence for stabbing a man who had been harassing him. At seventy-eight years old, it was likely that Sykes would spend his last days just as he had spent his early ones: bound and unfree. It was in this context that he related what happened to his cousin Jane while they were on the road to Asheville. "While we was there, the missus asked my cousin Jane to do the washing," Sykes recalled. Jane replied that she would do her own washing first and would get to the mistress's clothes afterwards.[15]

"You ain't free yet, I wants you to know that," the indignant mistress informed Jane.

"I knows that I not but I's going to be free," Jane snapped back.

The mistress took Jane's declaration of impending independence in silence, but she told her husband when he returned from town. It was then Jane learned just how far away she was from freedom. "Mr. Jim was mad and he takes Jane out on Sunday morning and he beats till the blood runs down her back," Sykes recounted. A few days later, Sykes's owner led William and the rest of the men on their journey, leaving Jane and the other enslaved women at the camp. William never saw any of them again. He did not speculate about what happened to the women, but it's possible they were left to be picked up by a trader and sold.[16]

Of course, Jane was right. Freedom would come eventually for those who would live to see it. In the meantime, refugees like William and Jane joined other freedom seekers on North Carolina roads. A contrasting group of wanderers were the bands of armed deserters from the Confederate forces who haunted the woods and swamps. Around twenty percent of North Carolina soldiers deserted at some point. As the war dragged on, the problem got worse. With the help of supportive kin and civilians who had grown tired of the war and the suffering it caused at home, the deserters avoided attempts by Confederate officials to round them up.

They also carried out violent reprisals against Unionist sympathizers, Black people, or anyone they might hold a grudge against. "The woods was full of runaway slaves and Rebs who deserted the army so it was dangerous to walk out," Jane Lee, who had been enslaved in rural

Wake County, southeast of Raleigh and less than fifty miles from the Joyner farm, explained.[17]

Freedom in North Carolina came in waves of overlapping, multidirectional movement: the Union Army washing in from the coast; enslaved people making their way from the inland areas toward the coast and the army; slave owners fleeing with their families and enslaved property inland toward the mountains; deserters, runaways, and Confederate guards circling one another in the woods and barrens. Regardless of any official emancipation policy from President Lincoln, slavery began to crumble under the movement of troops and refugees and slaves. As Kate Edmondson and her neighbors recognized as they watched their slaves leave for the coast by the hundreds, emancipation had been a fait accompli since the war began. With so many white men off fighting, there was no one left to stop their mass exodus. For many enslaved people in North Carolina and throughout the Confederacy, freedom came not by proclamation but through perambulation. They simply walked away.

Yet, even as they quitted slavery by the thousands, even after Lincoln issued a tardy but transformative proclamation, freedom remained fluid. In North Carolina, it ebbed and flowed like the tidal waters, surging only so far as federal troops ventured, then retreating with them back to the coast. Freedom might come suddenly like a flood. One minute a man in blue was telling you that you were free, that the place was yours to farm. The next minute your former master returned with rifle in hand and demanded that you get off his land. Without any soldiers there to protect you, what else could you do but leave? It seeped away so quickly. But nowhere did freedom flow that it didn't leave a watermark on everything and everyone it touched.

. —— .

WERE THE SLAVES GLAD TO BE FREE? The answer to this question from the FWP survey may seem obvious. Of course, they were glad to be free. Enslaved people rejoiced, feasted, sang, danced, and cried tears of joy when they learned that slavery was no more. Jeff Bailey was only "a little bitty old boy" when he learned he was free, but the memory was seared in his mind and on his tongue. He had been to town with his father that day, when they overheard people talking about slavery being over. When they returned home, their mistress confirmed it. "You're free," she told them. "Go on out in the orchard and get yourself some peaches." He had never been allowed to eat any of the fruit before. "Baby did I get me some peaches," he exclaimed.[18]

These jubilant moments are plentiful within FWP narratives, but they do not define those recollections exclusively. From the thousands of interviews collected, there emerges no single memory of emancipation. Instead, there are conflicting accounts of the war's impact on individual lives and the meaning of freedom as it emerged alongside the disruption and destruction of armed conflict. The experience of war varied from place to place. Enslaved people living in the path of either army or in close proximity to battlefields experienced war and freedom differently from those who lived in remote regions where soldiers rarely if ever appeared. Union soldiers brought the happy news of emancipation along with the terror that armies often bring to civilians. For those who never saw a bluecoat in the flesh out in the remote reaches of eastern Texas—where the news of emancipation only reached the enslaved community in June of 1865, months after the war was officially over—freedom remained a distant, hazy dream.

Timing also mattered. Freedpeople's experience of war in 1861, when Confederate spirits were high and white folks assured one another that their departing sons would be back by breakfast, differed considerably from what it would be in late 1864 or early 1865, when defeat hung frozen in the air like winter drizzle. White people's hope ran low then, but so did food and other necessities, which mattered as much if not more than any vague talk of freedom. Enslaved people had waited long and prayed hard for deliverance, but the moment of its arrival marked the decimation of the social and economic world they inhabited. Many quickly realized that slavery's downfall did not in itself signal freedom's ascendence. New institutions, political rituals, and a social ethos premised on the values of inclusion and consent, rather than exclusion and violent compulsion, would be needed to replace those that had girded the foundations of a society based on slavery. In the meantime, formerly enslaved people would be left to wonder: what did it matter that freedom came as an act of war?

Priscilla Joyner did not recall much of her wartime experiences except those centered on Rix and what she knew of his time in the Confederate army. Her small world in remote Nash County was spared much of the raid-and-reprisal violence that dissolved rural communities farther east. Although Burnside's raiding parties made it as far as Tarboro, the next county over, Union troops pushed that far inland only in the spring of 1865 as Sherman's March came to an end at the state capital in Raleigh. If any of Sherman's soldiers passed by the Joyner farm, Priscilla did not recall it. Other men and women interviewed by the FWP, however, had much more to say about the wider experience of wartime emancipation.

Like Priscilla, many of these men and women were children, some teenagers or very young adults, during the war. This is not surprising given the fact that a majority of the enslaved population—at least fifty-six percent of those enumerated on the 1860 census—were under the age of twenty, with thirty percent younger than ten. Their youthfulness may account for the discombobulation and apprehension apparent in much of the FWP testimony about the war. But youth alone does not explain why freedom was a disconcerting experience for many enslaved people. Other contemporary sources confirm that emancipation was such a life-altering event that it could leave a person struggling to cope with the severity of the changes surrounding them. And paramount among those changes was the presence of an army that brought liberation and destruction in equal measure.[19]

One of the most common shared wartime memories in the FWP narratives is of Union troops arriving on the plantation or farm bringing with them news of emancipation. The mere sight of Union troops, some of them Black men, could instill feelings of excitement, fascination, and fear.

"Their feets sounded like muttering thunder," was how Cheney Cross described the sound of the approaching Union Army.[20]

Nancy Washington said, "They look just like a big blue cloud."[21]

Alice Green, who was enslaved in Georgia, and Hannah Brooks Wright, enslaved in Mississippi, both described Union soldiers as "bluebirds" because of their uniforms.[22]

Frank Larkin treasured his memory of mounted Union soldiers riding tall and proud on their horses: "It was the prettiest sight I ever saw."[23]

The appearance of soldiers was a signal event that became seared in many people's memory, not simply for the sight and sound of troops, which was often dramatic, but also for what their appearance portended. "Just before freedom come about 50 Yankee soldiers come through our plantation and told us that the bull-whups and cowhides was all dead and buried," James Bolton of Georgia remembered.[24]

But the soldiers were not always sensitive to the trouble this information could cause enslaved people. Slave owners sometimes responded violently to this encroachment on their authority once the soldiers were gone. Margaret Hughes's owners hanged an enslaved woman for revealing to the Yankees where they had buried their valuables. A soldier told Eliza Evans not to let her master call her "nigger" anymore. Instead, he told her, she should insist that he refer to her as "Miss." When she did as the soldier instructed, not only did her master whip her with a switch but her own grandmother did, too, when she found out. In these circumstances, being formally emancipated didn't change much of anything. "You better hush, you'll get a whipping," Mary Jane Hardridge's mother scolded when she reported that a soldier had told her she was free.[25]

Slave owners were desperate to maintain control over enslaved people. While some tried to compel their bondspeople's loyalty through the lash, others tried to manipulate them psychologically. Enslaved children were told that Union soldiers were devils who would spirit them away in the night. Mittie Freeman recalled with some amusement how she believed that Yankees had horns, because they were devils, or so her mistress had told her. A bold girl, Freeman wanted to see for herself, so when the men in blue arrived, she asked one to take off his hat so she could see his horns. How disappointed she was to find out her mistress's stories weren't true. He was just a man.[26]

But men could be devils, and those in the Union and Confederate armies were no different than men in armies throughout history. Pillage and despoilation were and continue to be constants in world military history, and for much of that history, those behaviors were understood as not only inevitable but also legitimate acts of war. Only in the early modern period did human beings begin to imagine looting, targeting civilians, and rape to be outside the bounds of "civilized" warfare. In 1863, President Lincoln endorsed the Lieber Code, a military order codifying these new principles. Nonetheless, civilians remained vulnerable to depredations that seemed to be as integral to military operations as bayonets or bullets. And none were more vulnerable than enslaved people.[27]

Although emancipation had become the official Union policy by the time soldiers began to arrive on southern plantations in large numbers, not all of the "bluebirds" understood their mission as one of liberation—at least not the liberation of enslaved people. Sam Word's mother encountered a Union soldier who intended to liberate her property but nothing else. "Mother had lots of nice things, quilts and things, and kept them in a chest in her little old shack. One day a Yankee soldier climbed in the back window and took some of the quilts," Word remembered. When Word's mother spotted him, she called out, "Why, you nasty, stinking rascal! You say you come down here to fight for the niggers, and now you're stealing from them." The soldier quickly set her straight. "You're a goddam liar," he retorted. "I'm fighting for $14 a month and the Union."[28]

The Union soldiers were dirty and loud. They demanded to be fed. They rifled through the owners' personal belongings looking for valuables. They took what they wanted—jewelry, silverware, doodads and trinkets, leftovers from breakfast, the last hog. Sometimes they saw enslaved people as potential allies, but just as often they regarded them in much the same way most white people did—as servants, as inferior, as undeserving of much consideration or sympathy.

Lizzie McCloud understood that the Union soldiers' arrival meant she would soon be free, but she could not help but feel apprehensive. Her emancipation story was tinged with a sense of foreboding that suggests she anticipated the danger soldiers posed to her. "Oh God, I seed the Yankees. I saw it all."[29]

McCloud was so frightened of the troops when they appeared on her Tennessee plantation that she hid under the house. As she lay there, she listened to the soldiers calling out for her. "Come out, Dinah. Dinah, we're fighting to free you and get you out from under bondage!"[30]

McCloud noted how the soldiers called all the enslaved women "Dinah." In antebellum popular culture, Dinah had become a generic name for enslaved women, just as Sambo had for men. In May 1865, the *New York Times* published this admonition to newly freed people in the South: "You are free, Sambo, but you must work. Be virtuous too, oh Dinah!"[31]

In the Book of Genesis, Dinah was also the name of Abraham's granddaughter who was kidnapped and raped by the Canaanites, prompting her two brothers, Simeon and Levi, to massacre the Canaanites and plunder their city. Like the biblical Dinah, enslaved women endured rape and other forms of sexual violation at the hands of their owners and overseers. Sixteen-year-old McCloud, like all enslaved women by that age, was aware of her own sexual vulnerability. They had also been warned by their masters and mistresses that Yankee soldiers were devils who wished to harm or kill them, which is why, when the soldiers arrived, McCloud ran and hid under the house. From where she lay she could see the soldier's boots as he paced back and forth, and as he tried to coax her out from her hiding place, she heard him say, "We's a fightin' for you, Dinah!"[32]

What exactly did the soldier want from her? McCloud never explicitly says. But like many of the published ex-slave narratives, her interview exhibits what literary scholars describe as "undertelling" *around* the issue of sexual violence and trauma. The soldier's words lead us to believe he expected gratitude from McCloud for her liberation. We are left to imagine what form he wished that gratitude to take, but McCloud understood very well the threat encased within his ostensibly good-natured attempt to extend a hand of friendship to a young enslaved woman.[33]

While McCloud hid under the house, she could see the soldiers begin to set fire to the plantation. Seventy-five years after she lay there, watching the soldier's feet and listening to his appeals, this is the story she told the FWP interviewer when he asked her what she remembered about the war and when she knew she was free. "Yankees walked in, child, just walked right in on us," she told the interviewer. "I tell you I've seen a time. You talking about war—you better wish no more war come."[34]

Rape and the threat of rape constituted powerful tools in the arsenal of psychological warfare, and federal officers were not above using them. When the Union occupied New Orleans in the spring of 1862, General Benjamin F. Butler issued the infamous General Order No. 28, which proclaimed that any woman who insulted or assaulted one of his soldiers would be "treated as a woman of the town plying her avocation." The effect was immediate. Confederate women in the city ceased dumping their chamber pots on Yankee soldiers walking beneath their windows. Southern white women in other areas felt the threat of sexual violence when Union soldiers ransacked their bedrooms, rifled through their personal belongings, and ripped earrings or other jewelry off their bodies. The threat to white women was real enough, but court-martial records suggest that soldiers raped enslaved women more frequently.[35]

Sexual violence represented some hard truths about wartime emancipation. Slaveholders' warnings about Yankees looking to harm enslaved people were true in some cases. When Union soldiers raped an enslaved woman in full view of the plantation household, they sent a message to slave owners about their dwindling authority. "Such public acts of sexual violence served to demonstrate power over Black women, threaten white women, and mark southern defeat," explains historian Crystal Feimster. Rape was not simply a tragic consequence of war but a potent symbol of Union victory.[36]

As impressive and terrifying as the arrival of Union soldiers could be, the sight of a defeated master was also extraordinary. Hannah Austin was only about ten years old and admitted she was too young to understand what freedom really meant. But she remembered clearly the day her master, Mr. Hall, informed her mother that they were free. Eight decades later, she could hear him speaking. "His exact words were quote 'Liza you don't belong to me any longer you belong to yourself,'" Austin recalled. The words became seared in her mind because of what happened next. "I watched my mother to see the effect his words would have on her," she explained, "and I saw her eyes fill with tears." Then she looked back at Hall's face and saw he was crying, too.

The word "freedom" did not have any meaning for such a young girl, but the sight of her mother and the man she knew up until that moment as her master both crying, albeit for different reasons, let her know that nothing would ever be the same.[37]

. —— .

THE LARGEST UNION MILITARY INCURSION into North Carolina, after Burnside's coastal invasion in 1862, was General Sherman's Carolina Campaign in the last weeks of the war. Skirting Nash
County and the Joyner farm, Sherman's men pivoted at Goldsboro
about fifty miles south and swung northeast toward the capital at
Raleigh. Rumors of the march flew like startled birds, flitting from
farm to farm and town to town. The rancid smell of burning tur-
pentine factories, set ablaze by stragglers behind the main column of
troops, carried on the spring breezes. Thick black smoke could be seen
for miles from the pine forests, torched to ward against any last-ditch
Confederate ambushes. Beyond the crackle of blazing timber, the surrounding areas were quiet. No trains chugged into depots like the one
at Rocky Mount, not far from the Joyners' home. Union troops had
ripped the tracks from the ground and twisted them into the infamous
"Sherman's neckties," just as they had been all the way from Atlanta,
where the march had begun four months before. People stayed close to
their homes, guarding whatever food remained after the long winter:
a few sweet potatoes, a bit of sorghum, some old corn. Ann Eliza and
the older girls, Margaret and Mourning, probably drove any livestock
they hadn't yet eaten into the woods in the hope of rounding them up
later after the danger had passed. In normal times, fifty miles might
take three or four days to travel in a wagon over rough tracks. Thirty
thousand marching men could be there in two days; a fleet cavalry
unit in a few hours. The fear of them bore down on the Joyner farm
even if the men themselves never did.[38]

The only soldier Priscilla ever saw was her stepfather, Rix Joyner,
and that was more than enough. While other folks interviewed by the
FWP recalled many wartime stories of external intrusions into their
daily lives, Priscilla's wartime memories recalled the strained family
dynamics in the Joyner household. Rix spent more than a year and a

half at home recuperating from the wounds he received at Antietam. In that time, he managed to alienate Priscilla from the other children. The older girls, Margaret and Mourning, and their brother Robert— born in 1860 after Rix and Ann Eliza reunited —became their father's allies in his war against the mixed-race girl their mother claimed as her own. "You see," Priscilla explained, "Rix was doing all he could to poison the minds of his own children against me."[39]

Eventually the Provost Guard came for Rix. In the fall of 1864, he was forced to make his way back to Virginia. Somewhere along the end of a ten-mile U-shaped trench line that ran from Appomattox in the east to Petersburg in the west, Rix and what remained of the 1st North Carolina became the last line of defense between General Ulysses S. Grant and the Confederate capital at Richmond. There Rix spent a miserable winter huddled against the cold, mired in mud, and starving. A few wooden huts constituted the only shelter in the trenches. Most of the troops faced the freezing temperatures and rain without blankets, overcoats, or even shoes. After a sleet storm, one soldier had to crawl out of his frozen coat and leave it to thaw by the fire. Food shortages meant that the men's rations consisted mostly of turnips and cabbage. The main enemy of the "unwashed, uncombed, unfed, and mostly unclad" at Petersburg was not Grant's army, encamped almost within spitting distance on the other side of the trenches, but rather the cold. Frostbite and fevers attacked the Confederacy's last defenders daily. And everyone seemed to know that it was only a matter of time before Grant marched his army right over them. The only thing to look forward to in the spring was defeat.[40]

Those who could walk got up and left. The North Carolina border lay only fifty miles away, but most were too weak or too sick to attempt an escape from their frozen hell. At some point during the long winter, Rix probably took ill and was transported twenty-three miles north to Jackson Hospital in Richmond where most of the ailing North Carolina troops were cared for in the war's final two years.

One of no fewer than fifty-eight hospitals operating in the city during the war, Jackson was one of the larger medical complexes. Located on the city's western edge, Jackson boasted forty-nine buildings, a forty-acre vegetable garden, and a renowned library. Jackson Hospital at one time represented the best in modern American medical facilities. However, by the time Rix arrived in the early spring of 1865, Jackson, like the rest of the once vibrant city, was a ghost of its former self.[41]

Although shelter existed at Jackson, there was little else. Shortages of food, fuel, and medicine rendered the hospital little better than the trenches. Instead of turnips and cabbage, hospital staff and patients ate the rats that scavenged the dead and sometimes the living, too. Here among the rats Rix spent his last days, suffering from flu, dysentery, pneumonia, or some other deadly biological agent. Cold and alone, he died on March 10, just two weeks before the United States flag would once again fly over Richmond.

. —— .

As Sherman's men camped in and around Raleigh that spring, word came of Lee's surrender at Appomattox. The more than 350,000 newly freed people in North Carolina, as well as the 30,000 free people of color, now faced the daunting work of making freedom meaningful. As they labored to establish new economic livelihoods and engage with the law and local government as independent political actors, North Carolina's freedpeople also struggled to rebuild their families beyond the reach of the men and women who used to own them and who still felt it was their prerogative to control Black family life.

There were other trials, too. "When freedom come, folks left home, out in the streets, crying, praying, singing, shouting, yelling, and knocking down everything," recalled Patsy Moore, who had been enslaved in De Soto County, Mississippi. "Then come the calm. It was sad then."[42]

Moore explained that the war had destroyed so much of enslaved people's lives that the enormity of the change set people on their heels. "So many folks done dead, things tore up and nowhere to go and nothing to eat, nothing to do," she said.[43]

The hard realities of life in a war-torn country blunted freedpeople's joy at finally being set free. There was so much sadness—disquiet and restlessness, too—feelings that no proclamation, no constitutional amendments, no ballot box could assuage.[44]

Rix was buried along with most of Jackson Hospital's dead in the Soldiers' Section of Richmond's Hollywood Cemetery, the final home of Confederate luminaries like George Pickett, Jeb Stuart, and Jefferson Davis. He rests in the shadow of the Monument to the Confederate War Dead, a ninety-foot stone pyramid erected by the Ladies Hollywood Memorial Association (LHMA) in 1869. Pyramids invoked a sense of permanence in the face of death. Just as pyramids in the ancient world housed the bodies of the dead until the time for their physical resurrection, the Confederate monument at Hollywood housed the LHMA's memory of the Confederacy until it could be resurrected not as the traitorous slaveholding enemy of the United States it was, but as a noble embodiment of the true spirit of American liberty.[45]

Rix's decaying corpse helped give life to a new narrative of the Confederacy, a narrative that would, over time, help to reverse the revolution of emancipation and ensure that southern Blacks lived in a state as close to actual slavery as possible. The "Lost Cause" posited that southern independence had been an ill-fated but glorious project defeated only because the North was better resourced. No sooner had Rix's body been carted to the burial pit than southern politicians like Jefferson Davis began revising the history of secession to erase its leading cause—slavery—and recast the conflict as one of amorphous cultural and economic differences. Gone were the days when men like Alexander Hamilton Stephens, Davis's vice president, proudly declared slavery to be the Confederacy's "cornerstone." Soon others joined in this reimagining of the Civil War as the great American tragedy. Historians, journalists, novelists, and later, filmmakers, produced gilded images of stately, well-ordered plantations and harmonious relations between enslaved people and their owners that contrasted sharply with a turbulent, hostile, and often violent postwar period. And what lesson did the prophets of the South's new civic religion hope to convey to their audiences? The guardians of the Lost Cause aimed to convince anyone who would listen that the war had been a tragic mistake, emancipation a criminal one, and that the only way to rectify them was to restore the political power of those who had so recently fought to destroy the United States. For the LMHA and its successor, the United Daughters of the Confederacy (UDC), Rix Joyner became a hero, a martyr, a paragon of Confederate virtue.[46]

To Ann Eliza and the children, he was just gone. No one knew where or how he died. All they knew was that he had been taken away by the Provost Guard never to be seen again. Priscilla had heard a rumor that he had been shot as a deserter. Perhaps that is why no one ever took the trouble of trying to track him down. "I don't think Miss Ann Liza," as Priscilla referred to the woman who claimed to be her mother, "cared one way or another."[47]

If Ann Eliza thought Rix's death would bring an end to the turmoil in her home, she was mistaken. His older children missed him, even if his wife did not. They resented his absence and took their resentment and grief out on Priscilla. Ann Eliza, it seems, was incapable of correcting their behavior. Although Priscilla mentions Ann Eliza's attempts to comfort her when the white children had been cruel, she never says their mother admonished or punished them for abusing the girl who was supposed to be their sister. Isolated from other people of color in the neighborhood, denied the comfort that the people in "the quarters" might have given her, Priscilla endured the abuse from the white Joyner children with no support from within or outside the family.

When he was small, Priscilla took some pleasure in caring for her little brother Jolly, who had been born in 1863. "Jolly, the youngest, was my favorite," she explained. "He hadn't been old enough when his father lived to understand any of the things he had been told about me." But soon he joined the others. The siblings' commitment to Priscilla's exclusion, their unwillingness to accept their sister as one of their own, mirrored the broader world of emancipation-era America and its bloody contestations over the place of newly freed African Americans in southern society. In a sense, the Joyner family was America writ small, and in their family drama we catch a glimpse of the larger drama of the long emancipation.[48]

Priscilla's older sisters, Margaret and Mourning, continued in the work Rix had taught them, and now the younger boys joined in the game. Their taunts, which had once been simply mean, grew physical. "Robert and Jolly were growing up and sometimes it was all I could do to keep all four from jumping on me."[49]

Freedpeople across the South worried about being attacked and tried in vain to keep it from happening. The taunts, cussings, and beatings seemed unavoidable, given that nothing short of disappearing altogether would appease the most indignant white southerners. The mere fact of their presence, of being free and Black, meant that they would endure all the disdain and hatred white people could muster. That they could endure these physical and emotional abuses and still build families, communities, churches, schools, political coalitions, and bridges to a future they hoped would be better is a testament to the fortitude and determination of the charter generation. Those institutions, along with the hope and love they bequeathed to their children, grandchildren, and great-grandchildren, are their monuments.

FOUR

THE PURSUIT OF HAPPINESS

.———.

RECONSTRUCTION WAS A TIME of bewildering contradictions. On the one hand, it was a moment of confounding upheaval and unprecedented transformation. In only four short years, the nation's political system had been upended, slavery abolished, and four and a half million people emancipated. Congress, a body that before the war had bowed before "King Cotton," now considered confiscating the deposed monarch's land and dividing it up among the people he once forced to work upon it. Not only might freedpeople become landowners, they might also vote, hold elected office, testify in court, and exercise the same "civil rights and immunities" as the men and women who, just months before, had legally owned them. By virtue of their birth within the jurisdiction of the United States, formerly enslaved people would enjoy "the full and equal benefit of all laws and proceedings for the security of persons and property as is enjoyed by white citizens, and shall be subject to like punishment, pains, penalties, taxes, licenses, and exactions of every kind, and to no other." So declared the Civil Rights Act of 1866, which laid the foundations for the Fourteenth Amendment. Not a decade had passed since the

Supreme Court had ruled that Black people had "no rights which the white man was bound to respect." From slaves to citizens in just nine years—freedpeople sat at the helm of a legal revolution unmatched in world history.[1]

Life inside the former Confederacy, however, was mired in racial prejudice and violence. White southerners were determined to make sure that although slavery might be dead in name it would live on in the workings of their daily lives. Already masters of cruelty, they continued to hone the arts of intimidation and exact hardship at new levels of virtuosity. Their repertoire included: cussing, sneering, and belittling freedpeople at every opportunity; charging a family more for meager amounts of food and clothing than they made in wages; turning out tenants after the harvest but just before settling-up time; and when words came to blows, beating and sometimes killing a freedperson with impunity. These were just a few of the everyday acts of injustice that honored slavery's memory and violated freedom's vision. A group of Alabama freedmen, who had been cheated out of their earnings and threatened with violence if they complained, rightly concluded, "this is not the pursuit of happiness."[2]

The Declaration of Independence recognized three "inalienable rights" conferred on humankind by its Creator. In addition to life and liberty, the pursuit of happiness reflected the affective nature of the Founders' vision for an ideal democratic society. It affirmed the view that, in addition to life and liberty, human beings required some degree of emotional satisfaction. Born of the Enlightenment, the idea that individual happiness not only was a positive good in itself but should be the goal of government became a hallmark of the age.[3]

It also became the standard of the new United States. By the early nineteenth century, Americans had gained the reputation for being among the happiest people on earth. On her tour of the country in the 1830s, British writer Harriet Martineau found Americans to be surprisingly good-humored and was amazed at how well they could make her laugh. One of her companions "dropped some drolleries so new to me, and so intense, that I was perplexed as to what to do with my laughter," she noted. Jocular and joyful, the Americans Martineau met seemed to embody the hope and promise of a new age of human existence, one ruled by happy striving instead of dour suffering.[4]

Yet underneath the joviality lay an unfathomable despair. If the Declaration of Independence codified free, white men's right to pursue happiness, it did so on the backs of enslaved people. Relying as it did on enslaved labor, the expanding cotton economy enriched white men and women, enabling them to acquire land, capital, and many other material representations of happiness, including, most importantly, the time in which to enjoy those possessions. Even the New Yorkers who so amused Martineau with their jokes enjoyed leisures financed by slavery. Theirs was a happiness born of slavery. (Of course, that happiness was not available to all white people to the same degree; indeed, most poor, working whites no doubt would have thought the joke was on them.) The dissonance between the Declaration's stated aims and the existence of slavery in the United States became increasingly antagonistic as the years passed. By 1858, twenty years after Martineau penned her observations about American happiness, Abraham Lincoln, then a contender for Illinois's Senate seat, declared, "there is no reason in the world why the negro is not entitled to all the natural rights enumerated in the Declaration of Independence, the right to life, liberty and the pursuit of happiness." The Civil War might have brought the nation closer to realizing that ideal, but even then, happiness for the newly freed was elusive.[5]

According to the Alabama freedmen, it was not enough to merely survive—survival was the goal of an enslaved people, although to be sure, enslaved people found numerous ways to flourish and prosper even while wearing the yoke of bondage. But the Alabama freedmen believed that happiness should not be the exception, available here and there, for those unfortunate enough to have Black skin. It should be the rule for all free people, at least insofar as free people should possess the opportunities to pursue it. The Alabama freedmen argued that Reconstruction should open up space for Black people not merely to exist but to thrive. Their own land, fair dealings with whites, the right to testify in court, access to education—these were the preconditions for happiness they petitioned the Freedmen's Bureau, the quasi-military government organization set up to help ease the transition from slavery to freedom, to help them achieve.

But for others, happiness remained a more intangible goal than fair labor contracts or testifying in court. The sullen expectations white people placed upon freedpeople's emotional as well as physical lives often stunted their ability to reimagine the world and their place within it. So many of Reconstruction's battles took place in the realm of the imagination and involved the deployment of emotional weaponry like rage, sympathy, grief, and love. And happiness. Happiness was unpredictable. It might come in great waves, like when a mother found the child who had been sold away from her decades before. Other times it trickled down in small drops—a new dress, a wagon ride into town, sleeping under the same roof as your spouse. These were the moments by which a person measured their freedom.

And what about Priscilla's happiness? The war's end did not bring any peace to the Joyner household. As the white Joyner children grew older, they continued to single her out for abuse. Perhaps they saw how their white neighbors and family members treated freedpeople and did the same to Priscilla. Children learn the lessons of racial etiquette early, and Reconstruction no doubt reinforced ones they may have already learned about the necessity of violence to keep Black people in their place.

"I was pretty unhappy most of the time," Priscilla admitted, "except when mother would come in and talk to me at nights." Ann Eliza would hold her close and stroke her hair until Priscilla fell asleep.[6]

These moments were the few times Priscilla felt at peace. Although she often spoke with ambivalence about "Miss Ann Liza," the memory of these talks at night alone in her room stood out against the pain the other children caused. But we might still wonder why Ann Eliza was unable to control the other children's behavior and keep them from ganging up on Priscilla. Was she a poor disciplinarian, or did the children's mean treatment of Priscilla serve her purpose in some way by making Priscilla more dependent on her for what little love and affection she received? Whichever it was (and perhaps it was both), Priscilla's happiness was not to be found in the Joyner household.

She might not have found it among her own people either. Dora Franks was a mixed-race child whose father was the "young master"— the plantation owner's son, a fact her mother never kept from her. It would have been difficult to hide the fact that Dora had a different father than her mother's other children, who all had much darker skin than she did. Her mother's forthrightness may have saved Dora the uncertainty that bothered Priscilla so much, but both girls still experienced life as an outsider. "Lord, it's been my sorrow many a time," Franks recalled, "because the children used to chase me round and holler at me, 'Old Yellow Nigger.' They didn't treat me good neither."[7]

While the teasing and name-calling wounded Franks, it's not clear from her narrative if it was simply because the young master was her father, or if her white grandmother, the mistress of the plantation, favored her. "I stayed in the house most of the time with Miss Emmaline," Franks admitted. The woman taught the young girl how to spin and weave cloth, highly prized skills that would have elevated Franks's position in any slaveholding household. Although neither the grandmother nor other members of the white family openly acknowledged that Franks was their blood kin, they seemed to dote on her and "wouldn't allow nobody to hurt [her]." When the plantation cook, an "old black woman" as Franks described her, struck the young girl in the face when she asked for a piece of "white bread like the white folks eat," Franks immediately showed Miss Emmaline her bloody nose.

Incensed, Miss Emmaline ordered the cook to be whipped "so hard she couldn't walk anymore," according to Franks. This kind of preferential treatment, along with the fact that Franks used her favored position to exact punishment on another enslaved person, may have motivated the other children's meanness toward her.[8]

Franks's story highlights not only the manipulative power of white slaveholding women but also the ways that power could corrode relationships among enslaved people. Children can be spiteful. It's not difficult to imagine how Priscilla might have used her relationship with Ann Eliza in ways that encouraged the other children's negative behavior toward her. She may also have viewed the local Black community the same way Franks did the Black cook who denied her the piece of bread she wanted—as someone who was beneath her. Both Dora Franks and Priscilla Joyner were children pulled between two worlds and who suffered immensely because of their proximity to white slaveholding women.

· —— ·

Emancipation was nothing if not an existential crisis. As once proud enslavers questioned what good was life if they had to do their own cooking, cleaning, and planting, freedpeople wondered how good life might be now that they could do their own cooking, cleaning, and planting. There were so many new and exciting and terrifying possibilities. What should they do first? Where should they go? What if they made the wrong decision?

Some people seemed to know the answers to these questions instinctively, as if they had been planning their next steps for years. But many did not. Seventy-five years later, Mose Davis could still picture his father running into their cabin "waving his arms like a windmill," shouting, 'Boy, we is free—you can go and get yourself a job 'cause I ain't going to hitch up no more horses.'" Davis's father knew what he was *not* going to do anymore. But beyond that, some freed-people found it difficult to imagine the kinds of living they might do.[9]

Mary Lindsey had been owned by a woman who removed her from Indian Territory to Texas during the war. Far from her family and friends, she continued to work for her in exchange for room and board. One day a young freed boy came by and told Mary that he was going to work for a white family in Bonham, ten miles away, that would pay him $1/week. He told her of other local freedpeople she knew who had gone there for work. He encouraged her to go, too. But Mary couldn't seem to muster the courage she needed to follow him. She continued to work for her former mistress, but she couldn't stop thinking about Bonham. Each day, when her work was done, she walked to the end of the property and looked out toward the town, imagining she was there "or some other place," dreaming about the possibilities that might await her. This went on for a period of time. Finally, she decided to go. She threw her few clothes in a bundle and walked the ten miles to Bonham under cover of darkness, fearful of alerting her employer.[10]

Once she arrived in town, Mary continued looking over her shoulder. Maybe she expected the old lady to send someone after her, as she would have in the old days. Time went by, but no one came. Still, she couldn't shake the feeling that she had done something wrong and that she'd have to pay the price. Old thoughts, like old habits, died hard. "I keep on being afraid, because I couldn't get it out of my mind I still belong to Mistress," she confessed.[11]

Robert Glenn, a freedman in rural Butler County, Kentucky, also spoke of the difficulty in breaking those old ways of thinking when he was interviewed by the FWP. He spent several years figuring out what he wanted to do now that he no longer had to serve the man who once owned him. Should he go back to North Carolina, where he was born, to find his family? Should he try to get a job and earn some money, maybe in a city like Louisville or Nashville? Glenn couldn't make up his mind, so he spent his free time rambling in the

woods and thinking. The long walks helped loosen his mind gradually. "I took my freedom by degrees," as he put it.[12]

A little at a time—that seemed to be the safest way to do it. Glenn
had lived alone with his former owner since he was nine years old on
a small farm in a fairly remote, rolling part of central Kentucky. He
knew no other enslaved people. His former master was now elderly,
and Glenn felt the need to remain "obedient and respectful" to him.
After all, the man had taught him to read, a rare and precious gift
for an enslaved person. So, while Glenn "thoroughly enjoyed being
free," it was only when he was alone, walking in the woods or sitting
by himself late at night, that he could indulge in the fantasy world
of freedom. "After I retired at night I made plan after plan and built
aircastles as to what I would do." Glenn's evocative description of his
imaginative wanderings, both in the woods and in his mind, give us a
glimpse of a contemplative young man who by necessity had become
accustomed to solitude and found some measure of peace in it.[13]

Other freedpeople felt similarly about the restorative power of
movement. The very act of moving, of putting one leg in front of the
other, without need of a pass or anyone's permission, stimulated the
senses and ignited the imagination. The war had set in motion streams
of migration: soldiers, refugees, contrabands, deserters, freedom seekers of all kinds. The war ended, but the movement did not. "I remember so well, how the roads was full of folks walking and walking along
when the niggers was freed," recalled Robert Falls, a freedman from
Cleveland County, North Carolina. "Didn't know where they was
going. Just going to see about something else, somewhere else."[14]

Falls said it was common, when you met someone on the road,
to pause a moment and share in that not wholly unpleasant sense of
uprootedness. You'd ask where they were going. They'd shrug and say
they didn't know. You'd nod, they'd nod, and you'd both walk on.

Falls told the FWP interviewer that this wanderlust was a crucial precursor to a greater awakening in his own mind about what he

wanted out of life. The other people he met on his journeys alerted him to new opportunities, and soon he began to realize that things could be different from what he had always known. "And then something begins to work up here," he said, touching his finger to his forehead. "I begins to think and to know things. And I knowed then I could make a living for my own self, and I never had to be a slave no more." After all the walking and talking and thinking, without an overseer's say-so, without any interference from his old master, it clicked: he was his own person.[15]

A freedperson's ability to come to this conclusion, and the quickness with which it happened, depended on many factors. How isolated were they? Did they know other emancipated people who shared their knowledge of freedom and the broader world? How old were they? If in their teens or younger and without any family or friends, the more reliant they would be on others, and the more beholden they might feel to their former owners. (The same could be true of elderly freedpeople who were unable to work and support themselves.) Glenn was only fifteen years old when the war ended. Mary Lindsey was about twenty years old and still felt unsure of the direction she should take. In the end, we must account for the effect of individual temperament when it came to wrapping one's head around freedom. Some people are more self-assured and possess confidence from a young age. They proceed on instinct and gut reaction. Others are more hesitant, even timid, and wait for others to lead the way. Regardless of their personalities, they faced momentous decisions that would shape the rest of their lives. For some, the burden of those decisions was heavy.

· —— ·

As the war drew to a close, journalists flocked to the South to capture the state of conditions there as well as the mood of its people. John Trowbridge, an antislavery writer and novelist who was more sympathetic to the plight of freedpeople than some of his contemporaries, investigated former slaveholders' complaints that ex-slaves were enjoying freedom too much—so much so, in fact, that they were becoming sullen and undisciplined. They seemed to have expected, the planters explained to Trowbridge, that freedom meant they would not have to work anymore, or at least not work for a white man anymore, and that the government would provide for them. When they realized that the government was not going to give them land and that their former owners would not allow them to dictate the conditions under which they worked, the freedpeople became angry, even riotous, and refused to work at all, according to the planters. As slaves, the planters assured Trowbridge, they never complained about working conditions, or the amount of food they received, or the quality of the shelters they lived in. They never talked back or sassed their owners, or any white people for that matter. They never demanded anything more or better than what their owners saw fit to give them. They smiled more. They were more courteous. They laughed and joked and seemed . . . well, happier.[16]

Trowbridge doubted this rosy view of slavery. He knew full well that these were old lies slaveholders told themselves and everyone else in order to deflect both guilt and criticism for their participation in a system they knew within their hearts was morally abhorrent. He and other antislavery writers in the decade before the war had pointed out that if enslaved people *seemed* happy, it was only because they dared not risk revealing their true feelings and facing a whipping or worse. Trowbridge marveled at the depth of former slaveholders' self-deceit on this matter, so wherever he traveled in those first few months after the war, he made a point to talk directly with freedpeople and put to them the slaveholders' proposition that they had been happier as slaves.

As a result of his investigation, Trowbridge concluded two things. The first was that freedpeople had expected a certain amount of happiness to be theirs as a result of emancipation. "They believed that the government which had been their Liberator would likewise be their provider: the lands of their Rebel masters were to be given them, and their future was to be licensed and joyous," Trowbridge wrote.[17]

Trowbridge did not fault them for this assumption. Given that all they had ever known was unrequited toil, he did not find it unreasonable that ex-slaves should desire some joy out of life now that they were no longer compelled to work under threat of the lash. The problem, he thought, was that some pursued such pleasures in excess and thought their lives in freedom would be nothing more than "a Christmas frolic."[18]

Still, he found those who shirked honest work by turning to "vice and vagrancy" to be a small percentage of the whole, and certainly no worse than white people. "I am not aware that the negro has any more love for work than another man," he admitted.[19]

Trowbridge's second conclusion went to the heart of what he believed made freedpeople truly happy. Unlike the momentary pleasures that had accompanied freedom's first moments—one imagines Mose Davis's father hollering and waving his arms—Trowbridge concluded that once they expressed these initial raw emotions, the majority of freedpeople would settle down and come to embrace a joy that slavery had denied them. After observing freedmen working their own farms in Virginia, Trowbridge wrote: "Those appear most thriving and happy who are at work for themselves."[20]

Trowbridge's observations on the state of freedpeople's emotional lives are striking. He acknowledges that enslaved people expected to be happy once freed and rightly so. He also recognized that their ideas about happiness may have been different from what others, most notably their former owners, envisioned for them. But his constricted view of Black joy, or the more "sensuous" expressions of excitement and exaltation at the end of slavery, as frivolous and contrary to the real work of freedom, reveals an important insight into what white northerners thought should be the emotional work of reconstructing the nation. In order to remake the South's economic and political system in the image of the industrial, democratic North, freedpeople's emotional lives, their expectations for happiness, indeed their very understanding of what it meant to be happy, would need to be reconstructed, too. Even white allies like Trowbridge believed freedpeople's desires would have to be harnessed so that they could be driven in pursuit of the greater goals of reviving the South's large-scale agricultural production and its place in the lucrative and expanding global cotton market.

This meant that freedpeople would be expected to work the land for others in much the same way they had before emancipation. Of course, they would now be paid wages—a crucial break with the past that cannot be overstated. But freedpeople often had no choice but to work for white landowners. The Freedmen's Bureau oversaw a new system of contract labor whereby freedpeople agreed to perform farm labor on a part of the owners' land in exchange for a place to live and wages to be paid monthly or at the end of the year. Landowners tried to wring as much work out of freedpeople as they could in these arrangements, and they tended to write up the agreements as if slavery, in spirit if not form, still existed. Local contracts classed them "hands" by age and experience and paid differential sums accordingly.

It was not uncommon for owners to dock a sick worker up to twenty-five cents per day as well as levy unspecified "fines and forfeitures" for any other lost time. The cost of any seed, livestock, tools, or any other provision, including food and clothing, would be deducted from a worker's wages. Workers also had to pay to have their cotton ginned and bagged. By the time Christmas rolled around, when it was time to settle up, workers often found they owed the planters money instead of the other way around.[21]

Freedpeople at first relished the new cash economy. Although cash was scarce, wage labor enabled freedpeople to buy things: new clothes, good food, jewelry, household items, and perhaps most importantly, time to enjoy these things and each other. Long before freedom, enslaved people had cultivated a sense of individuality through consumer activities. In his analysis of plantation store ledgers, historian Ted Ownby notes how enslaved people who had earned money by selling garden produce or hiring out their time tended to buy nonutilitarian items often with "touches of the luxurious and fantastic." They were often drawn to novelty items or bits of finery that allowed them to express themselves, add comfort to their lives, and exercise choice outside of their owners' control. They also chose items to make their living conditions more comfortable.[22]

"Marster would let us work at odd times for outsiders and us could use the money for anything us pleased," Prince Johnson, who had been named in honor of Queen Victoria's husband, Prince Albert, fondly recalled. "My gran'ma sold enough corn to buy her two feather beds," he added.[23]

Planters and other white observers didn't always appreciate the importance of having money to spend and being able to choose what to buy with it. After the war, some freedpeople continued to enjoy buying inessential goods despite the constant admonitions from whites to save their money. A frustrated northern "carpetbagger" who had moved to Louisiana after the war to run a plantation reported that one of his field hands had spent all of his seasonal earnings ($150) within ten days of receiving it. To the planter's dismay, all the freedman had to show for it was "the greatest lot of trash you ever saw." He did not elaborate on what the freedman and his family actually bought, but he begrudgingly admitted that the freedman and his wife and children "were satisfied and happy." When the planter asked him why he didn't save some of his money, the freedman asked a different question: "What's the use of living if a man can't have the good of his labor?"[24]

To the freedman and his family, these purchases were little joys that brought some beauty, comfort, and pleasure into their lives. This essential difference in outlook always meant that freedpeople would seem unprepared for freedom in the eyes of most white people, even those like Trowbridge and the northern planter, who professed to be their allies. Against the odds, some freedpeople did, in fact, manage to scrape and save what money they could, and some even became landowners. Many others lost their life savings when the Freedmen's Bank, a savings initiative for emancipated slaves set up by Congress but plagued by mismanagement and fraud, folded in 1874. Yet the presumption that freedpeople were "unready" for freedom because they remained impoverished, or because they might, from time to time, choose to purchase "frivolous" items, shaped white perceptions of Black behavior and the larger problems of Reconstruction.

·——·

LIVING SO CLOSELY to the people who just recently owned you—and in most cases believed they still should—imbued routine, everyday interactions with alarming volatility. The archives of the Freedmen's Bureau are replete with reports of violence stemming from the most mundane things, such as walking down the road, going to school, or going to work. A cursory list of weapons used in some of the most common assaults against freedpeople attest to the way that violence could erupt almost anywhere: an axe, a hoe, a hoe handle, a four-pound weight, a fence rail, a shovel, a piece of board, a brick. White people attacked with whatever was at hand.

Many of these assaults occurred over questions of labor. When Sylvia Parker, a freedwoman living in Wilmington, North Carolina, ran into John Lawrence on the street, she took the opportunity to ask him about the money he owed her. Lawrence, a white man, had hired her to pick cotton in late summer. Now it was nearly January, and he still hadn't paid her. Lawrence denied that he owed her anything, but Parker insisted he did. She also told Lawrence twice that "he had not done right by her." The remark offended him greatly. Lawrence became so enraged that a Black woman had publicly impugned his integrity that he began beating her "upon the head and arms" with a stick he found lying nearby.[25]

Even something as silly as some teenagers throwing snowballs took on greater significance during Reconstruction. It rarely snowed in Wilmington. In early January 1867, however, the white stuff covered the ground. The local Freedmen's Bureau agent observed a "party of [white] boys & men" enjoying "the diversion of attacking everyone who passed white & Black with snowballs." Based upon testimony from many witnesses that day, the agent felt that the group was just having some fun.[26]

That is until Amos Spruill, a freedman, happened by and was hit by a snowball. He protested, and the gang began chasing him down the street, pelting him as he ran. When they caught up to him, several of the whites became violent, kicking and punching him. One even drew a pistol and threatened to shoot him. The agent's report concluded that Spruill "took offense and resented in abusive language which the defendants also resented by an unjustifiable assault." However, the agent placed most of the blame on Spruill for taking offense at what the agent perceived to be a harmless bit of fun. Although the snowball throwers may have overreacted by assaulting Spruill, the agent believed that if the freedman had just kept his emotions in check and his mouth shut, all the trouble could have been avoided.[27]

The agent's expectation that freedpeople should just silently endure white hostility was not unique. Both southern whites and northern men like those who worked for the Freedmen's Bureau were united in the belief that the biggest problem facing the postwar South was the emotional character of freedpeople. Charles Soule, an army captain in charge of overseeing labor contracts between freedmen and landowners in South Carolina, made this clear in a letter to his superior in Washington in which he explained the difficulties he faced. "Even where they are satisfied that the idea of freedom comprehends law, order, and hard labor," Soule wrote, "there are many whom the absence of the usual restraint and fear of punishment renders idle, insolent, vagrant and thievish."[28]

Insolence was a common complaint about freedpeople's demeanors. Encompassing a wide range of expressions and behaviors, insolence, along with impudence, signaled a freedperson's unwillingness to play by slavery's old emotional rules. An Edgecombe County planter demanded that the freedpeople he employed exhibit "prompt and cheerful obedience to the manager" and forbade "cursing and swearing." For others, freedpeople didn't have to say a word. "The town is becoming more crowded with 'freedmen' every day and their insolence increases with their numbers," complained one alarmed Georgia woman.[29]

Although she did not elaborate as to what exactly freedpeople were doing that worried her so, other white southerners complained that their former slaves met their gaze directly, refused to move off the sidewalk or path when they encountered each other on the street, or simply ignored them. These nonverbal cues petrified former slave owners who still expected Black people to be all smiles and deference. "Things are coming to such a pass that it is unsafe for ladies to walk on the street," the Georgia woman declared. "Every available house is running over with them, and there are some quarters of the village where white people can hardly pass without being insulted."[30]

These everyday interactions became the basis of a widespread movement to remove freedpeople from public life in the South through violence. In the late 1860s and early 1870s, what had begun as sporadic and largely unorganized episodes of intimidation became a full-fledged campaign of terrorism. Paramilitary organizations like the well-known Ku Klux Klan and the lesser-known White League, which supplanted the Klan in Deep South states like Louisiana and South Carolina in the 1870s, staged coups of Republican-led state and local governments and claimed hundreds if not thousands of Black lives. Led by former Confederate officers, these units rallied people in rural communities by manipulating the Georgia woman's discomfort with the way former slaves behaved toward her and other white people. Calling upon all white men to unite against "the supreme danger" posed by emancipation, the White League argued that only violence could correct the temperamental nature of Black people that so threatened the South's social order. "It is with some hope that a timely and proclaimed union of the whites as a race, and their efficient preparation for any emergency, may arrest the threatened horrors of social war, and teach the Blacks to *beware of further insolence and aggression*, that we call upon the men of our race to leave in abeyance all lesser considerations," declared the first White League organized in Opelousas, Louisiana.[31]

The White League in Louisiana would go on to murder, torture, and terrorize freedpeople and their white supporters throughout the state, culminating in the violent takeover of the state government, then located in New Orleans, in 1874. Although federal troops reinstalled the duly elected Republican governor for a brief time, the violence in Louisiana inspired similar campaigns in Mississippi in 1875 and South Carolina in 1876, both ultimately leading to the white "redemption" of those states and the end of Reconstruction.

White terrorism stripped emancipated people of what political power and economic independence they had managed to scrape up from the ruins of slavery. Despite the unforgiving circumstances facing them, freedpeople had gained the right to vote and exercised it with stunning efficacy, electing Ulysses S. Grant president not once but twice, as well as ushering in Black officeholders at the county, state, and national level. Many also managed to become landowners. In the eyes of the White League, this simply would not do. Acting as the strong arm of the Democratic Party in those states, heavily armed White Leaguers kept Black voters from the polls through intimidation and, when necessary, murder.[32]

The White League also hoped to cause an emotional readjustment for those who exhibited impatience, frustration, and anger at the way white people treated them as well as pride and happiness in their own accomplishments, families, and communities. The White League and their supporters were incensed as much about the way freedpeople felt as they were about how they voted. Their belief that Black anger imperiled white society reflected long-standing racial dogma regarding emotions.

For nearly five hundred years, Europeans had justified their kidnapping and enslavement of people of African descent in part on the idea that Black people did not feel the same way white people did. They did not love their children or each other as deeply. Their emotional attachments were shallow, simplistic, and fleeting. In *Notes on the State of Virginia*, Thomas Jefferson elaborated on what he perceived as the emotional differences between white and Black people. While Black people exhibited great "ardor" when it came to the physical expression of affection, their feelings fell short of the kind of committed love that white people exhibited for their spouses and families. "Love seems with them to be more an eager desire, than a delicate mixture of sentiment and sensation," he claimed.[33]

Any "griefs" slaves felt, and he surely witnessed many among the four hundred people enslaved at his home at Monticello, including several of his own children, were "transient." The loss of a spouse or child to death or sale might produce intense expressions of grief in the moment, Jefferson acknowledged, but they were "sooner forgotten" and thus, "less felt" by Black people.[34]

It doesn't really bother them. That's how enslavers assuaged any guilt they might have felt when they tore mothers from children on the auction block. If enslaved people were incapable of forming any deep and lasting personal attachments, then any grief they exhibited would be short-lived. Enslavers like Jefferson also conveniently overlooked how they restricted enslaved people's ability to express feelings that contradicted that myth. A woman who cried too hard or too long after a child was sold might be threatened with the sale of her other children. A man who could not find the strength to get up and go to the field after his wife died would be whipped. Parents dared not protest any punishment the master deemed suitable for their children. "Many a day my ole mama has stood by and watched massa beat her children 'till they bled and she couldn't open her mouth," recalled Caroline Hunter.[35]

Enslaved people had little choice but to silently endure whatever heartache came their way. Emancipation changed that. Now you could tell a white man he wasn't treating you right, as Sylvia Parker did when she ran across the employer who owed her money. But as Parker found out, such emotional release was not without its cost. Freedom altered the rules of emotional engagement in the South, and members of the charter generation often found themselves unsure of what they were.

Anger was a particularly dangerous emotion. There is a story within the FWP interviews, a folktale told by different narrators from different places, of a slave who made the mistake of cussing the master within his earshot. Usually another slave encouraged this behavior as a kind of prank. Ed McCrory brought the tale into the post-emancipation period. In his telling, two old freedmen, both named Joe, stayed on to work with McCrory's master, a man named Ed Mobley.

According to McCrory, one day Joe Murray let the cows get into the cornfield. The old master cussed him out before all the field hands as they came in to eat dinner. Humiliated, Joe Murray grieved about it to everyone once they sat down to eat. Joe Raines—the other Joe—gave Murray some advice: "Next time he cuss you, do like I do, just cuss him back. This is a free country . . . just give him as good a cussin' as he gives you."[36]

A few days later Joe Murray got his chance. The hogs got out of the gate, and as he tried to round them up, Ed Mobley "lit out on him." But this time, Joe Murray gave as good as he got. When he finished, Master Ed gave Joe Murray a "slavery time whippin'." After Murray related what happened, Raines pointed out his mistake. "You didn't cuss him right," Joe Raines told Joe Murray. "When I cuss Master

Ed," Raines explained, "I goes way down in the bottoms where the corn grow high . . . I looks east and west and north and south. I see no Master Ed. Then I pitches into him and gives him de worst cussin' a man ever give another man."[37]

The story was Ed McCrory's way of showing how little had changed since emancipation. Everyone still called Ed Mobley "Master." He could cuss you all day long, but if you cussed him back and he heard it, you'd get whipped. Former enslavers despised freedpeople for showing anything other than gratitude or what they called the "old attachment" enslaved people had ostensibly felt for their owners during slavery.[38]

"Do they still seem to retain any of their former attachment?" Charles Jones asked his mother when she wrote to him to complain about how many of the "servants" refused to stay on and continue working as before. The Jones family, prominent Georgia planters who owned three large cotton plantations near Savannah, was dumbfounded that their former slaves would choose to go elsewhere. They were particularly offended when they just up and left—no notice and no goodbyes.[39]

"Adeline, Grace, and Polly have all departed in search of freedom, without bidding any of us an affectionate adieu," wrote Jones's wife, Eva, to her mother-in-law. The freedwomen's refusal to participate in Eva Jones's emotional charade confounded their former mistress. They obviously felt no obligation to feign affection for Jones or to seek her blessing as they departed. No doubt wishing to avoid a confrontation with a woman who expected their continued deference, Adeline, Grace, and Polly packed their bags in the night and left while Jones slept.[40]

The women's behavior became evidence of the post-emancipation "mania" that whites feared had unleashed freedpeople's volatile tempers. A study of Black inmates in southern mental asylums after the

Civil War found that the vast majority of those people were institutionalized for exhibiting behaviors such as anger, aggression, and "excitability." Physicians and asylum wardens commented on the perceived increase in these behaviors among freedpeople and attributed their prevalence to "a bestial madness borne of freedom." In the last decades of the nineteenth century, as the study of human psychology slowly developed into a legitimate branch of medical science, professional understandings of diseases of the mind reflected the racial attitudes of American society at large. For instance, melancholia, the nineteenth-century term for depression, became a diagnosis reserved primarily for whites. Institutionalized African Americans, on the other hand, were more likely to be diagnosed with "mania"—the clinical term for what the White League called "insolence" and a crucial step in the criminalization of Blackness.[41]

With their emotional responses under such scrutiny, it is little wonder that many members of the charter generation interviewed by the FWP recalled feeling cautious and unsure about what to do. W. L. Bost, a freedman living in Asheville, North Carolina, put it this way: "After the war was over we was afraid to move. Just like tarpins [terapins] or turtles after emancipation. Just stick our heads out to see how the lands lay."

Susan High recalled how her father struggled to keep his family housed and fed after their former owner "turned him out with a crowd of children without a thing." The work and worry wore him down and tempered the feelings of joy that may have come with emancipation.

"Daddy said he was proud of freedom," she said, "but was afraid to own it."[42]

It took a while for some members of the charter generation to "own" their freedom and pursue it unreservedly. For Priscilla, who was still a young girl, it wasn't yet clear what owning it would mean. Regardless of her actual legal status before the war, as long as she stayed in Ann

Eliza's household, where the white Joyner children could torment and abuse her, freedom meant very little. She had no people. And being peopleless, whether enslaved or free, was one of the worst things that could happen to a Black person, especially in the lean, perilous years of Reconstruction. If Priscilla Joyner were to ever feel the joy of true freedom, she would have to find her people.

FIVE

FREEDOM HILL

. —— .

T HE NEWS CAME as a shock. Priscilla had no idea Ann Eliza had been thinking of sending her away. In all of their secret nighttime conversations, they had never discussed it. Ann Eliza was clearly upset it had come to this. The night before she told Priscilla the news, she had sobbed uncontrollably, but the girl didn't understand why. Ann Eliza probably worried about Priscilla's safety. The boys, Robert and Jolly, were getting older and were directing their aggression toward her. Even the girls, Margaret and Mourning, had not softened to Priscilla. It seemed she had no choice but to find a safe haven for the girl.

To Priscilla, though, it may have seemed that she was being cast out. Ten miles away from the Joyner place, Rocky Mount may as well have been the moon. With its stores and trains, hotels and saloons, the depot town could seem both alluring and terrifying. She knew no one there. Where would she live? What would school be like? None of the Joyner children had ever been to school. At twelve, Priscilla could neither read nor write. What would the other children make of her? Would they treat her any better than her own brothers and sisters? For all their bullying, her half-siblings were the only family she knew, and the little farm was her whole world.

Ann Eliza tried to convince Priscilla the move was for her own good, that she would have a fine time at school with other children *like her*, and that they wouldn't be mean to her. She assured Priscilla that she was doing this because she loved her, and that the farm would always be her home.

"And she told me a lot of other things—how I must not forget that I was as good as anybody else—how much she loved me—and how I was always to remember that this was my house," Priscilla recalled. "Then she told me that she was going to see to it that I was taken care of."

"The house and this place will be yours someday," Ann Eliza told her, "and you are going to have the biggest share of my money."

But Ann Eliza's assurances gave little comfort to Priscilla as she packed a trunk with her few belongings and faced setting off into the world on her own. It may not have been particularly loving or welcoming, but the farm was the only home she had ever known. Her thoughts may have drifted to a younger girl, possibly her sister, Ida, who had been born in 1866. Priscilla had not seen her for quite some time. Priscilla never mentioned her in the interview with Dunston, although she did name one of her daughters Ida. Like Priscilla, Ida was mixed-raced. Rix had died in the closing weeks of the war, leaving the identity of Ida's father a mystery to us, just like it was for Priscilla. Unlike Priscilla, however, it appears Ida did not live long with Ann Eliza, who was listed as her biological mother on Ida's 1948 death certificate. By 1870, she was living in neighboring Edgecombe County with a man named Jim Price and his wife, Roberta, and an eight-year-old boy named Duke. Whether Ida or Duke had biological connections to either of the Prices is unknown. What is known is that Jim raised Ida as his daughter and was listed as her father on her 1884 marriage license. Jim and Roberta Price were Black.[1]

The same questions about her true identity swirl around Ida just as they do for Priscilla. Was the girl Ann Eliza's biological daughter, or was she another Black child who had been bound out to her by the state? Forced apprenticeship remained a feature of post-emancipation labor, yet another way slavery's shadow cast darkness upon the light of freedom. Whatever Ida's true origins, it appears Ann Eliza thought about her upbringing differently than she had about Priscilla's. By the time Ida came along, Ann Eliza was no longer determined she could—or should—raise the child herself. A lot had happened since Priscilla had been born. Ann Eliza was now a widow. The war was over, but times were still hard. Ann Eliza's prized farm was now valued at a mere $198, and she claimed only fourteen dollars in personal property. The thought of another mouth to feed may have terrified the woman who was barely holding her life and family together. And with slavery now abolished and Reconstruction underway, the state authorities policed the apprenticing of Black children more than they ever had before. If a Black child's parents came forward to challenge a white person's claim on them or their labor, the Freedmen's Bureau would take the charge seriously.[2]

But other questions, many of them unanswerable, linger about her choice. How did Ann Eliza know the Prices? Was Jim Price Ida's father? Was he Priscilla's? Why in the course of her otherwise detailed interview does Priscilla never mention Ida? If Ann Eliza had given the baby away as soon as she was born, then Priscilla, who would have been eight at the time, may not have even realized what had happened. The silences in the historical record make this story a difficult one to piece together, and most importantly, they made it difficult for Priscilla and Ida to know who they were and where they belonged.

Ann Eliza had finally come to the decision that she could not give Priscilla what she needed, a decision possibly hastened by Ida's arrival and subsequent departure from the Joyner home. Even if Priscilla did not know about or understand Ida's situation, the move to Rocky Mount was upsetting. Ann Eliza's deceit compounded the sense of upheaval. Priscilla would not stay long in Rocky Mount, a fact she only realized some months later. When Jolly Bowen, who Priscilla described as "one of the colored men who stayed with us after freedom," drove her to town in the buggy, it was only to hand her off to her new guardian, a detail that Ann Eliza had not divulged.

"I later found out that mother had given me to Mrs. Harriett Dancy, of Tarboro," Priscilla explained.

Dancy and her husband, Glenn, a blacksmith, lived in the all-Black enclave known at the time as Freedom Hill, a settlement of freedpeople on land once owned by a prominent Edgecombe County slaveholder, L. L. Dancy. Many Freedom Hill residents were named Dancy, a testament to their ties to the land and their shared kinship. L. L. Dancy saw it differently. In his mind, they still belonged to him, by proximity if not by law.

It was spring when Priscilla arrived at the Dancys' home, and school would not begin until the fall. In the meantime, she would have to work for her keep. Despite Ann Eliza's claims of having money, she apparently did not have enough to pay the Dancys for Priscilla's lodging and board. The 1870 census listed Priscilla as a "domestic servant" in the Dancy household.

If Priscilla felt hard done by this change in her circumstances, she didn't say. There were other lodgers living with the Dancys, including an apprentice blacksmith named Henry Thompson and a twenty-one-year-old student named Robert Spaulding. Unlike Priscilla or Thompson, Spaulding held $200 in real estate. He may have also had money to support himself while living with the Dancys, as no occupation other than "attending school" is listed for him on the census. Where would a freedman get such financial support?

A look at Spaulding's life ten years later in 1880 gives us a clue. That year, Spaulding and his wife Annie were farming a small plot in Columbus County, about a hundred and seventy miles southwest near the South Carolina border. In 1860, there was only one slaveholder in

Columbus County with the surname Spaulding—Emmanuel Spaulding, who owned seven people, including a ten-year-old boy. Ten years later that boy, most likely Robert, would make his way to Tarboro, to live alongside the growing community of freedpeople at Freedom Hill and attend the school. If Emmanuel Spaulding gave young Robert the plot of land out of a sense of duty or guilt, or because Robert was his son, we cannot know. What is clear is that Freedom Hill beckoned to the young man, offering him the opportunity to better himself, to live and work among like-minded people. Harriett and Glenn Dancy welcomed Robert Spaulding into their home and eased his way into the new world of freedom. They would do the same for Priscilla.

. —— .

THE LITTLE COMMUNITY of Freedom Hill sat on the eastern bank of the Tar River where it bends southward on its meandering journey to join the wider Pamlico River before emptying out into the Atlantic Ocean at the Outer Banks. Incorporated in 1885 as Princeville, in honor of one of its founders, a carpenter and freedman named Turner Prince, it is the oldest Black town in the United States. But in 1870, when Priscilla arrived in neighboring Tarboro, less than a mile away on the other side of the river, to live with the Dancys, it was still just a loose settlement of freedpeople. Five years earlier, a New York cavalry regiment had occupied Tarboro for a few days as they made their way from New Bern to Raleigh at the end of the war. Some of the soldiers had camped along the banks of the Tar on L. L. Dancy's land. Local freedpeople earned money washing, cooking, and selling vegetables and milk to the troops. They listened as some of the officers read the Emancipation Proclamation and then advised them to stay put and work for their former owners, which many of them did, at least at first.[3]

While the overwhelming majority of its residents remained domestic servants five years after emancipation, Freedom Hill was also home to an impressive mix of artisans and skilled workers. Mary Carlyle made her living as a seamstress. Frank Dancy was learning how to be a blacksmith. Matthew Clark made mattresses. There were no fewer than ten carpenters and carpenters' apprentices living there, including town founder Turner Prince. David Harris was a brick mason. Within ten years, the ranks of craftspeople and entrepreneurs would grow to include a sawmill operator, several independent grocers, numerous washerwomen, painters, shoemakers, three nurses, and a prostitute.[4]

Like other "African villages" that sprang up in emancipated areas across the South, tents and shanties made of discarded materials dotted the landscape. Inside these makeshift shelters, however, freedpeople made the world anew. They organized schools and churches, prepared meals at communal "cook-houses," stabled their livestock, and created communities that missionaries and government officials admired for their "neatness, comfort, and order." Most remarkable, according to one official, were the gardens. Although the Black settlements usually rested on the poorest land, freedpeople's ability to coax an abundance of life out of the rockiest, sandiest soil astonished all those who witnessed it. "In some cases, their corn, fifteen feet high, quite overtopped their houses," wrote the federal officer in charge of the Trent River settlement at New Bern.[5]

As successful as some of these villages were, they were vulnerable. When Confederates attacked New Bern in 1864, the Trent River settlement was all but destroyed. Settlements that were part of a larger army encampment might be ordered to evacuate at a moment's notice when the troops moved on. With their tents pulled up, provisions cut off, and no protection from hostile southern whites who surrounded them, freedpeople who had tried to make a home in these refugee camps were forced to start again somewhere else. White officials told themselves and each other that the people were used to being rootless and suffered little from being forced to move again and again.[6]

"The negro is always jolly," wrote the Trent River superintendent, "and when he is driven out of one home, he will 'tote' his small inventory of household stuff upon his head, until he finds a place in which to establish another. He goes forth like Abraham, journeying for 'de promus land.'" Even the professed "friends" of the freedpeople were not above mocking Black speech.[7]

The Freedom Hill people were fortunate in one respect. They had not been part of an established army camp. The Union cavalrymen who first arrived on the Dancy plantation in early July 1865 moved on quickly. By the end of the month, the men who had read the Emancipation Proclamation from a small rise on the riverbank that gave the community its name were on steamers bound for New York City. Any supplies the army might have handed out to the freedpeople were gone, but so was the threat of violence that came from white soldiers contemptuous of anyone with Black skin, or the sickness, smallpox, or other "camp fevers" that armies often brought with them wherever they went. The Freedom Hill people were on their own, and it was probably for the best. All those carpenters and their apprentices got to work constructing permanent shelters and repurposing old ones. There were no meddling missionaries or imperious superintendents around to "supervise" the construction of homes and other structures. A twentieth-century architectural survey of Princeville would note the predominant "saddle-bag" house: two log buildings joined around a central chimney. Most slave cabins had been saddle-bag-style dwellings because they were cheap to build and could house at least two families. Eventually, the formerly enslaved people at Freedom Hill remade these multifamily dwellings into single-family homes.[8]

Just across the river sat Tarboro. An important inland port for cotton planters shipping their bales to market, the town enjoyed the wealth that the trade in cotton and slaves had brought it. Fine houses adorned with colonnades and porticos and wrought-iron railings embracing wraparound porches flanked both sides of the now

A typical "saddle-bag" house in Princeville.
COURTESY OF THE NORTH CAROLINA STATE HISTORIC PRESERVATION OFFICE

Princeville c. 1940. The homes pictured probably date to the town's early days. They have since been demolished.
COURTESY OF THE NORTH CAROLINA STATE HISTORIC PRESERVATION OFFICE

*Originally a cider press, this was converted to a cotton press by Isaac Norfleet around
1860 to meet the growing demand for cotton. It was documented in 1936 as part of
the Historic American Building Survey, another New Deal project.*
COURTESY LIBRARY OF CONGRESS

fifteen-acre town common. Shaded by giant oaks, the common was
once as large as fifty acres when it was first established in 1760. It was
a place for picnics and barbeques, or just to promenade, to see and be
seen. In 1938, during the time the FWP interviewers were traversing
the area looking for elderly ex-slaves to interview, the white citizens of
Tarboro decided to move an old wooden cotton press to the common
so everyone could admire this important piece of local history that
whites remembered as the good old days.[9]

Plenty of freedpeople continued to live in Tarboro, including the
Dancys. It was only about a half mile away from Freedom Hill, within
easy walking distance, and the two communities, Black and white,
blended almost seamlessly at times. Freedom Hill folks crossed the
bridge over the river to attend school in Tarboro at St. Paul's AME
Church. Tarboro folks crossed over to Freedom Hill to visit friends

and relatives, to buy groceries, or to attend services at the new Zion Primitive Baptist Church. Some moved there permanently.

It was within this vibrant milieu of burgeoning freedom that Priscilla entered her adolescence. Living in town where all this life and activity circulated around her must have been intoxicating. She met so many new people, like Robert Spaulding, the Dancys' studious boarder, and his teacher, Mr. Robert Taylor, who had been born in Jamaica. And there was that young man, Lewis, who lived across the creek from the Dancys. He quickly became a fixture around the Dancy house. He always seemed to appear whenever Priscilla went outside for anything. Not that she minded. He was sweet, and she liked talking to him. He didn't curse or drink like a lot of the boys in town. He was five years older than Priscilla, but even at seventeen had the seriousness of someone much older.

Priscilla would soon come to think of the Dancys and the rest of the Tarboro/Freedom Hill community as her people. There she would come to know the deep sense of kinship that bound the freedpeople together. The feelings of alienation she had experienced in Ann Eliza's household soon began to evaporate as the Black community welcomed her as one of their own. How the realization came that she, too, was part of that collective, whether it was gradual or if there was a singular moment when she realized that she was a part of "we," she didn't say. "There is no better word than *we*," writes historian Ibram X. Kendi in his explanation of how the collective identity of Black Americans as a people became a salve against racism, terror, and violence throughout the centuries. The knowledge that you were not alone, that there was kinship and belonging even if there were no blood ties, empowered individuals to endure countless hardships, and more importantly, to imagine alternative ways of being.[10]

Freedom Hill grew quickly. By 1880, it had more than three hundred residents and comprised two enumeration districts on the census. When it became Princeville five years later, it had a mayor, five commissioners, a clerk, a treasurer, and a town constable. And there were flowers. In the yard of every saddle-bag house there were flower and vegetable gardens that earned Princeville the local honor of being known as "a town of flowers." "There is scarcely a dwelling in the place without them," noted the Tarboro *Southerner*. "The honeysuckle seems to be the most popular, though there are not a few roses. At this time of the year the air is laden with perfume."[11]

If the white residents of neighboring Tarboro were comforted by Princeville's modest beauty, it was not for them that the residents planted and sowed. The vegetables fed their families and brought in some much-needed cash when there was a surplus. On its way to becoming a fully independent Black community, the people of Freedom Hill (and later Princeville) worked hard to ensure their town's self-sufficiency and longevity. This was where they were from, and this is where they would stay. "Back in the day, I reckon, the slaves knew and my great-great-grandmother knew. They knew what they were moving here for," explained a lifelong Princeville resident in 2003.

After a devastating flood in 1999, the Federal Emergency Management Agency (FEMA) proposed a buyout for Princeville residents. The government would purchase their property at market value and "move" the town to another location away from the river. Most residents rejected the proposal. Accepting the buyout would have meant giving up something invaluable, something that simply could not be relocated. "They know—they knew," the resident said, blurring the line between past and present. "This was the town. This was home."[12]

. —— .

Leonidas Lafayette Dancy—"L.L." in his official correspondence or just "Lafayette" to his friends and family—was not the kind of man who relinquished control easily or with good humor. Although he jokingly informed the census taker in 1880 that he was a "gentleman of leisure," he had stayed busy the fifteen years since the end of the war with various designs to reassert his authority over the people he once owned and who now lived on land he and another planter, John Lloyd, had ceded to them. It was not unheard of for former slave owners to sell or even give land to former slaves, but it was usually not the best land. Dancy and Lloyd were no exceptions in this respect. The land on the banks of the Tar River was equal parts sodden and rocky. It flooded almost yearly and never yielded anything of much worth. No doubt Dancy told anyone who asked why he gave away his land to slaves that he was glad to be rid of it. Good luck making anything out of it, he probably thought.[13]

The Freedom Hill people surprised him, though. Slowly but surely, they built a town, not some slipshod settlement but a vibrant, living community with homes, stores, and industry. If he expected them to give up and move on, he was disappointed. Their efforts to stake a claim to the space he once ruled over like a feudal lord were relentless. But if they were tenacious, so was he. Eschewing the military traditions represented by both his namesakes, Leonidas Lafayette Dancy avoided Confederate service but nonetheless continued to act like he was a master. Never mind that in 1865 his only remaining taxable property was a carriage for which he owed the federal government one dollar. Like a drowning man clings to a life raft, Dancy clung to the belief that he alone had the right to define freedpeople's family relationships and dictate when and where they made homes, and that they owed him their labor, if not perpetually, then at least for a time.

He demanded their deference forever. In early January 1866, Dancy's attorney wrote to the local Freedmen's Bureau officer requesting his help in obtaining the return of a thirteen-year-old boy named Frank, one of his former slaves. Dancy explained that he had seen to Frank's care since his mother, a woman named Kate, had died when the boy was only two. Although the boy was now free, Dancy declared that he was "entitled"—his lawyer used that word several times—to

Frank's labor until he was twenty-one, as the state's apprenticeship laws allowed. However, Frank's sister, Lucy, and her husband, Ben, had other ideas. They had taken Frank to a nearby farm where they now worked and refused to return him to Dancy, despite their former owner's repeated entreaties. In his letter, Dancy's lawyer dismissed the notion that Lucy and Ben truly cared for young Frank or had any affective attachments to him. They only wanted his labor, the lawyer claimed without any hint of irony. He did not explain the source or the depths of his client's purported concern for the child's welfare, other than to say he had had the boy for eleven years since the mother had died. Was the child Dancy's son? Possibly, but he couldn't very well come out and say so. Short of declaring that he was, in fact, Frank's father, Dancy had little to convince the Freedmen's Bureau agent that he had legal rights to the child. No documents exist to say if Lafayette Dancy regained custodial authority over Frank, but it's unlikely given the efforts of the local Freedmen's Bureau agents to support Black families in similar situations.[14]

Dancy held no formal apprenticeship papers on Frank, which placed him at a disadvantage when it came to making his case to the Freedmen's Bureau. Other freed children were not as fortunate as Frank. Although Dancy seemed disinclined to apprentice any Black children himself now that he was a "gentleman of leisure," he appeared as a witness on behalf of white planters in no fewer than eight apprenticeship cases in the late 1860s and early 1870s. All of these children were listed as "orphaned" except one. In that case, the mother, Hetty Dancy, signed her mark to bond allowing her "illegitimate" daughter, Harriet, eight years old, to be apprenticed to Matthew Savage, a local farmer. By signing the affidavit attesting to the terms of the agreement, Lafayette Dancy swore that Hetty gave her daughter willingly and that neither he nor Savage had put any undue pressure on the woman to relinquish custody of the child. North Carolina law gave Edgecombe County the right to apprentice any child it deemed to be a burden to the state. Just as it had been before emancipation, orphaned and indigent children, illegitimate children, and Black children became targets for this still-legal form of unfree labor. It could be that Hetty felt she had no choice. With no money and no one to speak on her behalf—no lawyer, no white friends—what could she say? Who would listen?[15]

In at least one case, the Freedmen's Bureau interceded on behalf of Black parents like Hetty Dancy. In November 1866, a freedwoman, Emma, went to the home of David Sloan to demand that he release her four children. When he refused, she went to the local Freedmen's Bureau office in Sampson County and complained. Sloan insisted that the children had been bound out to him legally by the county court. The agent, however, ordered Sloan to deliver the children to Emma "at once." If he refused again, Emma was to report it to the agent "without delay." There is no evidence that Emma had to return to the office.[16]

. —— .

WHY DID THE Freedom Hill people choose to stay so close to their old plantation and to their former owner, a man who devoted himself to making their lives as difficult as possible? There is no evidence that Dancy was a particularly caring or generous slave owner. Aside from being a single man with no family of his own, Lafayette Dancy operated a plantation that resembled most other midsize plantations in the antebellum South. With real estate valued at $10,000 in 1860, and personal property worth $35,000, his was neither the smallest nor the largest plantation in Edgecombe County. His personal property had consisted mostly of thirty-nine enslaved people ranging in age from a month old to sixty-five.[17] Dancy was heavily invested in his enslaved workers' ability to have children; of those thirty-nine people, twenty-two of them were under the age of twelve. With such a young workforce, Dancy undoubtedly looked forward to years of profit and

growth. Nothing short of war would have stopped him from perpetu-
ating the system of brutality necessary to do so. Like other farming
operations, both large and small, that operated in the slave South
from the seventeenth through the nineteenth century, Dancy's might
be considered part of what some historians now term a "slave labor
camp," where forced labor and sexual exploitation organized daily life
in ways that the more genteel terminology often used to describe slavery in the United States masks and deflects.[18]

But what did the Freedom Hill people call it? Like freedpeople
throughout the South who chose to stay and build their lives on or
near the site of their enslavement, the Freedom Hill people called it
home. An important document that survived the tumult of Reconstruction reveals just how important it was for some freedpeople to be
able to call their old plantations home. In 1865, just months after the
war ended, a group of freedpeople on Edisto Island, South Carolina,
part of the Sea Islands of the southeastern coast, petitioned the government to allow them to stay on their old plantations even as their
former owners sought to evict them. Early in the war, the white owners
had fled the Sea Islands to escape the arrival of Union forces, leaving
most of the enslaved population behind. For more than three years,
those people had continued to farm, growing cotton for the federal
government and food for themselves. Once the war was over, however,
the original owners returned and insisted that the people either turn
the land back over to them or leave. In their petition to the superintendent of the Freedmen's Bureau, the Edisto Islanders explained their
attachment to these sites despite the cruelties they had endured there.
They laid claim to the plantations not simply because their former
owners had been disloyal and abandoned the land, but also because it
was *their* home, too. "We Have property In Horses, cattle, carriages,
& articles of furniture," they wrote, noting how their possession of
certain household items legitimized their claims of home.[19]

They had household objects, but they also had people—generational ties made them hesitant to leave, something they alluded to when they spoke of their desire for "land enough to lay our Fathers bones upon." The land of the plantation housed kin, both living and dead, and this fact often made freedpeople reluctant to leave.

"[L]and was not separate from the ex-slaves' sense of community," notes historian Julie Saville, and "attempts to maintain a link with particular land led some freedpeople to plant a patch on the old 'home place' after they took up residence elsewhere; others made the reverse arrangement." *Home place* was the term many freedpeople used when they talked about the land on which they had been enslaved.[20]

When the Edisto Islanders complained of being driven off the land, they feared not only the loss of their crops and livestock but also the dissolution of their families and their connections to the past, a past that was rooted in a particular place. "This is our home," they declared, "where we have toiled nearly all our lives."[21]

The Edisto Islanders' petition reflects a predicament among freedpeople who longed to make a home in the only place they had ever known, the former slave plantation. The land represented their economic livelihood. On it sat their physical shelters, which contained all their worldly possessions. This was where their kin, both living and dead, resided. This place held the memories of loved ones as well as the myriad traumas slavery inflicted upon them: forced separations, physical punishments, and unrequited toil. As enslaved people, the Edisto Islanders had been chained to the land, unable to leave, to choose to be elsewhere. Now, as freedpeople, they had a choice, but to them it seemed like no choice at all. "Their dilemma reminds us," writes Saville, "that they reckoned severance costly, even when part of freedom's price."[22]

Despite their best efforts to establish a new life elsewhere, some freedpeople found severance too costly. In his testimony to the FWP, Warren McKinney spoke of his mother's restlessness after they left their home place in South Carolina and made their way first to Augusta,

Georgia. Only a boy when the war ended, McKinney initially found all the moving chaotic. Life in Augusta was overcrowded and unpleasant. Times were hard; there was not enough work. The deprivation he had endured on the plantation near Winnsboro did not compare to the poverty he and his mother encountered in Augusta. As the stream of country migrants flowed into town, Augusta soon became plagued with consumption and cholera, and McKinney recalled seeing hearses stacked with half a dozen or more coffins going by outside the tenement where he and his mother lived with other refugees. All the death obviously left an impression on him. As white supremacist violence increased in the 1860s, people once again took to the road.[23]

More than anything, Warren McKinney wanted to settle down. Eventually, he and his mother made a home in Arkansas, where McKinney found plenty of work and even "voted some." It was a striking contrast to their life in Augusta. Despite this stability, McKinney's mother was dissatisfied. So, when their former master got in touch, he was able to persuade her to return to South Carolina, a decision McKinney never fully understood. Something pulled her back to the plantation to work for the same man who, McKinney recalled at the start of his interview, used to whip her until she cried. McKinney offers no explanation for his mother's decision to return to South Carolina. Perhaps she longed for the familiarity of the old place. Whatever her reasons, her son felt compelled to accompany her. He remained at her side for "four or five years" until she died, at which point he moved back to Arkansas and picked up his life again. He had lived there for the intervening fifty-six years until the FWP interviewer arrived at his door.[24]

McKinney's mother may have been pulled back to her home place in much the same way that later generations of southern Blacks who migrated to the urban north felt compelled to return despite the knowledge that little had changed in their absence. The ties that bind southern Blacks to the region often seem to "defy full human comprehension," writes anthropologist Carol Stack, who charted the reverse Great Migration among natives of the Carolinas in the latter half of the twentieth century. She estimates that across the region more than 100,000 Black Americans made the journey home. When asked why they gave up good jobs and decent housing in Philadelphia or New York to return to an economically stagnant rural area that seemed to offer so little in the way of inducement to return, the migrants spoke of a kind of "soul searching" that led them back home in search of community, history, and redemption. But their ruminations were anything but romanticized. The decision to return to the South was not an easy one and was made with the full understanding that it would entail considerable sacrifice. "Home is a hard fact," Stack explains, "not just a souvenir of restless memory, and for the people . . . who made the journey away and back, home is a hard land—hard to explain, hard to make a living in, hard to swallow."[25]

Perhaps Warren McKinney's mother returned to her former owner because he was her father or grandfather. Or perhaps he manipulated her feelings of pity or obligation like so many enslavers did in the aftermath of emancipation. Maybe she missed her kinfolk who had stayed and wanted to reunite with them toward the end of her life. Whatever her reasons, the decision to stay with her son in Arkansas or go back to the man who had once owned her involved intricate calculations that weighed competing motivations. Among these, the plantation's status both as a household and as a home place, a site of social and emotional relationships as well as economic ones, kept many ex-slaves rooted to places in ways that may seem unfathomable to twenty-first-century minds.

Like the Edisto Islanders and Warren McKinney's mother, the men and women of Freedom Hill were "home place people." Their community was based not only on blood but also on an expanded notion of kinship. Emancipation necessitated such an expansion, as freedpeople took in nieces, nephews, cousins, aunts, uncles, and other more distant relatives who needed shelter and support. Households grew to include many nonblood relations, too. The language of family shaped postwar labor relations on plantations as work crews often presented themselves as families in order to gain a foothold in a particular labor market, and employers likewise encouraged workers to invoke family connections as a way to expand their workforce.[26]

This sense of kinship confounded some white relief workers who worked among the freedpeople during and after the war. Elizabeth Botume, a Massachusetts-born woman who traveled to the Sea Islands to work as a teacher among the freedpeople, recalled an incident where the plantation women organized on behalf on an unwed expectant mother who faced ostracism from the northern whites there, including Botume, who held her in disrepute. The women wanted to gather a layette for the new baby and pressed Botume for assistance.

"What is she to you?" Botume asked the women, wondering why they put themselves out for another who was not blood kin. "Dey's all massa's niggers," the women replied. The shared experience of life on the plantation created a bond among plantation people forged in slavery but still useful, and even necessary, in freedom.[27]

As home place people, the residents of Freedom Hill and neighboring Tarboro nurtured a broad understanding of what it meant to be *kin*. Harriett and Glenn Dancy took in Priscilla as well as the two other youths. Harriett and Glenn Dancy's neighbors, the Sparrows, shared their home with two schoolteachers, W. T. Mabson and John W. Spaulding, possibly Robert Spaulding's older brother. A few houses down, two teenage sisters, Charietta and Harrietta Hyman, lived as domestic servants with the wheelwright John Lawrence and his wife. Like Priscilla, the sisters were most likely helping out in their host household until school began in the fall.

This broad conception of family had a profound effect on Priscilla. She may not have been their daughter, but the Dancys obviously cared for her a good deal. They bought her new clothes and made sure she was clean and presentable when she went to school. Priscilla's appearance made an impression on the Joyners back in Nash County when she would return for Christmas. "The children were all very polite to me," she said, noting the change in their behavior toward her. They "used to admire my starched dress and hair ribbons, and so on."

Dresses and ribbons were no small things to freedpeople. Former slaveholders often scoffed at their desire for little fineries. Even white missionaries who sincerely desired to assist the charter generation in their efforts to make a free life felt less than charitable when freedpeople refused castoffs and hand-me-downs. Mary Ames, a northern teacher who worked among the freedpeople in South Carolina, was shocked when a young girl returned a donated dress Ames had given her because it wasn't the right size. "Ma says it don't fit, and she don't want it," the girl told her. "It was rather larger and short," Ames admitted, "but she was very dirty and ragged, and we told her she must keep it."[28]

The desire for a nice dress that actually fit, however, was anything but frivolous. Enslavers used clothing to visually convey the debasement of the enslaved; coarse cloth dyed in drab colors signified undifferentiated lowliness. Tattered, poorly fitting garments, handed down and passed around from countless wearers, negated individuality. Alterations or adornments might help make an old dress one's own, but in this case, the young girl and her mother wanted something better. Their dignity and happiness demanded it. They no longer had to settle for what some white person saw fit to give them. Ames and other white people overseeing the transition from slavery to freedom might deny that freedpeople had a right to their desires, but as Priscilla's experience demonstrates, a new, clean dress, adorned with a colorful sash or bow, and a velvet ribbon in your hair could make a world of difference, not only in how other people saw you but also in how you saw yourself. This was the gift that the Dancys, and by extension the community of freedpeople in Tarboro and Freedom Hill, gave her.[29]

. —— .

NOT ONLY DID Priscilla look different, she acted different. She could read and write now, skills that Ann Eliza's white children still lacked. The creation of a free, state-sponsored public school system in the South was one of Reconstruction's greatest accomplishments. North Carolina had been a few steps ahead of many other slaveholding states where education was left to churches and private academies. The first state-funded "public" schools in North Carolina had opened in 1840, but of course, these weren't open to free Black students. All but a handful of those schools shut down during the war. Then in 1868, the new state constitution provided for the creation of a public school system that would be free to all children between the ages of six and twenty-one, including Black children. To fund this new system, the state levied local taxes, yet another reason many whites resented Reconstruction. They were indignant that their tax dollars would pay for Black children to go to school. And they flatly refused to send their children to school alongside the children of former slaves, so the progressive new school system quickly became racially segregated.[30]

The school Priscilla attended was one of many freedmen's schools established not by the state but by private missionary and aid societies. The Freedmen's Bureau assisted these schools by providing funds to rent school buildings, transporting teachers to school locations and helping them secure accommodations, and offering protection for students and teachers when they came under threat from the white community. The schoolhouses symbolized emancipation in many ways, so it was not surprising when hateful whites burned them to the ground, or when they set upon schoolteachers to terrorize them into giving up their posts. A teacher in Granville County found a freshly dug grave with his name inscribed on a makeshift headstone one morning as he walked to school. No teachers, no schools. No schools, no freedom.[31]

White southerners also used less violent methods to subvert freed-men's education. A self-styled "committee" of local people surrepti-tiously bought the building being used for a freedmen's school near Tarboro. When the teacher became ill and fell behind in the rent, the committee demanded that he pay up or get out. Unable to collect enough money to cover the rent from the students' impoverished families, the committee chained and locked the doors. Without a schoolhouse, the students "now have to wander about until I can get a place for them to go to school in," the teacher wrote to the Freedmen's Bureau.

"Must things go this way?" he pleaded.[32]

The teacher lamented the local white population's "depraved desires" that led them to rejoice in seeing eager pupils locked out of their classroom. The superintendent sympathized, but there was lit-tle he could do. The bureau's meager budget was not enough to keep the school's doors open. He might write a strongly worded letter to the committee, discouraging their obstruction and pointing out the benefits of a better-educated class of workers. He might appeal to their sense of Christian charity. He might even suggest that the bureau step in to correct their misbehavior, but he knew—and the committee knew—that it would not. The committee had violated no federal laws. They had only adhered to the principles of free enter-prise, which demanded that property owners be reasonably compen-sated for the use of their buildings. If freedpeople had a right to education, then the building's owners also had a right to do with their property as they saw fit.

Money for education was scarce. The donors who had eagerly sup-ported the northern aid societies' school missions with money, books, and teachers during the war and immediately after began to tighten their purse strings as Reconstruction ground on. Many expected the government in the form of the Freedmen's Bureau now to pay for the costs of educating the freedpeople. Time and again, the North Caro-lina superintendent of education informed the societies that he had no money to purchase supplies such as books or blackboards, nor did he have funds to pay teachers or to rent school buildings. No, there were no suitable buildings where they wanted to establish a school. No, there were no qualified local teachers who were willing to take on the job. No, there weren't any white families who would house a northern teacher. They would have to board with a Black family. Yes, he knew the books were torn and falling apart. No, he didn't have any more of them. "Best wishes for your success," he closed all of those replies.[33]

As white resistance to Black education grew, the hardest supplies to come by were teachers themselves. The superintendent wrote to the American Missionary Association (AMA), the largest and most vigorous supporter of Black schools in the South, that the people in Harnett County, sixteen miles from Raleigh, were in search of a teacher to open a school there. "It is in the country—no village there—population mostly colored," he warned. Northern white teachers often had high expectations, and he needed to disabuse them of any romantic notions they might harbor about life in the South. It was a hard job, made even harder by the poverty of their students' families and the hatefulness of their white neighbors.

"They would prefer a colored man, who would preach to them Sundays. If he cannot be obtained, they would like a colored female teacher," the superintendent wrote, pointing out the freedpeople's preferences for a teacher of their own race. "If neither," he concluded, "a white lady will do, but I would not recommend sending the latter."[34]

Despite the local community's preference for Black teachers, northern white women composed the bulk of teachers in freedmen's schools, and many did their best to advance the cause of education and racial equality under desperate conditions. Countless freedpeople, both children and adults, learned to read and write under their tutelage. However, as one female teacher in Northampton County demonstrated, they could be a little obtuse at times. "We didn't assist your school last year because you did not send in any <u>petition</u> for aid," the exasperated superintendent replied, drawing a dark line under the word "petition," when she admonished him for neglecting her pupils.[35]

There was only one officer for the region, which included Nash and Edgecombe counties, and he was tasked with not only overseeing schools but also supervising freedmen's courts and adjudicating labor disputes, among his many other duties. And hers was not the only school in his jurisdiction. How was he to know she needed help if she didn't tell him?

In fact, they all needed help. Everywhere the schools struggled to find buildings, teachers, and supplies. In many places, the only educational institutions that existed were "Sabbath schools" that met every Sunday to teach pupils, both young and old, rudimentary lessons in reading. "They are very poor and humble, being taught in almost all cases by col'd men, who can just read a little, and held in private houses, or in open, rough, unfurnished and unplastered col'd churces, not fit for stables," wrote the Freedmen's Bureau agent in Elizabeth City.

"Yet they are doing good work," he insisted.[36]

Even without the necessary materials or the training that northern teachers might have, these teachers were dedicated to sharing what knowledge they possessed—most importantly, the ability to read. If, as Frederick Douglass argued, learning to read "ruined" a slave and made him "forever unfit" to be subjugated, then it was a crowning achievement for a person now free. At the Jackson Freedmen School in Tarboro, sixty men, women, and children attended classes on a regular basis. Only four of them had been free before the war. Of those sixty pupils, fifty-seven of them scraped together money for tuition. The principal, Jason H. M. Jackson, along with this wife, Fannie, collected a total of $6.74 for the term. That was an average tuition of twelve cents per student. It's not clear if the Jacksons asked for a set amount from each student, but most likely each one paid whatever he or she could. Almost everyone paid something for the opportunity to learn to read and write and, in addition, study geography, arithmetic, and for the girls, needlework.[37]

Priscilla did not attend Jackson's school or the one taught by her neighbor, Robert Taylor. According to her interview, she attended school in Rocky Mount. It's unknown why the Dancys sent her there instead of ones closer to their home, but whatever the reason, she most likely experienced a similar curriculum.

"I was way behind the other children," Priscilla recalled of her first term at school in the fall of 1870. She had never been to school before. Ann Eliza could have taught her the alphabet and to write her name, but perhaps with the family turmoil and the war, she neglected to pass on any of her own literacy skills to her children. In any case, Priscilla initially felt out of place in school, but it wasn't long before she caught up to the other children. "I learned fast," Priscilla told Dunston.[38]

Like most of her fellow students at freedmen's schools across the South, Priscilla learned to read by using *The Lincoln Primer*, a beginner's textbook written specifically for the newly free. As the preface explained, teachers in the freedmen's school had found the many excellent primers used in northern schools to be insufficient for the task of educating the charter generation. So, in 1864, while emancipation was still unfolding, the American Tract Society (ATS), an evangelical publishing organization based in Boston, put together a reading manual that was better suited to what northern missionaries believed were the special educational needs of ex-slaves. "While intended to aid in teaching them to read and write," the ATS wrote, "it is also designed to afford them instruction in religious truth, and in those various domestic, social, and civil duties to which freedom has introduced them."[39]

The primer began with the basics: a two-page spread of the alphabet with both upper- and lower-case letters, a chart of long and short vowel sounds, followed by examples of hard and soft consonants. Then the lessons began with simple, two-letter words like "go" and "do."

Next, students moved to three-letter words. As the words gradually acquired more letters, the lessons acquired a moralistic tone.

Put no rum or gin in a cup.

Students read a short story entitled "The Lie," where Tom and Jem both eat some nuts that weren't theirs to eat. When Tom is asked if he ate the nuts, he lies. Eventually, once he realizes it is a sin to lie, he confesses, but he remains confused because his friend, Jem, has told him to lie.

Jem is a bad boy. Do not be as he is. He is in the way to a bad end.

One bad act will lead to more.

A bad boy will make a bad man.

These didactic lessons aimed to impress upon freedpeople the values of hard work, thrift, sobriety, and cleanliness—values missionaries perceived were lacking in them, if not due to their innate inferiority, then because of the lingering effects of slavery. Either way, to twenty-first-century ears, these lessons sound condescending, at best.

Try to be neat as well as good.

Do not be rude or talk loud.

God made all men to work.

At least one Freedmen's Bureau agent found fault with the moralizing he read in the *Lincoln Primers.* William Stone came from an abolitionist Boston family, and after the war he settled in South Carolina to work with the bureau and later became the state attorney general. He married a Quaker teacher from Pennsylvania whom he met in his duties overseeing the freedmen's schools in his district, so Stone was well versed in the typical curriculum taught in the schools. Upon receiving a box of five hundred *Lincoln Primers* from the ATS that he was to distribute to the area schools, Stone was disappointed with what he found inside. A fervent supporter of Radical Reconstruction and a rare soul who believed that freedpeople were ready for equal rights *now* and not at some unspecified time in the distant future when they had learned how to talk, dress, and comport themselves like white people, Stone bristled at the *Say yes, sir, and no, sir* admonitions contained in the primers. "They taught a doctrine which I could not accept," Stone wrote.[40]

But he had little choice other than to give them out. He had witnessed firsthand the violence with which local whites reacted when their former slaves failed to observe the unwritten rules of racial etiquette and conform to their expectations of deference. Stone admitted that these kinds of lessons appeased southern whites and were the only kinds of books they would allow in the schools. And if it kept them from burning down schoolhouses, then perhaps it was worth it.

With the help of Mrs. Dancy and her teachers, Priscilla came to embody the ideal Black girl that emerged from the *Lincoln Primer* and other pedagogical materials aimed at Black children in the late nineteenth century. Priscilla mastered not only the spelling, grammar, and arithmetic lessons, but also the instructions about dress and comportment. The downtrodden girl who had left Nash County that spring was gone. Her siblings hardly recognized the girl who had taken her place when she arrived back at the farm for Christmas.

The confidence she had acquired at school from the lessons of uplift and self-discipline, though bourgeois and at times even paternalistic, set Priscilla apart from the rest of the white family with whom she was raised. This psychological distance gave her some perspective on their fraught relationship. If Priscilla had not begun to question Ann Eliza's story before she left Nash County, she certainly would have begun to do so once she had settled in with the Dancys in Tarboro. The nurturing she received from the Dancys would have stood in stark contrast to the way she had been treated at Ann Eliza's. She would have learned what good mothering was as she watched Harriett Dancy care for her family. She would have seen the determination and devotion with which the Freedom Hill people reconstructed their families and homes. She would have learned how important it was to have a people, that it enabled you to become a whole person who could feel free as well as be (legally) free. In Tarboro, she finally belonged. Those five years were the turning point in her life. "After getting to live with and understand *my people*," Priscilla told Dunston, "I used to look forward to going back [to Ann Eliza's] less and less."[41]

Soon, the final break with Ann Eliza would come.

SIX

ROOTS OF LOVE

· —— ·

Every year at Christmas, Ann Eliza would send Jolly Bowen in the buggy to pick up Priscilla and bring her home for a visit. Each year, she would see how much the girl had grown since the last time. The Dancys were taking good care of her, of that Ann Eliza could be sure. Her dresses were clean and fitted. Her hair was neatly combed and adorned with bows. She smiled as Margaret and Mourning admired her clothes and ribbons. For once, Priscilla seemed happy. Ann Eliza surely noticed the change in her and may have been pleased to see the girl blossom. But she may have also worried that she was losing her. That realization became unavoidable in Priscilla's fourth year away, when it was time for her to come home again.

"In 1874, when mother wrote me, I told her that I was not able to come that year without giving any definite reason. The reason, though, was partly that I didn't want to go and partly because—well, I had a beau," Priscilla explained.[1]

Her beau was a soft-spoken young man named Lewis Joyner who lived across the creek from the Dancys. He had asked Priscilla to stay in Tarboro for the holiday instead of going back to Nash County. Over the holiday, Lewis applied for a marriage license.

Priscilla and Lewis Joyner married on June 2, 1875. Lewis was twenty-one, Priscilla only sixteen. At that age, she would have needed a parent or guardian's permission. Priscilla informed Thelma Dunston that Mrs. Dancy had given her consent, but on the marriage license she gave her age as twenty-one, suggesting that her guardian's permission had not been immediately forthcoming. This might explain the long period between getting the marriage license and marrying. Priscilla turned seventeen in January, and soon she would realize that her childhood was quickly coming to an end. In September, almost nine months to the day after she and Lewis received their marriage license, she would give birth to Frank, their first child. By June, it would have been apparent to everyone that she was expecting, and Mrs. Dancy would have realized that her efforts to get them to wait had been for naught.

When Priscilla spoke of their courtship to Dunston, she told a story of a reliable man who would not let her down. "He was a good level-headed, sober-minded man," she said when asked about her husband.[2]

Those few words reveal a lot about how Priscilla may have judged her young suitor. Unlike her stepfather, Rix, who had failed to provide for his family, Lewis was a steady worker. He was cool and even-tempered, unlikely to make rash decisions. He took the warnings she had read about in her *Lincoln Primer* to heart and avoided alcohol. She believed she could depend on him. And it is also possible that, as she looked back on her youth with the wisdom earned over eight decades, the old woman speaking to the interviewer may have recognized something in Lewis that her much younger self did not. Priscilla spoke with the confidence of a woman who knew she had chosen the right man.

Even at sixteen, Priscilla knew that marriage could make her life easier in some important ways. She had grown up watching Ann

Eliza struggle without the help of a steady, hardworking man, and she understood the economic benefits marriage provided. She also knew all too well the importance of legitimacy. Ann Eliza may have given birth to two mixed-race, illegitimate children. It's not difficult to imagine a sixteen-year-old Priscilla, pregnant and unmarried, determined not to repeat her mother's decisions, determined her children would know their father. She likely shared this conviction with Lewis, who was also fatherless.

Aside from his calm demeanor and clean living, Priscilla told the interviewer little about what she loved about Lewis. She did not tell the story of how they met, or if the Dancys disapproved of the five-year age difference between them. The details of their courtship, of the dreams shared and promises made when they could find a few moments alone, Priscilla kept to herself. "We had 'got acquainted by happening,' as they used to say," was all she told Dunston.[3]

But when it comes to our ability to contemplate the bond between Priscilla and Lewis, what she didn't say may be as important as what she did. Lewis had people. He was the eldest son of Romanda Joyner, a formerly enslaved woman who lived near Ann Eliza with her sons General Grant and Colfax. These were Lewis's younger brothers, named in honor of the Union war hero elected to the presidency in 1868 and his vice president. Romanda was no doubt a steely woman to have chosen these names. One can imagine how it would have made her former owners, a member of Rix's extended family, feel to hear her call her sons across the fields that now separated her home from theirs. By the time Priscilla moved to Tarboro in 1870, Lewis was living across the creek from the Dancys. But he had always lived in close proximity to Priscilla. In keeping the girl close to her and away from the "colored people," however, Ann Eliza had made sure they had little or no connection.

Born in 1853, Lewis had been enslaved. We cannot know for certain who his father was, but his marriage license gives us a possible clue. As was common practice at the time, a white man named Jordan Joyner applied for the marriage license on Lewis's behalf and most likely paid the bond. Jordan Joyner was one of four men by the same name born between 1795 and 1836, all of whom had been Nash County slaveholders. Possibly a cousin of Rix's, he was a member of an extended kin network who lived, worked, and intermarried with each other throughout the nineteenth century. They also shared naming practices. Rix's grandfather was also named Lewis.[4]

Jordan Joyner was likely Romanda and Lewis's former owner. He may also have been Lewis's father. Lewis's older sister Louisa, who died in 1915, had told her son (Lewis's nephew) that her father was Jordan Joyner. The nephew informed the coroner of this information, who listed it on Louisa's death certificate.[5]

But in 1875, when Jordan Joyner was still alive, this kind of public reckoning was not possible. On their marriage license, Lewis's father is listed as "unknown." So is Priscilla's. But they were differently fatherless. If Jordan Joyner was his father, Lewis probably knew it. Louisa obviously did, and passed on that knowledge to her son. Enslaved people often knew if their father had been a white man, and who that white man was. "I hate to say these things," confessed one ex-slave from Tennessee who knew his father was his first owner, "but they often happened this way back in those days. The masters were often the fathers."[6]

The closest Jordan Joyner would come to claiming Lewis as his son might be to sponsor his marriage license. These open secrets surrounding paternity could have devastating effects on enslaved people's sense of self. One freedman recounted the day he felt compelled to get off the Nashville streetcar when it reached the gates of the cemetery where his father, the plantation owner's eldest son, was buried. "I started cussing—'Let me get off this damn car and go see where my God damn father is buried, so I can spit on his grave, a God dam son-of-a-bitch,'" he recalled.[7]

His anger was palpable as he recounted living with and caring for his former mistress—his grandmother—until her death. She left him a house in town, where he still lived, but that was not the inheritance he wished for. It wasn't about property or money. It was about recognition. Neither his father nor his grandparents had ever acknowledged him as their blood. The thought of it still enraged him so many years later.

"I got no mercy on nobody who bring up their children like dogs," he continued. "How could any father treat their child like that? Bring them up to be ignorant like they did us. If I had my way with them all I would like to have is a chopping block and chop every one of their heads off."[8]

"The white folks never tell me who my father was," said Alexander Robertson, but he had his suspicions. "I have to find out that for myself, after freedom, when I was looking round for a name," he explained. He had heard rumors about his parentage, and as he was light-skinned, he put two and two together. "From all I hear and 'pear in the looking glass, I see I was half white for sure, and from these things I hear, I conclude I was a Robertson which have never been denied." He felt satisfied with his choice of surname, but he still wondered what his father's first name might have been. If he guessed, he didn't tell the interviewers. "Maybe it best just to give no front names," he concluded.[9]

When it came to her father's identity, Priscilla had neither a front name nor a back name to go on, but like Alexander Robertson, she suspected who he might be.

"[S]omehow I've got the notion it must have been the carriage driver whose duties took him in and out of the house, day and night," but even as she told this to Dunston, she second-guessed herself. "You understand, now, this is before I was born, so it's just an idea that got into my head about the coachman."[10]

If her suspicions were correct, or if they were just the fanciful imaginings of a fatherless child, Priscilla shared with Lewis, and with so many others in the charter generation, a desire not only to know who their fathers were but also to have loving relationships with them. Lewis may have known who his father was, but what kind of relationship did he have with Jordan Joyner, the man who enslaved him for the first twelve years of his life, the man who likely raped his mother? Did he crave the acknowledgment and fatherly concern like the unnamed man from Nashville did? Perhaps the fact that Jordan stood up for him in court and signed the bond for his marriage license gave Lewis enough recognition to stave off that kind of anger and resentment. But we must wonder, even though Lewis knew who his father was, did he still feel robbed of the daddy he knew other children had?

Like many other members of the charter generation, Priscilla and Lewis shared "an imprecise sense of their family history and their family members' experiences in slavery." Silences surrounding their fathers' identities and the circumstances of their conceptions and births left gaping holes in their sense of self. Feelings of anger, betrayal, and shame often accompanied the half-light of truth surrounding the circumstances of their parentage and likely bound the young couple together. So did their longing to create for their own children the kind of family that slavery had denied them both. They may have missed the presence of their fathers, but their son Frank's arrival started a whole new line of people, a line that would eventually include twelve more children (although not all of them would live to adulthood). Now Priscilla would belong to them, and they to her.[11]

Marriage provided Priscilla with an increased sense of belonging and rootedness, just as it did for other members of the charter generation who found tremendous joy in formalizing old relationships and forming new ones in the wake of emancipation. Marriage became a marker of freedom in a number of ways, not least of which were the legal benefits it bestowed on families. However, when the FWP interviewers asked the charter generation about their marriages, they did not recall stories about the legal rights they gained by becoming someone's wife or husband. Instead, they talked about what it felt like to be in love, to feel and give affection freely, without the interference of a slave owner. They told stories about how it felt to be surrounded by all your people as you pledged your love and loyalty to one another. They recalled the difference that love made in the face of continued hostility from those who sought a return to the days when Black people could not choose their mates or, if they did, hope to hold on to them. Being free meant being able to feel love and express it fully, or to be done with it altogether if such emotional encumbrances were not to your liking. Above all else, for so many of the men and women who lived with the trauma of displacement and separation, love meant finding a home in another person and putting down roots with them in a place of your own choosing.[12]

. —— .

IF PRISCILLA HARBORED any doubts about Lewis and their marriage in 1875, the cultural imperative to be married and start a family likely overrode them. Unable to legally marry prior to emancipation, many freedpeople rushed to legitimize old relationships and establish new unions during Reconstruction. They did so for a number of reasons: economic security, legal standing, and respectability.

"We must harmonize our feelings," advised the president of the State Convention of the Colored People of North Carolina in September 1865. The meeting brought together the leading representatives of the state's Black community at that time, many of whom had been freeborn in cities like Raleigh and Wilmington. They urged freedpeople to proceed cautiously and earn the respect of the state's white citizenry. The convention's president, Rev. James Walker Hood, an AME minister and native Pennsylvanian who came to North Carolina during the war, placed the onus of harmonizing feelings squarely on the freed community.[13]

"Respectful conduct begat respect," Hood instructed.[14]

There was nothing more deserving of respect than traditional marriage, an institution that had been denied enslaved people, leaving them unable to claim authority over their own children or establish independent households. *Until death or distance do you part* had been the wedding vows enslaved people made to each other. Couples joined by informal marriage ceremonies understood that their unions were conditional. When their owner needed to settle a debt, he could sell or trade husbands from wives, mothers from children. When he died, his heirs could divide the estate and the families that comprised it. When his children married, he could give the young couple a cook or a housemaid to start them out on their own plantation. Slave marriages had no legal standing. Parents had no claims on their children. The comforts and joys of family life were always dampened by the dread of separation.[15]

The inability to legally marry also left freedpeople vulnerable to charges of sexual immorality from whites, who saw the absence of marriage as evidence that former slaves were unfit for freedom and self-governance. Hood understood that marriage was a fundamental civil right, and that without it, freedpeople could never hope to attain full citizenship. As their enslavement depended upon their inability to legally marry, so too would much of their freedom depend on their ability to choose and wed a spouse. Having a legally recognized marriage enabled formerly enslaved couples to challenge apprenticeship laws like the ones Lafayette Dancy used to exert his control over the families he once owned in Edgecombe County. It also bolstered their ability to negotiate with employers when signing labor contracts. The wives of Black Union soldiers would find it much easier to claim a widow's pension if they could provide the Pension Bureau with an official marriage certificate. By providing useful economic and political benefits, marriage was a tool freedpeople could use to carve out something resembling a free life.[16]

But it could also be used as a cudgel to reinforce their inferiority. The tiresome proselytizing by missionaries and government agents about the importance of living up to their manly obligations and upholding female chastity was more than just an annoyance. The speeches like the one Reverend Hood gave to the convention in Raleigh reflected the deeply racist assumptions many whites, even those who professed to be freedpeople's allies, possessed regarding their familial relationships. While celebrating the emancipatory vision of free families, these calls to marriage played a familiar white refrain: freedpeople must emulate white, middle-class family ideals, but they would need to be compelled to do so since they did not *feel* the same way whites did about their spouses and children. Furthermore, whites typically viewed Black desire, whether it was a desire for a new dress or a desire to remain single, as a threat to the reconstruction of the South's moral order and therefore needed to be restrained. The expectations for freedpeople's marriages were heavy, and at times they seemed impossible to fulfill. In fact, historian Tera Hunter argues that "no other group in U.S. history faced such an aggressive campaign to remake its most intimate relationships."[17]

Given the overbearing imperatives from the government, schools, churches and their missionaries, how much freedom would couples like Priscilla and Lewis have to define their own ideas of marriage and family? How could they resist the overwhelming impetus to conform to the government's idea of how they should feel and live? Could marriage provide them with the kind of respect and elevated status that Reverend Hood believed was possible?

When Hood urged freedpeople to "harmonize our feelings," he spoke not only to the great political importance of marriage but also to the immense emotional work of freedom. Getting married is one of the most consequential and emotionally charged acts human beings engage in. So much is at stake—not only your personal happiness but also the happiness and well-being of your family, particularly any children who might be born to the union. Marriage has always been a social act involving not just the two people being wed but also their kin. This was true for the charter generation, just as it had been for their enslaved parents and grandparents, as well as for their masters' families. Marriage is a blending of many overlapping social worlds, and sometimes the blending is seamless; other times it is uneven or incomplete. The emotional labor required to merge families and establish social networks, while simultaneously making space in which their own intimate attachments could develop, could be taxing for any newlyweds. But for Priscilla and Lewis, and for other members of the charter generation, the added pressure of the political implications of their marriages and the racialized assumptions about their ability to love, stretched them even further.

Yet freedpeople embraced marriage, not just for the political and economic benefits it often conferred or for the social respectability it might give them in the eyes of others. They married because they were in love.

. —— .

THE IDEA THAT PEOPLE should marry for love is a relatively recent development in the history of human social relations. Until the Enlightenment, when notions of individual free will began to challenge established hierarchies of power and authority, people married for many reasons: to maintain or improve their economic standing or social status; to forge alliances between families, principalities, kingdoms, or nation-states. "For centuries, marriage did much of the work that markets and governments do today," historian Stephanie Coontz reminds us. People married because their parents told them to. They married because not to do so meant setting themselves apart from the rest of their society, to be considered odd, at best, or a pariah, at worst. For those who were without means, especially women, whose entire legal and social status derived from their marital status, staying single was simply not a respectable option, unless one became a nun. Without a husband, a woman was at the mercy of male relatives to support her, and if there were none, or if they refused, then the only choices left to her were the convent, the poorhouse, or the brothel. Such were the choices available to women, and indeed to most people, when it came to marriage. Of course, that's not to say people didn't feel love toward their marriage partners; it simply wasn't required or, according to most authorities on the subject, even desirable. Love clouded your judgment and got in the way of making a "good match." When it came to marriage, love was not just irrelevant. It was an impractical, selfish, and dangerous distraction.[18]

But by the mid-nineteenth century, the old ways of looking at marriage had changed. The ancient customs that proffered marriage as a tool for cementing political alliances or economic advantage had been replaced by the belief that couples should marry for love. Sermons, advice books, and popular sentimental novels testified to the belief that the ideal marriage was one where affection and mutual attraction bound man and wife together and insulated them from the pressures and temptations of the outside world. Sexual and spiritual intimacy, culminating in lifelong devotion, became the hallmarks of an ideal Christian marriage.

In the United States, this ideal emerged despite the fact that southern slaveholders cruelly flaunted its conventions. While some allowed their bondspeople to nominally choose their mates, and sanctioned their unions with formal if minimal wedding ceremonies, others routinely forced enslaved people to engage in sexual relations in what survivors described as "breeding" programs like the ones used for farm animals.

"My father said that they breeded good niggers—stud them like horses and cattle," recalled J. F. Boone to the FWP interviewer. Boone's father, Arthur Boone, who had lived most of his life enslaved, told him how the system worked. "Good healthy men and woman that would breed fast, they would keep stalled up. Wouldn't let them get out and work. Keep them to raise young niggers from," Boone's father explained to him.[19]

As debates over slavery grew more raucous in the 1840s and 1850s, antislavery writers began to argue that, in fact, slave marriages represented the truest form of romantic love. While legal marriages between free people might be strategic or instrumental, marriages of enslaved people bore no such taint. Slave marriages represented pure expressions of affection and devotion. In works like *Uncle Tom's Cabin*, where enslaved spouses chose to love each other despite the heartbreaking fear of sale and separation, their commitment to the ideal of romantic love was made stronger by their inability to uphold their commitment to each other.[20]

"Why does the slave ever love? Why allow the tendrils of the heart to twine around objects which may at any moment be wrenched away by the hand of violence?" asked Harriet Jacobs as she reflected on her own failed efforts to marry the young carpenter whom she desired "with all the ardor of a young girl's first love." Her enslaver, who desired to keep Jacobs to satisfy his own lascivious desires, denied her beau's request to marry her, leaving her heartbroken.[21]

Slaves loved, as Jacobs reminds us in her autobiography, because slavery could never dampen human emotions and desire completely. Slaveholders worked diligently to convince themselves that Black people did not—could not—love as white people did, that their emotions were shallow and uncomplicated. Jacobs's owner rebuked her for having "high notions" that led her to believe she ought to be able to choose her own mate, and threatened to kill her suitor if he ever saw him again. But such "high notions" provided enslaved people a source of comfort and a means of defiance against the dehumanizing attempts of enslavers to reduce them to a source of labor. Those high notions continued to comfort newly emancipated people who found themselves legally unbound but still struggling to live freely.[22]

"When I was fifteen, I marry Bill Moore," recalled Sena Moore in her interview. At eighty-three years old, Moore's memories of her wedding had not dimmed. She painted a richly detailed scene for her interviewer that spoke to the singular importance of that day in her life story. "Stood up with him, that day, in a blue worsted dress and a red balmoral over a white tuck petticoat, and under that, a soft piqu[é] chemise with no sleeves," she said of her wedding ensemble.[23]

Moore's description of her dress reveals the importance the day held for her, not just as an old woman looking back fondly on her youth, but as a young, newly free girl declaring her love publicly. It was elegant and colorful. First, she had acquired a delicately woven—and probably expensive—undergarment. Piqué weaving often featured a basketweave or honeycomb pattern that made plain cotton fabric softer and more elegant, unlike the rough calico typically used for enslaved people's clothes. On top of the chemise, Moore had managed to procure a decorative second layer made of red wool with black stripes draped with ties over the white base, with neat, parallel folds decorating the bottom of the garment—a balmoral petticoat, so named for its originator, Queen Victoria's, love for her Scottish estate. In the 1860s, balmorals were highly fashionable pieces of ladies' wear that were commonly worn by well-to-do white women. Perhaps Moore's balmoral was a castoff from her former owner. Or perhaps she managed to save enough money from her wages to buy one. However she came by it, the balmoral signified how important the marriage was to Sena Moore and her desire to look beautiful for her groom.[24]

"I had sweet shrubs all through my hair," she recalled, "and it held them all night and next night, too. Bill make a big laugh 'bout it, while nosin' in my hair and smellin' them sweet shrubs." With fragrant, wine-colored blossoms in her hair, Sena Moore stood proudly beside Bill as they became man and wife. The lightheartedness and joy they both felt in 1868 floats up from the pages of her 1937 interview.[25]

These beautiful memories of Sena and Bill's marriage stood in sharp contrast to the heartbreaking memories of marriages that were passed to descendants from older generations who had been enslaved. The joy Sena Moore felt at her wedding was so strong in part due to her knowledge of her mother's marital heartbreak, the details of which Sena told in conjunction with her own love story. Before recounting her wedding to Bill, Sena remembered how her mother cried when the slave owner sold her husband, Sena's father. Her tears had little effect on her owner, who dismissed her sorrow with a cliché:

"Plenty more good fish in the sea, Phillis," he said.

Eventually, her mother found another partner, but the way Sena Moore spoke of the pairing leaves the question of her mother's choice in the matter open. "She take up with a no 'count nigger named Bill James," and soon she gave birth to a son. Did Sena's mother "take up" with this man because she wanted to, or did her owner pressure her to find another man so she could have more children and increase his wealth?[26]

Choice was an important theme in Sena Moore's emancipation story. She contrasted her ability to choose Bill with her mother's inability to stay with her chosen husband and the likelihood that she was forced to "take up with" another man she did not love and who did not treat her well. Emancipation meant that she would not have to endure the same heartbreak as her mother, but the power to choose brought with it new pitfalls. Before she married Bill, Sena Moore was confronted by an offer from a different suitor. "A Yankee want me to go off with him but I tell him no! Then when I refuse him," she explained, "he persuaded another gal to love him and leave with him. Her come back to the place six months later and had a baby by that scamp man."[27]

Moore's narrative reminds us that although the ideal of love in marriage was now held in great esteem, there were still practical considerations that might take precedence over matters of the heart. Not only did you have to be on the lookout for the sweet-tongued suitor who made promises he wouldn't keep, you also had to be able to discern which men would provide you with stability and security. Looking back, Sena Moore knew that she had made the right choice, and that knowledge comforted her. But the importance of the romantic ideal to Moore's story cannot be overlooked. It was revolutionary for a newly freed woman like Moore to be able to claim that kind of love as her own.

. —— .

PRISCILLA'S MOTHER-IN-LAW, Romanda, most likely had been raped by her owner and prohibited from choosing her own mate. By 1880, however, she had married Berry Joyner, another freedman from among the many Joyners, Black and white, of Nash County. Berry had been living with Romanda in 1870, but at the time he was only a boarder, the last member listed on the census in a household Romanda headed. By the next time the census taker came around, Berry was the head of household and Romanda was listed as his wife. In the intervening decade, either their relationship had evolved into something more, or Romanda and Berry decided to legalize a long-standing intimate partnership, as did many formerly enslaved people in the post-emancipation years. In the files of the North Carolina State Archives are hundreds of "cohabitation records" that document these relationships. Some couples had been together for only a few years, others for many more. Gloss and Zilpha Jones, "both of whom were lately slaves and now emancipated"—and, according to their cohabitation record, had been living together as husband and wife for thirty years—asked Edgecombe County to recognize them as legally married.[28]

Romanda Joyner was unable to freely choose or reject Jordan Joyner

Cohabitation certificate for Gloss and Zilpha Jones, Edgecombe County, North Carolina. COURTESY NORTH CAROLINA STATE ARCHIVES

when she was enslaved, but as a free woman, she could decide for herself if Berry Joyner would remain a boarder or become her husband. While her decision was in line with the government's admonitions to freedpeople about the importance of marriage, others thought differently and chose differently.

"I am my own woman and will do as I please," Dink Watkins informed her husband when he found her having sex with another man. She felt no obligation to stay faithful to him. Perhaps a liaison behind the Baptist church (where her husband caught her in the act) thrilled her. In his divorce petition, Watkins's husband claimed this was not the first time she had been unfaithful. Whatever the reason she chose to violate her marriage vows, her determination to do as she pleased subverted the middle-class ideal of how a respectable woman should behave. Dink Watkins operated by a different set of rules: her own.[29]

"I been married one time, and that was one time too much," Charity McAllister declared. Although McAllister married shortly after the war, she kept her maiden name, an unusual choice at the time.

McAllister was her mother's name. She knew her father's name was Blalock, and she had belonged to a man named John Greene, but she chose the name her mother took "when the surrender came," and she stuck with it. She may also have harbored doubts about her marriage to Richard Bogers, which had not been a good one, although she did not elaborate about why. Bogers had "been dead a good long time," McAllister said, but she had never remarried. Like Dink Watkins, she found marriage to the wrong man, if not marriage in general, to be a wholly unsatisfying institution.[30]

It is important not to romanticize freed marriages. While women like Priscilla Joyner and Sena Moore found steady, lifelong partners whom they loved and who loved them in return, others did not. In June 1867, Chainy Woodard asked the Freedmen's Bureau agent in Nash County for protection from her husband Sterling's violent temper. The next month Rose Whittaker told the same agent that she could no longer live with her husband, Hilliard, who "abused me by words and blows." She had left him and taken her two children to her mother's house, but she said her husband was threatening anyone in the neighborhood who might help her. She also reported that he and three other men even tried to kidnap her, but she had escaped. Showing Rose a letter he claimed was from the Freedmen's Bureau agent, Hilliard Whittaker had told her that the government wanted her to return to him. Whether or not this was true or just another ploy by a man desperate to regain his wife is unclear. Rose couldn't read and had only Hilliard's word to go on. So, she set out for the agent's office in Nashville "to give her side of the story." The agent took down her complaint and filed it away. It's not clear if he ever acted on it. Similar accounts of marital discord and brutality exist throughout the records of the bureau in North Carolina and beyond, reminding us that marriage, at its worst, can be a soul- and even bone-crushing experience.[31]

For some freedwomen, though, violence was a part of married life they learned to accept. When she spoke to the FWP fieldworker,

Tanner Spikes recounted a mostly loving marriage to her husband, Frank. He called her "honey gal," and they were married for over fifty years before Frank died just a few months before the interview. Tanner knew almost as soon as she met him that he was the one for her. "Other boys come to see me but I ain't love none of them but Frank," she said. Then she added, "He ain't never whupped me but once and that was for sassing him, and I reckon that I needed that."[32]

It was difficult to live in contradiction to convention, even if your husband abused you and your children. Black women and their families faced intense scrutiny of their relationships and living arrangements. Although they recognized this scrutiny as racist and unfair, it made subsequent generations hypervigilant when it came to issues of sexual propriety. The respectability politics that shaped much of Black political culture in the late nineteenth and early twentieth century, premised on Victorian ideals of the nuclear family and selfless motherhood, had little room for the Dink Watkinses and Charity McAllisters of the world. The charter generation lived with the knowledge that, regardless of their choices, their lives would always come up short in the eyes of many white people.

Tina Johnson recounted how her mother had married a man named John Curtis several years after the war, and it was a real church wedding held at the Baptist church in Augusta. Sometime later a white man teased her by asking if she knew if her mother and father were married before she was born. The insinuation was, of course, that they were not, that Johnson was illegitimate, and that her mother was loose. The fact that her parents had been enslaved and could not legally marry when Johnson was born did not matter to the man asking the question. Johnson countered with a question of her own. "I says to him that I wonder if he knows were his mammy and pappy married when he was born."[33]

If she was irritated by the FWP interviewer's question, Johnson didn't show it, at least not in the tone of her voice or the expression on her face, since the interviewer transcribed her story with no additional comment. But by choosing to recount a story in which she "pulled a good one on a white man" who had asked the same question years before, we can imagine Johnson also asking the interviewer *do you know if your parents were married when you were born?*

Questions of paternity and legitimacy bore down hard on formerly enslaved people as they embarked on their freedom journeys. Surely there were many women like Dink Watkins and Charity McAllister and Rose Whittaker, women who found marriage too restrictive, their husbands too demanding, or violent, or boring. Seeking redress, through either abandonment or divorce, carried consequences even if the Dink Watkinses of the world seemed not to care. Respectability sometimes reined in a woman's desires and slowed her stride toward freedom.[34]

. —— .

BUT FREEDPEOPLE DIDN'T GET MARRIED or stay married just because it was the respectable thing to do. They got married because they were in love and wanted to create families and homes with the person they loved. By the end of the Civil War, most people may have accepted love as the primary motivator in marriage, but that realization only gets us so far in understanding the role it played in the charter generation's evolving sense of what it meant to be free. Some emancipation stories made subtle yet important connections between love, marriage, and a feeling of rootedness and connection, both geographically and socially.

Like Sena Moore, who balked at a suitor's plan to move her away to a new location, Martha Colquitt was also hesitant to leave the home place. She chose a husband with strong ties to the local community, a man who was known and respected around the neighborhood. Traverse and Martha Colquitt spent their entire lives in Oglethorpe

County, Georgia. Unable to afford an elaborate trousseau, Martha Colquitt's sense of romantic love extended far beyond the clothes she wore (in fact she never mentions them, unlike Sena Moore). Instead, in her testimony, she focused on the important social function marriage and weddings played in the lives of the charter generation as well as those who came before. When asked about her marriage, Martha focused on the multiple celebrations put on by both the bride's and the groom's families. After the "big wedding" at her sister's home, Martha and Traverse celebrated again with his people. "The next day my husband carried me to where he was born, and his ma give us another big fine dinner. She had a table longer than this room, and it was just loaded with all sorts of good things," Martha recalled. Both families were involved in the wedding celebrations and went to great effort to ensure that the young couple was properly feted.[35]

Marriages and weddings retained much of their social function for the emancipated, just as they had for the enslaved community. Communal gatherings, dinners, and "frolicks"—music and dancing— marked the continuity across space and time. And just as slave owners attempted to exert their control over slave marriages by deciding whether to grant their permission or by holding ceremonies in their parlors where they served as witnesses, white people continued to play a role in some post-emancipation weddings. "The white folks that my husband had used to work for had sent some of the good vittals" for Martha and Traverse's wedding party, she told the interviewer.[36]

Likewise, Georgia Johnson's former owners gave her a big surprise on her wedding day: a full-on feast like the ones they gave white couples when they married. "Out in the big house yard was a long table just loaded down with everything good—chickens, barbeque, pies, and a great big wedding cake, what my old Mis'tess done baked for me her own self," Georgia fondly recalled. Her husband's former owners had also given them a celebration. But all their apparent good will was not without its price. The man held the groom's apprenticeship papers and informed him that because he was only nineteen, he "owned him" for one more year. The couple had to remain there and work for the man until the term of service had expired.[37]

Former owners tried to insert themselves however they could into freedpeople's personal lives, but their blessing at a wedding proved meaningful in some of the FWP emancipation stories. When Martha Colquitt recalled how Traverse's former owners had provided some of the food at their wedding, that information conveyed her sense of her husband's good reputation and his rootedness in the neighborhood. The couple would spend their married lives together in the vicinity around Athens, Georgia, and their connections not only to the community of former slaves but also to their former owners and employers seemed to give Martha a sense of security. Even in the 1930s, she still maintained a relationship with the elderly daughter of a man she had worked for after freedom. Martha often visited Mamie Bacon, who was about her age, to "talk about old times, and to get her to advise me how to get along."[38]

"I surely does love Miss Mamie," Martha declared.

Colquitt's declaration of love for this white woman might have reflected the influence of the white interviewer's expectations within the broader context of the Jim Crow South. As a former slave, Colquitt might have been so conditioned to praise white people and defer to their expertise and beneficence—a conditioning only reinforced by the racist segregation and violence she continued to live under—that she reflexively spoke of her love for Miss Mamie without really meaning it. Or she may have consciously said it out of fear that doing otherwise might put her or her family at risk.

But what if Martha Colquitt's expression of love for Miss Mamie reflected her basic need for rootedness? Philosopher Simon May argues that a feeling of "ontological rootedness," or a desire for the kinds of deep connection to others and the places we inhabit in ways that validate our own existence, drives much of human behavior and may help us understand not only why Martha Colquitt expressed love for Miss Mamie but also why she chose to marry Traverse. "If we all have a need to love," May writes, "it is because we all need to feel at home in the world; to root our life in the here and now; to give our existence solidity and validity; to deepen the sensation of being . . ."[39]

For better or worse, Miss Mamie represented a thread of continuity in Martha Colquitt's life that anchored her in time and place. Both women grew up in the same area, knew many of the same people, and had been acquainted with each other for a long time. As the daughter of Colquitt's former employer, Mamie Bacon may have assumed her father's prescribed role in Colquitt's life as an authority figure and possibly as a source of financial support. When Colquitt asked Bacon for advice about "how to get along," she may have been seeking advice, money, or work. Bacon's ability and willingness to provide that support may have inspired Colquitt's proclamation of love, in part. But like Traverse, whose roots in Clarke County were as deep and lasting as his wife's, Mamie Bacon's continued presence may have validated Martha's sense of being and lent her life the kind of "indestructable" experience that May argues is universal.[40]

Colquitt was not alone in this regard. Other FWP narrators spoke of the importance of rootedness to their sense of self as well as to their marriage choices. One marriage that exhibited such permanence was that of Richard and Cora Weathers. "I have been right here on this spot for sixty-three years. I married when I was sixteen and he brought me here and put me down, and I have been here ever since," Cora Weathers told her interviewer. When the fieldworker interpreted this to mean that her husband, Richard Weathers, had abandoned her, Cora quickly corrected him. "No, I don't mean he deserted me. I mean he put me on this spot of ground," she explained.

Cora's marriage to Richard had marked the beginning of her attachment to her neighborhood in Little Rock, Arkansas, and she recalled how it had grown up from just a few tiny houses after the war. It was where she and Richard had raised their six children and become part of a close-knit community. She drew a mental map of the place and its people, walking the interviewer through it street by street. There were the two Georges, George Winstead and George Grey, who both lived near the intersection of Chester and Eighth. Dave Davis lived one street over on Ninth and Ringo. Rena Lee lived at 906 Chester. Down near Ninth and Broadway, past the only little store they had at the time, John Peyton, an enterprising fellow with a green thumb, ran a little nursery selling flowers out of his small log house. Many of the people she knew when she and Richard first moved to Little Rock were dead and gone. Their ramshackle houses were gone, too, replaced by more permanent structures. Richard had also passed away, but Cora was still there, on the same spot where they had lived together for so many years.[41]

The search for home and love defined the freedom years for so many in the charter generation. Despite the intense scrutiny their marriages and families received, or perhaps because of it, freedpeople embraced romantic love as an emblem of their emancipation. Those intimate relationships and the meanings they gave to the lives of their participants far exceeded the worth placed on them by the government, missionaries, and their former owners, many of whom did not accept the charter generation's ability to love—at least not in the ways white people did. And, in fact, they did love a little differently. They loved because their mothers and fathers had their hearts as well as their bodies broken by slavery. They loved because it was now possible to do so under the protection of law. They loved, because what good would freedom be without it?

SEVEN

THE HOUSE ON SECOND AVENUE

· —— ·

PRISCILLA AND LEWIS started their life together in the summer of 1875, and settled near Stony Creek in Nash County, not far from Ann Eliza, Romanda, and other extended family members. Their own family grew quickly. Their oldest child, Frank Lewis, was born later that year, followed by Hattie in 1877 and Hyman in 1879. More children arrived at regular intervals in the coming decade: Jencie (1883), Isabella (1885), Eliza (1886), and Mamie (1888). During the early years of marriage, Lewis worked as a "farm laborer," an occupation that denoted he did not own the land he lived and worked on. The nearest "farmer," or landowner, was Reuben Joyner, whose family occupied the household immediately preceding Lewis and Priscilla on the 1880 census form. Reuben Joyner's father was Jordan Joyner, the white man who had applied for the wedding license on Lewis's behalf and who was probably his former owner and father. This meant that, in all likelihood, Reuben was Lewis's older half-brother.[1]

Lewis either earned a wage for the work he performed on Reuben's farm or a share of the crop he produced. The latter system, known as sharecropping, came into favor with white landowners and Black farmers alike during the lean postwar years, when cash was hard to come by. Landowners often lacked the money to pay wages, and similarly, freedpeople lacked the money to buy their own land. Instead, they settled for working on a farm owned by someone else in exchange for a portion of the crop, which they could then sell themselves. Although they were still beholden to landowners, sharecropping, as it emerged after the war, had its advantages. Unlike the gang labor system that had characterized cotton production under slavery, sharecropping allowed Black farmers to work more or less independently, free of the constant surveillance of overseers. A cropper's family had a garden plot, where his wife and children grew vegetables to supplement their diets or to sell for cash. They also might keep chickens as well as a milk cow. With some luck, a few good crops, and a boss who was inclined to deal fairly when it came time to settle up at the end of the year, a sharecropper might save enough money to eventually buy his own place.

But the promise of autonomy soon evaporated. The white supremacist "Redeemer" governments—which sought to end Reconstruction and restore white southerners to political power in the 1870s—dismantled many of the legal protections freedpeople had gained in the previous decade. In the wake of the devastating financial panic of 1873, which precipitated a long economic depression in both Europe and North America, cotton prices plummeted. Rather than diversify, landowners demanded that their tenants produce more cotton, not less, which meant abandoning their garden plots and, in some cases, planting the crop right up to the cabin door. The only collateral sharecroppers had access to was their future crops, and they had little choice but to use it to buy their seed, tools, and now much of their food, from the plantation stores landowners operated to supplement their farming operations. After the crop was sold and their debts paid, sharecroppers typically still owed the landowner, so moving on to a better place was out of the question. They would have to borrow more seed, feed, and flour from the store in advance of next year's crop. And so the cycle began again.[2]

Nash County sat outside the Deep South "Black Belt," where a much-reduced King Cotton still reigned, but landowners like Reuben Joyner would continue to pay tribute to its tarnished majesty. The economic fortunes of every southern farmer, large or small, rose and fell with cotton regardless of how much of it he raised. Like landowners and tenants in Georgia, Alabama, and Mississippi, Reuben and Lewis were locked in the grip of a system they both disliked and neither controlled.[3]

Yet, even as that system forced Reuben's hand in ways he may not have wanted, he possessed powerful things Lewis did not—namely, land. We cannot know if the half-brothers had a good relationship, working or otherwise, but even if they did, Lewis was unable to climb the socioeconomic ladder in the years he worked for Reuben. With a growing family, Lewis and Priscilla had to stretch their resources further and work harder for longer. They were bound to have felt frustrated, and Lewis in particular must have felt stifled as he watched Reuben accumulate enough wealth and land to pass on to his children.

Lewis may also have been dissatisfied with the way their economic situation intruded on his marriage. Despite the fact that most women like Priscilla had to work outside their home to some degree, freedpeople largely adhered to a traditional view of marriage governed by a rigid gender hierarchy. Although husbands and wives were presumed to occupy distinct if overlapping spheres of authority that created a rough equality between the sexes, men assumed the final say on most aspects of family life. The more sharecropping pulled a wife away from her prescribed role as wife and mother, the more tension it created in the marriage.

Nate Shaw, a sharecropper from Alabama, struggled to keep his wife, Hannah, out of the fields. A woman who was used to chopping cotton and milking cows, Shaw's wife expected that she would continue with these duties, but her new husband thought otherwise.

"When I married her I cut her loose from the field to a great extent. I didn't try to take her teetotally out," Shaw explained, "but the work she done in the field weren't enough to wear her down."[4]

Even if Shaw allowed her to continue with farm work so long as it wasn't too taxing—Hannah, like Priscilla, gave birth nearly every other year—there was one job he flat-out refused to allow Hannah to do. "I didn't allow her to go about washin' for white folks," Shaw said. "I didn't want any money comin' into my house from that. . . . There was plenty of [white folks] would ask her and there'd be a answer ready for 'em."[5]

Taking in washing was a common way for sharecroppers' wives to earn much-needed cash. In fact, labor contracts often stipulated that a tenant's wife was responsible for the landowner's washing as part of the arrangement made for the family's use of a cabin or other accommodation. Whites expected Black women to work regardless of their marital status or family obligations. As a tenant on Reuben Joyner's farm, Priscilla likely did some of his washing as well as her own and may have sold her services to other white families in the neighborhood. Was this a sore spot for Lewis as it was for Nate Shaw? Did it gall him to think of his wife scrubbing his half-brother's dirty clothes?

To add to Lewis's likely unhappiness about his and Priscilla's working conditions, racial violence hit close to home in the spring of 1887. In early May, a nineteen-year-old Black man named Ben Hart was accused of attacking a sixteen-year-old white girl in Tarboro. Newspaper accounts of Hart's alleged crime varied wildly. Some reported him to be forty-seven years old, much older than the alleged victim. One report described him as lying in wait, naked, in some bushes, for the girl or girls (in some reports there were two) to walk by on their way home from school. When they neared him, he jumped out and grabbed one of the girls, threw her on the ground, and beat her. Others left out these salacious details and noted only that Hart had "attempted to assault" a white girl. The discrepancies were not uncommon in accounts of the alleged assaults by Black men that whites used to justify lynchings in the late nineteenth century. Sexual innuendo and racial paranoia combined to create a perfect storm of violence against thousands of men and women, whose main—and often only—crime was being Black. We will never know if Ben Hart and the unnamed girl were young lovers caught out by one of the girl's friends who saw them together, assumed her friend was being attacked, and made the accusation against Hart. Or perhaps the young "victim," horrified by the prospect of her sexual relationship with a Black man being revealed, did what many other white women in her situation did: she accused him of rape. It's also possible that there was no connection at all between the young white woman and Hart, and that Hart found himself accused for no reason, or at least no reason we can know.[6]

What is certain is that a mob forced Ben Hart out of jail and hanged him. Calling themselves the "People's Committee," the lynch mob posted a note to Hart's corpse that read:

> We hang this man, not in passion, but calmly and delib-
> erately, with a due sense of the responsibility we assume.
> We take executive power in this case, and hang this man in
> accordance with the unwritten law of the land, because the
> written law provides no penalty adequate to his crime: and,
> be it understood, we who have done this act will repeat it
> under similar provocation.[7]

Lewis would have understood the note's warning and its implications for Black boys like his sons, Frank and Hyman, who might grow up and overstep any of the South's deadly racial boundaries. Priscilla understood it, too. Her own father, whoever he was, may have once been a young man like Ben Hart.

Ben Hart's murder reminded every Black person in Nash and Edgecombe counties of an important fact that had emerged since the end of Reconstruction ten years before: the law would not protect them. Although the local authorities had placed Hart in protective custody by moving him to a jail thirty miles away from Tarboro, they left a lone jailer in charge. When the mob arrived, he surrendered his key to them.

And when the county coroner, a Black man named Charles Lewis, called for an inquest to find those responsible for the hanging, the local papers dismissed his efforts. "This paper has consistently denounced lynching," wrote the white editors of the *Carolina Watchman*. "So do the laws of this state, but under our present lax system in respect to dealing with criminals like Ben Hart, it don't amount to much."[8]

It was in this milieu of repression and violence that talk of leaving the South began to circulate among the charter generation. Maybe they should go out west to Indian Territory or Kansas, somewhere where land was still plentiful and white people a little less so. Or maybe they should get out altogether, go to Haiti or even to Africa, anywhere but the hateful and bloody land that drained their hope and energy like the fields soaked up the few drops of July rain that fell on the parched, cracked earth. *Go. Go now. Before it's too late.*[9]

Lewis and Priscilla would not go as far as Africa, or even Kansas, but they went far enough to extricate themselves from the tangled Joyner family tree. They were an example of the way that rootedness could choke your life instead of fueling it. Members of the charter generation circulated through and out of the South, seeking new places where their roots might grow deeper and stronger, and where old ties might be stretched and even broken. The restlessness that had led many newly emancipated people to take off to find themselves or lost family members in the weeks and months after the war now took on a new urgency as they faced the darkening reality of life under Jim Crow. Yet the possibility of something new, even the act of moving itself, infused some of them with hope. The desire for rootedness and the feelings of restlessness sat uneasily in their hearts and would shape the history of Lewis and Priscilla Joyner, along with much of Black America, for the coming century.

.——.

WHEN PRISCILLA AND LEWIS packed up their growing family and left Nash County in 1888 or 1889, they joined the rear guard of a great migration of emancipated people that had begun twenty-five years earlier. While later migrations in the twentieth century would take southern Blacks to northern cities like Philadelphia, New York, Chicago, and Detroit, this earlier migration saw the charter generation move mostly around and throughout the South. With its beginnings in the dislocations of the Civil War, the first Great Migration cracked the foundations of the plantation system and enabled freedpeople to stretch their imaginations as well as their legs. These years witnessed an increase in the South's urban Black population. In Union-occupied cities like New Bern, New Orleans, and Atlanta, the presence of federal troops and the creation of refugee camps nearby drew people in from the countryside. Here federal troops handed out rations and offered freedpeople some protection from hostile whites. There was work, too. Freedpeople set up businesses trading, baking, and washing clothes. When large-scale migration to southern towns picked up after the war, whites simultaneously feared the large numbers of Black people congregated together and the depletion of their supply of farm labor in the rural areas.

But town life did not always provide the safety and better living that migrants sought. Although Warren McKinney's mother hoped to find work in Augusta, Georgia, she and her young son found mostly sickness and death upon their arrival. McKinney remembered the stacks of coffins nearly eighty years later when he spoke to the FWP interviewer. Although McKinney didn't know it, the cause of all those deaths was most likely cholera. In 1866, an epidemic hit most of the major urban areas in the United States, and even smaller cities like Augusta became a breeding ground for the waterborne intestinal disease. Located on the Savannah River, where many of the migrants washed, defecated, watered their animals, and gathered cooking and drinking water, Augusta was a prime "cholera field." The tail end of a three-year global pandemic that claimed hundreds of thousands of lives, the 1866 cholera outbreak in the United States staggered a nation still reeling from the Civil War.[10]

Charter generation migrants reckoned with the unknown and weighed the potential benefits of moving to town against the likely costs. Like those who went before them, the Joyners did not make the decision lightly. By the time they left in 1888 or 1889, Priscilla had given birth to six more children. They needed to be relatively certain that they could quickly put together a functioning household. Like other members of the charter generation, they set out for an urban area that promised better opportunities: Suffolk, Virginia. About a hundred miles from Nash County, Suffolk was home to a number of profitable industries, including shipping and rail transport, oyster packing, and lumber. According to Priscilla, Lewis had been offered a job in a lumberyard, an opportunity he may have found through friends and neighbors who had previously moved there.[11]

Lewis and Priscilla had likely heard tales of the perils of town life. Country folk often harbor deep suspicions of town folk and the lives they lead or are forced to lead. But as the turn of the century approached, the lure of better jobs and higher wages, as well as a possible respite from the terrors of the southern countryside, proved too tempting to resist any longer.

The Joyners' move to Suffolk from their rural life in Nash County took a leap of faith, but it also required extensive planning and deliberation. Their hard-won successes in the years after their arrival in the Tidewater region are a testament to the foundations established by the city's growing Black community from which Priscilla and Lewis drew but to which they also contributed. In other words, their ability to prosper, to support a large family (another son, Harry, was born in 1889, the first of five children born in Virginia), and to achieve a level of economic success that so many of the charter generation aspired to but never attained was not simply a matter of luck. Yet, for all they achieved, insecurity remained a constant in their lives. New vulnerabilities emerged that could be just as lethal as the lynchers' rope.

. —— .

THE 1890 CENSUS RECORDS were destroyed by fire, so we cannot check to see where the Joyners lived when they first moved to Suffolk, but the 1900 census lists them living in the borough of Holy Neck. Holy Neck had been an enclave for free Blacks before the Civil War and continued to be a gathering point for freedpeople after emancipation, including many North Carolina transplants. The Joyners' next-door neighbors, Archer Wright and his wife, were North Carolina natives. So was Ed Hall, who lived two houses up the street. Henry Burr, Thomas Green, John and Sallie Milton, and Robert and Lucy Williams, all of whom lived within spitting distance of the Joyners, were Tar Heels. A conclave of Carolinians, the Joyners' neighborhood in Suffolk likely provided Lewis and Priscilla important information and material support as they made the transition to city life.[12]

There are few sources we can use to understand how the Joyners adapted to their new surroundings and made a life for themselves in Suffolk, but we can glean some important clues from the census and a few existing city directories. In 1900, Lewis told the census taker that he worked as a drayman, a job that could earn him up to $1.50–$2.50 a day. A skill he had honed through years of farmwork back in Nash County, his ability to handle a team of horses was a marketable skill in Suffolk, a hub of lumber production since the end of the Civil War. By 1870, lumber was the top "New South" industry and employed more Black workers than any other trade. While textile mills, the South's other leading industry, hired white workers almost exclusively, the dusty, dirty, and dangerous world of lumber production was open to Black men. Jobs like the one that tempted Lewis Joyner to Suffolk became a way out of the trap of tenant farming and sharecropping, and thousands of men like him made their way to the Atlantic and Gulf coasts to make the first real money in their lives and, in the process, hopefully build new lives for their families.[13]

In the 1880s and 1890s, the lumber business boomed in the Virginia Tidewater. Trade journals advertised the high quality and seemingly inexhaustible supply of North Carolina pine, tons of which arrived weekly by train to be processed in the mills along the Nansemond River, which runs inland to Suffolk from the James River and the Chesapeake Bay. Lewis would have spent long days hauling loads of pine logs between the railyard and the mill, and then transporting the finished boards back to the railyard to be shipped all over the country. Driving had long been a popular profession among freedmen; the records of the Freedmen's Banks, organized briefly after the war to encourage former slaves to save their money and buy property, lists the various driving professions (hack drivers, teamsters, carriage drivers, and draymen) more than any other occupation. The steady wages Black draymen earned enabled some of them to buy property. In neighboring Norfolk, several Black draymen accumulated considerable property holdings, becoming some of the first free Black property holders in the area. At the same time in Holy Neck, the first Black property owners included brick masons and carpenters. In total, fifty-three Black residents of Holy Neck owned their own property in 1870, including thirty-five farmers in what was still a mostly rural area on the outskirts of town.[14]

By 1910, that number would rise to 338, nearly six percent of the district's total population, Lewis Joyner among them. Some of these property owners worked "odd jobs," as Lewis did by this time, or they were factory laborers. Others worked for themselves as carpenters or house painters. There were still farmers who owned their own land; their continued influence gave rise to the formation of the Nansemond County Farmer's Conference in 1909 to bring local farmers together, provide them information on new techniques and agricultural news, and celebrate their successes.[15]

The picture of Lewis's working life—and the working lives of his neighbors—that emerges from these scant sources is one of diligent striving and slow accumulation in the face of growing efforts to restrict their opportunities for doing so. A state constitutional convention in 1901 cemented white Virginians' two-decades-long efforts to disenfranchise Black Virginians, eliminate their political influence, and dominate their role in public life. Speaking at the convention, Lynchburg representative Carter Glass, who would later become a United States senator, made no pretense about the purpose of adopting a new state constitution. "Discrimination!" he declared in a speech advocating disfranchisement. "Why that is exactly what we propose; that is exactly why this convention was elected—to discriminate to the very extremity of permissible action under the limitations of the Federal Constitution with the view to the elimination of every Negro who can be gotten rid of, legally, without materially impairing the white electorate."[16]

To achieve this craven agenda, the convention adopted an "understanding clause" that required potential voters to read and answer questions about a passage from the Constitution. Additionally, registrants were required to pay a cash-only poll tax of $1.50 for three consecutive years. Glass predicted that it would take approximately five years for these measures to "eliminate the darkey as a political factor." It only took two. In cities like Norfolk, where Black voting had been strong since 1868, the Black electorate decreased by two-thirds almost immediately. By 1910, only forty-four Black citizens in that city had paid the poll tax.[17]

For a man who could neither read nor write, Lewis Joyner had little hope of registering to vote or joining Suffolk's small but grow-ing middle class of Black merchants, entrepreneurs, teachers, doctors, and ministers. He had to take what jobs he could find. As he aged— by 1910 Lewis was fifty-one—the manual labor he relied on to sup-port Priscilla and his four children still living at home would become increasingly difficult for him to perform. The 1910 census returns sug-gest that Lewis and Priscilla needed help to get by. That year, both of their teenage daughters, fifteen-year-old Lizzie and thirteen-year-old Ida, were working in a factory. Given that the city's first high school for Black students would not open until 1939, there was little option for the girls but to enter the workforce. Their wages helped support their parents and younger sister, ten-year-old Priscilla, who still lived at home. Their older brother, David, who was out of work at the time, also lived at home.[18]

Despite these obstacles, Lewis and Priscilla accomplished some-thing truly extraordinary for working-class African Americans in the Jim Crow South. Sometime in the decade between 1900 and 1910, they became homeowners. Their house on Second Avenue was valued at $500, which could be worth as much as $15,000 in today's market. But a home's cash appraisal is only part of its value. In some places, holding the title to your own property meant you were eligible to vote. This wasn't the case in Virginia, where other restrictions virtually eliminated that possibility, but homeownership nonetheless enabled families to avoid landlords (almost always white) who could raise rents at will and evict without notice. Property could be passed down to children and grandchildren, binding the generations together, giving them a home place. And for a formerly enslaved man like Lewis Joyner, a man who was once someone else's property, owning his own home symbolized so much about his life. In this house, there was no white half-brother to answer to, no wondering if you'd come out all right at year's end. Whites still liked to tell you where you could and could not walk, ride, sit, eat, and drink—but not in your own house. It was the shingled manifestation of all his and Priscilla's freedom dreams.[19]

The house on Second Avenue most likely resembled one of the few remaining structures from the period that still exist in the area today. Although the place where Lewis and Priscilla's home would have sat is now a grass lot, a contemporary structure built at the turn of the century sits a few doors down the street. The style of the house is representative of what architectural historians call an I-house. With two stories, this wood-shingled house is two rooms wide and one room deep. Over the years, the front porch was enclosed and an extension built off the back to increase the living space. This house, along with the others on Second Avenue, sits on a relatively large lot, large enough for a sizable yard and the large flower garden that Priscilla would become famous for keeping. Unlike the typical cramped housing afforded urban Black workers in the early twentieth century, the houses on Second Avenue, which sat on the semi-rural outskirts of Suffolk, allowed families some space and privacy. A far cry from the ramshackle tenements that haunted Warren McKinney's memories of post–Civil War Augusta, the little neighborhood on Second Avenue bore a striking resemblance to the settlement that began at Freedom Hill and was by that time known as Princeville, North Carolina.[20]

Priscilla had been keeping house for nearly three decades, so when she set up the house on Second Avenue she did so with the skill of a seasoned homemaker. It was a labor of love but labor nonetheless. Cooking and cleaning for such a large household took considerable effort, and no doubt the older Joyner girls helped their mother in her daily work. Over the years, Priscilla most likely had acquired the equipment necessary to keep the place running: a washtub and washboard, cooking pots and utensils, linens, and perhaps even a set of good china where most of the pieces matched. In this respect, her home was a far cry from what the mothers and wives in Freedom Hill had to work with at the dawn of emancipation, or even many of her sharecropping counterparts in the country. But, like rural Black women who sold eggs or vegetables from their garden to supplement their families' income, Priscilla sold her flowers, which would come to take up most if not all of the outdoor space.

Homemaking took on special significance for Black mothers of the charter generation. They had watched as their mothers and grand-mothers made homes out of practically nothing after working long hours in the fields or keeping house for their enslaver's family. These women entered the long emancipation with a keen sense of what it meant to be able to wash and mend a husband's shirt, put a meal on the table, or make a dress for a daughter to wear to school. These simple acts of domesticity were precious because they made a hostile world more inhabitable. Black domestic successes seemed to particularly enrage white people who resented their achievements and saw them as evidence that freedpeople did not know "their place." John W. De Forest, a Union army officer and Freedmen's Bureau agent, had called freedwomen's efforts to keep house "female loaferism" because they were spending less time in the fields. "Myriads of [Black] women . . . now have aspirations to be like white ladies and, instead of using the hoe, pass the days in dawdling over their trivial housework," De Forest wrote in his memoir.[21]

But housekeeping was anything but trivial. As scholar Koritha Mitchell points out, "homemaking has long defined who is and who is not a citizen." Those whom mainstream white society deemed to have "inferior" homes and family structures—Black and brown fam-ilies, nonnuclear families, queer families—have long been excluded from the larger national family. In fact, the negative portrayals of Black domesticity, and particularly of Black mothers, from De For-est's "female loafers" in the 1870s to the "welfare queens" of the 1970s, have served as the antithesis of hardworking white American citizens: promiscuous, lazy scroungers who refuse to work and expect govern-ment handouts.[22]

It was within this atmosphere of disdain and hostility that Priscilla kept her house and grew her flowers. Filled with the knowledge that nothing she could do would be good enough for whites to accept her or her children as equals (even those white ladies who admired and bought her bouquets), she kept her house anyway. She refused to capitulate to the negative views of her efforts, to give up on her dreams of a lovely home, and to just let things go. Only many years later, when poor health slowed her down, would her efforts slacken.

. —— .

THE PICTURE OF the Joyners that emerges from the census records is of a hardworking family struggling to achieve security in a place that afforded them an opportunity for advancement if not prosperity. If the Joyners and the other residents of Holy Neck managed to transform segregation into congregation—as historian Earl Lewis found was the case among the Black residents of neighboring Norfolk—they did so in the churches, schools, and businesses that nurtured their community. They also found togetherness in the safe spaces of their homes and in the neighborhoods they formed: the front porches and backyards, the pathways along the railroad tracks that separated Holy Neck from the rest of the town, and the banks of the Nansemond River where children fished, swam, and splashed away from the watchful eyes of parents and grandparents, momentarily free from the worries of the older people who felt Jim Crow's hold on their lives grow ever tighter.[23]

Priscilla and Lewis's children grew up in a world shaped by segregation. By the time they were teenagers, as they were in the 1910 census, David, Lizzie, and Ida Joyner had learned their "place" in southern society. Looking back on his own education in racial etiquette, Walter White, chairman of the National Association for the Advancement of Colored People (NAACP), recalled "a great awareness" that emerged within him after witnessing a white mob terrorize his Atlanta neighborhood when he was thirteen. "I knew then who I was. I was Negro," White wrote in his 1948 autobiography. Other Black southerners recalled learning similar lessons. Whether it was being sent to the back of the streetcar or to the smoking car on a train, or suffering the ridicule of white children laughing at their dark skin or curly hair, the feelings of humiliation, fear, sadness, and anger left deep impressions on their young hearts and minds. The rules of racial etiquette applied not only to physical spaces—where they could go and where they could not—but also to how far they might hope to rise in society. Even little Priscilla, at ten years old, was learning quickly how to walk, talk, look, dress, and act like white people expected her to act. Her life might well depend on her ability to play her part convincingly.[24]

The Joyner children's parents, teachers, and ministers would also school them on the proper emotions they could display in public. These lessons were meant to protect them from the volatile and unpredictable tempers of white people, but what was intended to empower their survival could also stunt the development and expression of their sense of self. For the writer Richard Wright, who grew up in Mississippi at the same time as the Joyner children, this meant learning to live with an overwhelming sense of dread. He was haunted by the fear of saying something wrong and not even knowing he had done so, of making a mistake that might result in a beating or worse. Talk about white people made him anxious, and he felt as if he were "continually reacting to the threat of some natural force whose hostile behavior could not be predicted." This stress and anxiety were inescapable. The younger Joyners must have experienced it to some degree, but like most of the children of Jim Crow, they left no written record of their feelings.[25]

Not everything about life in the Jim Crow South was bleak, however. Children and adults alike found respite and renewal in a variety of forms. Suffolk's Black residents, segregated from white society, found and expressed joy in each other. Urban areas like Suffolk nurtured spaces where Black people convened, talked, joked, danced, dreamed, and played. The streets of Black Suffolk were lined with Black-owned restaurants and stores where the residents could relax and have someone serve them for a change. Every year beginning in 1911, local Black businessmen in Suffolk organized the Tidewater Fair. Like white county fairs, the Tidewater Fair exhibited local farmers' prize livestock and their wives' vegetables and flowers. For a small admission fee, spectators could watch horse races, listen to speakers on various subjects, enjoy the carnival and circus acts, and eat ice cream. While white fairs sometimes had "Negro Days," the Tidewater Fair was open to all Blacks for five full days. The Tidewater Fair Association purchased the fairgrounds, ensuring that the festivities remained free from white interference or surveillance.

Churches also were important spaces of collective respite, where congregants embraced each other and were soothed by the messages of salvation and justice they heard. Segregated schools also became "centers of Black public life and vehicles for spreading history that contradicted white historical wisdom" despite oversight from white administrators and school boards. Black teachers instilled pride through lessons in Black history and culture that gave students alternative views of the past. Black students would have learned about Crispus Attucks, the Black martyr for American independence; Frederick Douglass's heroic escape from slavery in Maryland and his lifetime of agitation for abolition and equal rights; Harriet Tubman's perilous journeys as a conductor of the Underground Railroad; and Sojourner Truth's tireless work for Black and women's rights. Some Black history textbooks even included lessons on Nat Turner and John Brown, two men who struck back violently against slavery. Black-authored texts also contained chapters on white violence after the Civil War, including the Ku Klux Klan and lynching.[26]

Both the church and the school were places for respectable types of Black community, but often folks found joy in less reputable forms.

While upper-class Black urban residents enjoyed eating fancy hors d'oeuvres and discussing art, books, and politics at social clubs with names like the Douglas Literary Club and the Smart Set Social Club, working-class Black city dwellers were more likely to frequent saloons and barrooms, where they rubbed shoulders with pimps, gangsters, and sex workers, to drink, gamble, and dance their troubles away. Sometimes the "smart set" would slum alongside the "saloon set." Almost everyone would slide into the church pews on Sunday morning together with their aching heads bowed as the minister admonished the sinfulness of the previous night's amusements.[27]

Educators, pastors, and other guardians of Black respectability often lamented the way that young people, girls in particular, behaved in public. Silas Xavier Floyd, the son of enslaved parents, was one such guardian dedicated to instilling the values of modesty, politeness, and decorum to Black children. A newspaperman from Columbus, Georgia, he penned *Floyd's Flowers* in 1905, a kind of etiquette manual for young people. In it, he denounced the "loud girl" who dressed inappropriately and cavorted with her friends. To demonstrate his point, Floyd related an encounter he had with a group of young girls on a streetcar in Atlanta. The girls wore "boys' hats" and brightly colored jackets adorned with large buttons and belts. Floyd clearly did not approve of these outfits, which included "a most conspicuous plaid skirt." The girls were sharing a box of candy, and their raucous enjoyment of it disturbed Floyd, especially the loud voice of the girl whose candy it was. The girls devoured the candy, arguing over who got the best piece, and laughing at each other's attempts to get their share. At one point a piece went flying and landed in a nearby lady's lap. As a Black passenger tried to maneuver to the back of the car where he was required to sit, he nearly tripped over the girls' feet, which were sticking out in the aisle. Eventually the white conductor reprimanded the girls, but they were not chastened. Instead, their "giggling and tittering" continued for the remainder of the ride.[28]

Embarrassed by what he considered to be the girls' coarse behavior, Floyd used this incident as an example of how lower-class Black girls lacked the "delicacy" he believed they needed to demonstrate in their public behavior. He recognized that white people were always watching and judging Black behavior, and he wanted these girls to understand how their comportment reflected on the entire race. In his rush to silence the "loud girl," he interpreted her joy as a lack of self-respect and an affront to the message of racial uplift to which he and other middle-class professionals ascribed. But the girls on the streetcar cared little for what some stuffy preacher thought of them. They seized their moments of joy and flaunted them for everyone to see. Their determination to take up space and stand out, rather than shrink themselves to fit into the confines allotted them and blend in, represented an act of open rebellion against both the rules of Jim Crow *and* Black respectability.

Were Lizzie, Ida, and Priscilla Joyner loud girls? Did they rush around the streets of Suffolk talking and laughing too loudly? Did they eat in public and wear bright clothes? It's possible. They were working-class girls, the kind of girls who tended toward such behavior, according to Floyd. Both Lizzie and Ida earned money in factory work, and eventually Priscilla would join the working world as a domestic. What money they did not give their parents they may have used to buy trinkets and candy, boys' hats and brass belts. Like their parents' generation who found pleasure in participating for the first time in a consumer culture that allowed them to buy material items they desired instead of saving their money like the Freedmen's Bureau agents advised, the Joyner girls, and other working-class Black girls in Suffolk, most likely spent their pennies on things that did not contribute to their future financial security but nonetheless made them feel good—made them feel alive. If so, it was just as well since their time to wring whatever joy they could find out of life was short.

· ——— ·

WHEN DAVID JOYNER first became sick sometime in the spring of 1912, his symptoms may not have seemed like anything serious. He would have felt exhausted, but he worked long hours as a laborer, possibly alongside his father, and tiredness came with the job. David and his parents, with whom he lived, may have dismissed these initial signs of illness as just being worn down. If David thought he would be better in a few days, his mother, Priscilla, may have worried something more serious plagued her son. She had already lost one child: Glenn, "the baby," as she referred to him in her interview. He was most likely named after Glenn Dancy, the husband of the woman who took young Priscilla in after she left Ann Eliza's farm. The baby died very young, most likely when he was an infant and prior to 1910 when states uniformly began registering deaths, although if the baby was stillborn, his death may not have been formally recorded. His name never appeared in any public records related to the Joyners, but he had a name, one that honored the man who may have acted as a father figure to Priscilla in her adolescence. Black infant mortality remained heartbreakingly high in the early twentieth century, so the fact that Priscilla had experienced such a loss is not surprising. She carried the grief of little Glenn's death with her, tucked away and invisible to most, but the pain of his loss undoubtedly resurfaced when she was faced with the death of another child.[29]

Priscilla's worries would have intensified as the days passed and David's condition worsened. Within a few days, he was barely able to sit up on the side of the bed and take a sip of the water or milk that his mother brought him. He ate little and began to rapidly shed weight. The violent coughing left him breathless and hoarse. By mid-April, they had called a doctor for him. The doctor collected some of David's sputum to test for bacteria, but no results were needed to confirm what everyone already knew: David had pulmonary tuberculosis and would soon die.[30]

For much of the first half of the twentieth century, tuberculosis ranked among the top three causes of death for Black urban residents. In 1900, TB accounted for fifteen percent of Black mortality in the United States. After 1920, when targeted public health campaigns aimed at improving sanitation and living conditions among city dwellers began to take effect, the mortality rates began to inch downward. But it was only after World War II, when new antibiotic treatments halted the progress of the disease, that the fatalities finally dropped below ten percent. During these years, TB deaths were high among whites, too, but never as high as they were among African Americans. White mortality from TB never topped ten percent.[31]

The reasons for this disparity can be summed up in two words: Jim Crow. In cities and towns like Suffolk, Black residents often lived and worked in cramped, poorly ventilated buildings. Communicable diseases like TB, transmitted through close contact with infected individuals, thrived in such environments. Overwork, exhaustion, and stress compromised urban Black residents' immune systems, making them susceptible to illness and infection. Poor nutrition further weakened bodies strained by the hand-to-mouth existence many Black urban dwellers were forced to live. Medical treatment was expensive; physicians expected their patients to pay in cash, something poor people had little of. The fact that Lewis and Priscilla called a doctor for David is evidence of how seriously ill he was and how worried they were about him. In 1912, there were no Black physicians serving Suffolk, so Lewis and Priscilla had to call a white doctor, whose surname happened to be White. He saw David alive only once, on April 15, when he diagnosed him with TB. The next time Dr. White dealt with David's case was on June 15, when he signed his death certificate.[32]

To Dr. White, David Joyner was just another Black man with TB. Since the end of the Civil War, when emancipated people began their first migration to southern cities and towns, white southerners had used the increased prevalence of TB (then called consumption) among the newcomers as evidence of Black inferiority. Labeled "the negro servants' disease," TB represented a host of white anxieties about the post-emancipation world. Not only were they concerned about the growing population of urban Blacks who were more difficult to surveil and police than they had been on southern plantations, but also white southerners decried the transformation of the southern labor market now that Black workers had gained some power to negotiate their pay and the conditions of their work. In cities across the South, as white families opened their doors to Black domestic workers, the fear that these women posed a hidden danger to white households began to take shape.[33]

Consumption had always been racialized to some degree. Prior to the Civil War, it was widely known as the "White Death" because of the pale, wasted physique of its chronic sufferers. Romanticized as the disease of poets and painters, it was believed to heighten their artistic and spiritual abilities. But in the American South after the Civil War, consumption became associated with poor Black urban workers almost exclusively. Even after German physician Robert Koch discovered the bacteria that caused tuberculosis in 1882, white southerners continued to believe that it was Black people's racial inferiority—and their emancipation—that spread the disease.[34]

Writing in a Virginia medical journal, a white physician from Petersburg elaborated on the myth that enslaved people had been immune to disease and ill health. An epic fabrication belied by the evidence presented in slaveholders' account books and diaries—where enslaved people's diseased and disabled bodies were accounted and doctors paid to treat them—the idea that slavery had fortified and enlivened its victims echoed throughout the post-emancipation period. "Physically, under good care, wholesome diet, prompt medical attention, and the restraints upon roving at night and other dissipation, the negro had developed before his emancipation into fine specimens of manhood," wrote Dr. John H. Claiborne in his pseudo-scientific plantation fantasy.[35]

The Civil War, however, had opened a "Pandora Box of ills" that claimed the lives of freedpeople, according to the doctor. Claiborne listed—without evidence—a number of ailments, including "consumption, scrofula, cancer, syphilis," that enslaved people did not previously suffer but emancipated people did in great numbers. Claiborne relied on his own unassailable authority as an expert and the equally unassailable common sense that all white people supposedly possessed about the contagion that Black people carried in and on their bodies.[36]

The white medical community perpetuated theories of contagion based in "scientific" thinking that resembled superstitions of a much earlier era. Like their sixteenth-century ancestors who blamed crop failures on witchcraft, nineteenth- and early twentieth-century physicians like Dr. Claiborne, and most likely Dr. White, the physician who treated David Joyner, looked to equally spurious explanations for Black illness, particularly TB. Even when white physicians acknowledged that TB was a public health problem for *all* Virginians, they continued to insist that the epidemic originated among Black people and spread due to their ignorance and lack of personal hygiene. The Virginia State Tuberculosis Commission, organized in 1914, reported that the disease killed more Virginians, white or Black, than smallpox, diphtheria, typhoid, measles, scarlet fever, and whooping cough combined. In step with public health measures across the country, the commission called for a comprehensive campaign of prevention, which included early diagnosis, treatment, and home-sanitation measures. They also acknowledged that TB was not just an urban problem but that the rural death rate "was not far below" that of city dwellers. Yet, despite these acknowledgments, the commissioners declared, "Tuberculosis in Virginia cannot be controlled except by controlling tuberculosis in the negro race."[37]

However, not all scientifically trained, educated people succumbed to the racialized way of understanding TB. Writing in the *Southern Workman*, the journal for Hampton Institute, a leader in

Black education since the 1860s and only a few miles from Suffolk, physician Joseph France dismissed the idea that Black inferiority caused TB, and instead pointed to the harsh working and living conditions of Black urban residents as well as their lack of food, inability to keep their clothes or living quarters clean, and the lack of sanitary regulations in the "Black" sections of towns. Likewise, Black sociologist W. E. B. Du Bois, in his study of Black Philadelphia, concluded that it was not racial inferiority but poverty and the segregated "social conditions" of urban life that accounted for the high infection and death rates from TB and other preventable diseases.[38]

Neither France nor Du Bois denied that Black people suffered from TB disproportionately, or that racial determinants in Black health and mortality existed. Where they differed with Claiborne and other white medical professionals was in their conclusions about why those disparities existed and what should be done to alleviate them. France proposed the creation of a committee on TB prevention and the use of visiting nurses to train Black families in the care of TB patients and the methods of sanitation that would prevent the spread of the disease. France noted that the traditional forms of care for consumptive patients, namely the use of sanatoriums to provide sufferers with rest and recuperative treatment, were nonexistent for Black TB patients. It wasn't until 1917 that the Piedmont Sanatorium in rural Burkeville, Virginia, opened; it was the first sanatorium for Black TB patients in the United States.[39]

Piedmont came too late for David Joyner and his sister Mamie, who died of the disease two years later in 1914. But in all likelihood, had it existed when they became ill, it would not have made much difference in their outcomes. Both David and Mamie exhibited signs of an aggressive secondary TB infection for which there was little treatment. Most likely they had been exposed initially in early childhood. These primary infections sometimes showed no symptoms or quickly cleared up on their own. The bacteria would lie dormant in the body's tissues, sometimes for decades, before emerging in its most virulent form in adulthood. In the most vulnerable patients, infants and the elderly, or those who were already sick or with weakened immune systems, the disease would escape the lungs and quickly spread throughout the body, infecting the skin, joints, bones, intestines, kidneys, bladder, and brain. Death was certain although not always swift. David Joyner lingered for two months. Mamie died within two weeks, but how agonizing must those weeks have been for Priscilla, forced to watch her daughter gasp for air as she drowned in her own bodily fluids, knowing there was nothing she could do to save her?[40]

It would not be the last time Priscilla had to hold the hand of one of her dying children. In 1917, three years after Mamie's death and five years after David's, TB claimed the life of Priscilla and Lewis's thirty-four-year-old daughter, Jencie, who worked as a domestic in Suffolk. Two years later, Lizzie, who had married and was living in North Carolina, died from uremia, a condition often caused by kidney failure. She had just given birth to a daughter, Della, who came to live with her grandparents in Suffolk. They cared for the baby as best they could, but she succumbed to TB the following year, in 1920. Della's death from TB calls into question the cause of death listed on her mother's death certificate. Infants usually contracted the disease through their mothers in utero and developed the ravaging miliary form of the disease shortly after birth. It's likely that Lizzie's primary cause of death was also TB, which had spread to her kidneys. Later that same year, Priscilla's youngest child, named for her mother, died from TB. Like her sisters Jencie, Mamie, and Lizzie, she worked as a domestic. She was twenty years old.[41]

The Joyner girls all died from the "negro servants' disease," and their deaths, much like their lives, went nearly unrecorded except for the death certificates issued by the states of Virginia and North Carolina. These documents can give us important clues about their lives that we would not otherwise know. Death certificates list not only causes of death but also occupations, names of spouses and parents, and burial locations. What they cannot tell us, however, was the emotional toll illness took on the women and their families, how deeply it must have pained Priscilla to nurse five of her children and one grandchild with little hope that they would recover.

The death certificates also cannot tell us what indignities Lewis and Priscilla might have endured from the white doctor they called to tell them what they probably already knew: their child was dying. They would have ignored the silent or not-so-silent judgments he made about their home and its cleanliness. Regardless of how it appeared when he visited the house to see David and his sisters, he would have assumed her home was dirty and that she was a poor housekeeper. This negative assumption about Black women and their homes was the foundation for the myth of the "negro servants' disease" as it emerged after emancipation. The home Priscilla and Lewis worked so hard to buy and maintain, the center of their family life and a symbol of their ability to shed the yoke of servitude, was, in the eyes of the white doctor, a pest house. But they would have swallowed their pride and implored him to help their son and daughters and baby granddaughter—to ease their suffering if he could not save their lives.

He took their money and left, no doubt scrubbing himself when he got home and ordering his Black maid to boil his clothes, thinking all the while about how the Joyners epitomized the tragedy of emancipation he and his white colleagues lamented on a weekly if not daily basis. The doctor most likely blamed Priscilla for the sickness that plagued her children. As he bathed and put on a clean suit, Dr. White might have given the Joyners one last thought. *They should have stayed in the country, on the plantations and farms, where they were happy and healthy.*

· —— ·

AFTER DAVID AND HIS SISTERS and niece died, Suffolk's only Black undertaker came to the Joyner home to tend to their bodies. Founded in 1909, Crocker and Boykins Funeral Home offered the area's Black residents a respectful, dignified "homegoing" in an era when white undertakers relegated Black bodies to the basements of their funeral parlors, overcharged for their services, and routinely used cheap or substandard coffins and embalming materials for their Black customers. Before they began the embalming process, either Wiley Crocker, his brother William, or their partner John Boykins would have hung a black banner or wreath on the front of the Joyners' house to alert neighbors that solemn rituals were taking place inside. After ushering the family members into another room or out into the yard, they would begin the process of draining the blood from the body and replacing it with embalming fluid. This ensured that the body would last for a funeral that might be delayed a week or more to allow for far-off relatives and friends to travel home to say goodbye. Most of the Joyners' relatives lived in North Carolina, but it still might take several days for everyone to gather in Suffolk. Something about the preservation of the corpse also comforted family members who shuddered at the thought of their loved ones starting to decay before their eyes. Embalming made the body less rigid and restored some color and fullness to the flesh. With careful attention from a trained undertaker, who would apply makeup and rouge as well as arrange hair and clothing, families could see their loved ones whole and at peace, no matter how much they had suffered in death.[42]

Black undertakers and funeral directors like the Crocker brothers and John Boykins were an important part of the growing Black middle class. Along with Black barbers, tailors, and other small businessmen, Black undertakers provided an important service to their people and became pillars of their communities. Wiley Crocker founded the Tidewater Fair Association and soon expanded his business interests to real estate. With other local Black businessmen, he founded the

Nansemond Development Corporation and oversaw the development of Black residential and commercial real estate projects in Suffolk and the surrounding areas. Like Black undertakers in other cities and towns, Crocker became a wealthy man.[43] But success did not come easily. When the first Black undertakers began competing with white funeral homes, they encountered hostility and veiled threats. In Hattiesburg, Mississippi, a white undertaker passed out handbills to local Black residents warning them against using the new Black undertaker in town. "Don't patronize these niggers, we can give you better service," the handbill read.[44]

White undertakers did not, in fact, provide better service. Elijah Cook, a member of the charter generation and a carpenter living in Montgomery, Alabama, noticed that white undertakers treated Black corpses roughly and hauled them in ordinary wagons without much in the way of respect or pageantry. Soon after the Civil War, Cook bought a hearse and started offering dignified funeral services to Montgomery's Black community. Within twenty years, he had amassed a sizable fortune and became one of the town's leading citizens. Other Black funeral directors marketed themselves as conscientious, trustworthy, fair, and compassionate—qualities white funeral directors often lacked when it came to dealing with Black customers.[45]

Not everyone approved of the growing importance Black people placed on "funeralizing," the term scholar Karla FC Holloway uses to describe the business of burial and memorialization. As the number of Black funeral homes grew, so did the level of services they offered. Hearses drawn by teams of meticulously groomed horses, rivers of flowers, and caskets made of mahogany and other expensive materials, adorned with satin, lace, and other fineries, drove up the costs of funerals and led many families to take on the added expense of cash premiums for burial insurance. Some race leaders, like W. E. B. Du Bois, worried that Black people wasted money that could be better spent on buying a home or educating their children.[46]

Hortense Powdermaker, a white sociologist who studied rural Black communities in Alabama in the 1930s, noted the lengths poor families would go to ensure their kin a proper burial:

"Burial insurance is usually the first to be taken out and the last to be relinquished when times grow hard. It is considered more important by the very poor than sickness or accident insurance. No Negro . . . can live content unless he is assured of a fine funeral when he dies."[47]

What can explain this seeming preoccupation with death and dying? Why place such importance on having a funeral if it meant depriving your family of basic necessities? The answers to these questions lie deep in the past. During the antebellum period, enslaved people viewed death not only as loss but also as liberation and escape, a permanent reprieve from the endless toil and brutality of the slave regime. Death fulfilled the promise of return held in the spirituals, the chance to "fly away" and to be reunited with those lost to time and sale. Slave funerals were expressions of collective grief and hope but also conducted under the watchful eye of overseers and owners. Most slave funerals were brief, unadorned affairs. They rarely allowed time for lengthy goodbyes.

The cursory fashion with which most enslaved people were put to rest, the absence of reverence or ceremony, the unceasing nature of slave labor that denied any time for grieving, the lack of control enslaved people had over the burial of their kin—these conditions shaped how the charter generation and the generations to come viewed funerals. The desire for a better send-off, even for a grand display of respect and love, would not be seen as a wasteful extravagance. The ever-present threat of violence and death that has haunted Black people since slavery has shaped their relationship to death and their funerary practices, resulting in a culture that expects death and celebrates the dead in ways that white culture does not appreciate. Black funeralizing says, "These lives were precious. These lives should be mourned," to a world that so often has refused to see Black lives as worthy of grief.

Black educator and charter generation member Booker T. Washington put it another way. Although he would eventually come to applaud the ingenuity of Black undertakers like Elijah Cook, he couldn't help but feel troubled about the mindset that allowed men like Cook to rise so far. "The trouble with us," Washington remarked, "is that we are always preparing to die."[48]

Not everyone cared for the new, professionalized funeralizing practices. Georgina Cassibry, an ex-slave living near Mobile, frowned upon undertakers and "big funerals." She wanted nothing to do with them. "There's something else I want to tell you," she said to her interviewer, "when I die I don't want no undertaker putting his hands on me. I believe if one would touch me I believe I'd get up." It's not clear if Cassibry thought undertakers were too eager and might embalm a person who was not yet dead, or if a stranger's handling of the body might somehow interfere with that person's ability to pass over. Cassibry appreciated the earlier rituals that involved families more directly in the funeral preparations. "If you want to see a good show, just go to a big funeral," she continued. "I don't believe in them," she said, referring to modern funerals. "Why, years ago people tended to their own dead and bought their coffins and put them in it."[49]

As members of the charter generation, Lewis and Priscilla may have shared some of Georgina Cassibry's disapproval of large and expensive funerals. But having lost so many children in such a short period of time, they would have appreciated the care and attention Crocker and Boykins gave their boy and his sisters, as well as their little granddaughter Della. The house on Second Avenue, once a source of pride for Lewis and Priscilla, a manifestation of their hopes and a symbol of their hard-fought journey from slavery, had become a house of death. There, David, Mamie, baby Della, and young Priscilla had suffered and died. There, Lewis and Priscilla had watched and waited, helpless to stop their decline or ease their pain. After they were gone, was Priscilla able to make the beds without seeing her dying children lying in them? Did she internalize the racist narratives about cleanliness and TB and blame the house, or herself, for causing their deaths?

These questions cannot be answered by the existing documentary record. Yet asking them is necessary if we are to begin to comprehend the personal costs of the continued discrimination and neglect formerly enslaved people faced in their struggle to make freedom real. The home that Priscilla and Lewis worked so hard to make, a place to shelter their children, also housed their worst pain. It represented all of Priscilla's hopes and desires, but it also represented her fears, her sorrows, and possibly her shame.

. —— .

ANN ELIZA JOYNER had one final wish: to see Priscilla one more time. It was the winter of 1920, and Ann Eliza, then eighty-four, had been bedridden for almost a year. The cause of her death, when it came on February 7, would be listed as "chronic myocarditis" or, in layman's terms, heart disease. It was an unsurprising diagnosis in someone of her advanced age. By the standards of the time, when the average white woman born in 1850 could expect to live forty years, Ann Eliza, who was born in 1836, had lived over twice as long. She had experienced much change in her lifetime, including the dissolution of the family she attempted to build with Priscilla and her other children. When Ann Eliza chose to send twelve-year-old Priscilla to live with the Dancy family in Rocky Mount in 1870, the move marked the beginning of an estrangement, at first physical but soon emotional as well, that would characterize their relationship for the rest of their lives.[50]

In the Dancys' home, Priscilla found comfort and acceptance with an adopted family who cared for her physical needs, provided her with a safe place to lay her head, and saw to her education. In Tarboro and neighboring Freedom Hill, she met formerly enslaved people and watched them build communities in the shadow of slavery. There she learned that a new life was possible. Contentment, even happiness, could be hers, but, she felt, only if she cut ties with Ann Eliza. Soon Priscilla dreaded the yearly Christmas visit to the Joyner farm, and it wasn't just because of the teasing and abuse she may have continued to receive from Ann Eliza's other children. Priscilla had never felt a part of the family, but before her move to Tarboro she had no other experience by which to judge her feelings. Now she did.

It's unknown how many times Priscilla may have traveled back to Nash County to visit Ann Eliza in the intervening years. From the time she and Lewis moved to Virginia in the late 1880s until Ann Eliza's death, Priscilla had given birth to ten children, set up a house that she and Lewis owned, established the garden that would make her famous in Suffolk, and buried at least three of her children. There was not much time for visits to North Carolina, although Ida, the daughter Ann Eliza gave up shortly after her birth in 1866, still lived there, as did many members of both Priscilla and Lewis's extended family. But Ann Eliza's worsening condition brought her back one final time for a heart-wrenching visit that Priscilla recalled to Thelma Dunston nearly twenty years later. "She cried and sobbed and told me how much she regretted the wrongs she'd done me," recalled Priscilla, who did not elaborate on the details of what Ann Eliza said in their last meeting.[51]

Perhaps Ann Eliza was sorry for not giving her up at birth, as the enslaved people in the neighborhood had wanted her to do—or for taking her from her people in the first place, if that is what she had done. Or perhaps she regretted taking Rix back and allowing him and the other children to torment the girl. Maybe she wished she had never sent her away to the Dancys'. But there was one thing she did not regret. "[I] told her there was one thing I'd always wanted to know—the name of my father," Priscilla said. But her mother was not ready to make her confession. "She closed her eyes and turned her head away," Priscilla recalled.[52]

Priscilla pressed her again, but Ann Eliza was adamant. After all these years, even though the man was long dead, she would not reveal his identity. "He was a good man, Prissie, and you're a lot like him," was all she would say.[53]

Despite her unwillingness to give her daughter the one thing that mattered most to her, Ann Eliza wanted Priscilla to believe that she had only wanted the best for her. "Just remember that I'm your mother," she said, "and I love you as much as any mother ever loved a child."[54]

Ann Eliza had promised to leave the biggest portion of her estate to Priscilla when she first sent the girl to live with the Dancys. Now she repeated that promise. But Priscilla was not interested in the farm or any other material possession her mother might leave her.

"I told her I didn't need nothing, and that she didn't owe me a thing. I told her how happy I'd been with Lewis and my children and that it had been the best thing in the world for me to be put with my own people." But nothing eased Ann Eliza's gnawing regrets or Priscilla's desire to know her father's identity.[55]

When the visit was over, Ann Eliza's eldest son, Robert, drove Priscilla back to the train station in Rocky Mount. Priscilla recalled that both he and Jolly had been very cordial to her. Their families, however, were another matter. Their reception was chilly, to say the least. Their wives and children barely spoke to her the whole time she was there.

Not long after she returned home, she received a letter from Jolly telling her that Ann Eliza had died. Jolly also informed her that his mother had left no will, and that she had transferred the farm to Robert years ago. Priscilla knew he was lying, but she didn't care. What did that farm, the place she had spent the unhappiest years of her life, matter? She couldn't have the one thing she really wanted. Ann Eliza had taken it with her to the grave.

Priscilla's eldest son, Frank, felt differently. He viewed the farm as restitution for all the heartache his mother had endured while living there. No doubt, she and the rest of the family could use the money its sale would bring. Every time he came down from New York to visit her, he tore the house up looking for Jolly's letter, which Priscilla claimed to have lost. She told him not to worry about it. She had everything she needed right there where she was.

"I have my own place here and my flowers," she told Dunston.[56]

EIGHT

NO COUNTRY FOR OLD AGE

· —— ·

FOR MOST OF ITS HISTORY, the United States has not been a haven for old people. Historians disagree about the extent to which colonial Americans venerated the relatively small elderly population who resided mainly in New England prior to 1790, and precisely when the "denigration of old age" began. They also disagree about why early Americans began to see old people as a problem instead of as a valuable resource. Was it because there was no systematic way to care for them as their numbers began to grow after the American Revolution? Was it because industrialization in the early nineteenth century altered family structures in such a way that old people who could no longer work became burdens to their kin as well as to the state? Did the elderly's frail, disabled, and often diseased bodies come to signify failure, dependence, and corruption—attributes considered anathema to a Victorian culture that prized success, vitality, and purity? The answer to all of these questions is yes. A culmination of interrelated social, economic, and cultural transformations altered both the status of old people and the experience of being old in America.[1]

But one thing is certain: old people rarely enjoyed the mythologized esteem that we might believe they deserved or wish they were afforded. For many, particularly the poor and marginalized, advanced age was not a blessing but rather a curse, a continuation of the hard conditions under which they had lived and labored during the preceding years of life. For Priscilla Joyner and the other members of the charter generation, advancing age brought little respite from work or worry. In fact, freedom exacerbated the precarities of age and the inequalities of race in unforeseen ways.

This was because age functioned as a tool to reinforce gendered and racial hierarchies in the United States. Two examples of this stand out in the history of the charter generation's long emancipation. In the first, apprenticeship laws used age as a marker to ensure racial control. Black children were routinely indentured for longer periods than white children; Black boys until they were older than Black girls. This was true both before and after slavery in states like North Carolina, where Priscilla was born. When it came to making Black children obedient and pliable, "age was the device that lawmakers used in order to create what they hoped would be the most useful raced and gendered servants."[2]

A second example involves Civil War pensions. Many Black Union veterans and their widows who had been enslaved faced a nearly insurmountable obstacle to receiving a pension: providing proof of their birthdate, or the birthdates of their children. These facts often went unrecorded in plantation records, and therefore became unverifiable in the eyes of the federal bureaucracy. If an applicant could not prove their age, or prove that the children they claimed as dependents were, in fact, of dependent age (younger than sixteen in most cases), then the Pension Bureau would likely deem the case an example of age fraud.[3]

Members of the charter generation experienced age as yet another way the systems of American governance eroded their hopes for freedom. Even those programs that many post-emancipation lawmakers and reformers saw as race-neutral, such as the pension system, penalized former slaves unfairly and rendered null their most basic claims to citizenship. When the federal government began rolling out New Deal relief programs in the 1930s to combat the effects of the Great Depression, many ex-slaves lived in poverty so dire that FWP fieldworkers commented on their living conditions in interview transcripts. Some interviewers, living on a meager federal paycheck themselves, even bought their elderly subjects food.

Priscilla Joyner was better off financially than many others of her generation. Although Lewis died of kidney failure in 1926, she owned her home and brought in money selling flowers. She also had grown children to help support her. While other FWP narrators spoke openly of generational conflict with their children or grandchildren, Priscilla's testimony only glanced at the loneliness and isolation she felt as an elderly widow, a fatherless child, and a self-identified ex-slave. Although she had found "her people" among the community of former slaves, she shared with them a growing sense of difference that only increased with age and shaped their sense of who they were and what their lives had meant. This internal struggle marked what was for some the most enduring phase of the long emancipation.[4]

Toward the end of their conversation, when Thelma Dunston asked Priscilla about how she was getting along, Priscilla answered with a question of her own. "What more could an old woman want?"[5]

This was not just a statement about her own relative good fortune, a modest way of saying, "I'm alright." It was also rhetorical. Priscilla's question contained within it a myriad of possible answers that stretched far beyond her own individual life to touch on the lives of other charter generation members during the Great Depression. Their stories reveal not only what it was like to be old and Black and formerly enslaved in the United States but also what it means to take stock of your life and what you want as you enter your final years. What more could I want? What more could I have accomplished if not for the circumstances of my birth? What other paths might I have chosen if they had been open to me? What have I learned from the life I have lived? These questions did not appear on any suggested list provided by the FWP. But they lived in the minds of the narrators as they attempted to put their memories and feelings into words.

As the interviewees worked to articulate the meaning in their own lives, others sought to define them in ways that distorted their experiences. White nostalgia for the Old South, its popularity soaring during the Great Depression, drained the charter generation's lives of the vibrancy that becomes readily apparent when reading the interview transcripts. By the 1930s, former slaves had become ciphers for white anxiety about their own economic vulnerability, the nation's impending collapse, and growing racial tensions. As Black Americans' support for President Roosevelt and his New Deal policies increased, their historical alliance with the Republican Party—the party of Lincoln and emancipation—began to erode. This political realignment would make the majority of Black voters Democrats and coincided with increasing militancy among Black leaders, such as A. Philip Randolph, a former Pullman porter who organized the first March on Washington in 1942 to protest racial discrimination in federal employment. Just as America entered World War II, President Roosevelt responded with Executive Order 8802, guaranteeing that all persons regardless of color would be allowed to fully participate in all defense-related work. It was a time of rapid change, and the idea of the ex-slave as a symbol of loyalty, submissiveness, and timelessness soothed many white Americans who found the changes unsettling.

·——·

IN 1859, EDWARD POLLARD was returning to his Virginia birthplace after several years away working as a journalist. He had spent most of the past decade in California, where he witnessed the aftermath of the Gold Rush. The onslaught of settlers hungry for riches, the disorder and lawlessness of mining towns, the violent clashes between greedy prospectors and Indigenous people, the drinking, the unbridled avarice, the filth—all of it convinced Pollard of the insidious rot at the heart of a free labor society. He longed for the tranquility of the South, an essentially feudal society, as he saw it, supported by the virtue of chivalry and the natural hierarchy of slavery. On the train as he neared his boyhood home near Charlottesville, Pollard saw "the first unadulterated negro" he had seen since leaving the South years earlier. The sight of the old man nearly brought Pollard to tears. "He looked like *home*," Pollard wrote. "I could have embraced the old uncle, but was afraid the passengers, from such a demonstration, might mistake me for an abolitionist."[6]

The old man stirred in Pollard memories of his carefree boyhood on the plantation, fishing with his "sable playmates" and wandering the acres of his family's slaveholding domain. To the writer who later would coin the term "Lost Cause" to describe the Confederacy's doomed attempt to become an independent slaveholding republic, the elderly Black man represented all that Pollard thought of as good and noble about the South, and slavery, and himself. He was a symbol of Pollard's fading youth, and of the slave South's imagined invincibility. But in reality, the image of the loyal, elderly slave was little more than a figment of the white South's racist imagination.[7]

In their political propaganda, slavery's apologists touted the presence of elderly enslaved people on southern plantations as evidence of the institution's benevolence. Contrary to what abolitionists claimed, slaveholders like Pollard insisted that enslaved people were well treated and enjoyed long lives under the care of masters who rewarded years of loyalty and service with good homes, plenty of food, and medical care. In fact, enslaved people of advanced age often endured the same physical brutality and neglect they had faced in their younger days.[8]

By and large, the fantasy of slaveholder paternalism, the long-heralded values of caregiving, mutual obligation, and respect for the aged enslaved, evaporated with the dawn of emancipation. There were some former enslavers who believed they had a responsibility to care for the elderly people they had once owned who were now incapable of working and supporting themselves. "Old Amelia and her grandchildren I will spare the mockery of offering freedom to," promised South Carolina planter Henry Ravenel. "I must support them as long as I have anything to give."[9]

But for every Ravenel who vowed to support the aged people he once claimed ownership of, there were countless others who turned their backs on the old and broken. A northern journalist touring the South after the war was shocked to run across an elderly ex-slave on his way to Richmond. He paused to talk to the old man, who had stopped to rest along the roadside. The old man told him he had walked all the way from Dinwiddie County, a distance of about fifty miles. Why in the world would he embark on such a long and arduous journey? The elderly freedman explained that his master had turned out everyone on the plantation, including the sick and elderly.

"I knowed I was old and wore-out," the old man explained, "but I growed so in his service. I served him and his father before nigh on to sixty year; and he never give me a dollar. He's had my life, and now I'm old and wore-out I must leave." Dejected but not defeated, the old man accepted this hardship as the price for freedom, however little time he had left to explore it. When the journalist asked if he had not been better off in slavery, the old freedman rejected the idea. "I'd sooner be as I is to-day," he declared, as he picked up his bundle and made his way onward to Richmond.[10]

Elderly ex-slaves did not necessarily expect to stay on with their former owners; nor did they want to. South Carolina slave owner Grace Elmore reeled from her elderly nurse's decision to leave her. "Old Mary" had cared for Elmore when she was a child as well as all of Elmore's children, one of whom was still an infant. No sense of "duty" bound Mary to her former mistress or the baby, a fact that appalled

Elmore, who called her "the most pampered and indulged old woman" one could find anywhere.[11]

As indignant as former slave owners like Elmore were, it wasn't long before elderly ex-slaves became celebrated figures in white American culture. In songs, stories, and later cinema, white Americans celebrated elderly slaves and ex-slaves as symbols of what had been lost in the passing of slavery and the brutal ruptures of the Civil War and its aftermath. Not only did sentimental songs like the Stephen Foster classic "Old Uncle Ned" remain popular throughout the late nineteenth century, southern writers capitalized on the image for new audiences. Southern writer Joel Chandler Harris created Uncle Remus, a fictionalized elderly slave who told folktales about Br'er Rabbit and his exploits in a heavy dialect that made Black southerners appear comedic and simple. Between 1881 and 1907, Harris published six volumes of Uncle Remus tales. Three more collections appeared after his death in 1908. The last one appeared in 1948, testifying to the enduring appeal of these plantation tales well into the twentieth century. In 1946, Walt Disney produced a live-action and partially animated musical based on Chandler's stories. *Song of the South* premiered in Atlanta, just as *Gone with the Wind*, another Lost Cause celluloid success, had seven years earlier. With a bluebird perched on his shoulder, Uncle Remus sang the film's catchy Oscar-winning theme song, "Zip-a-Dee-Doo-Dah," teaching audiences for generations that everything in the antebellum South was "satisfactch'll."[12]

As these stories and images saturated American culture in the decades after the Civil War, the charter generation became tokens of white nostalgia—the same kind Edward Pollard peddled in the years leading up to emancipation. "If there were no other evidence of the care and kind treatment of the slaves by their masters, it would be found in the sturdy constitution and the long life vouchsafed to many of them," began the introduction to a pictorial "character study" of elderly former slaves published in 1915. The book's major theme was loyalty: the loyalty of the enslaved to their masters, and of masters to "their people."[13]

Author Essie Collins Matthews, the daughter of a South Carolina slaveholder, combined her sentimental prose with carefully composed photographic portraits of ex-slaves to make this argument. Entitled *Aunt Phebe, Uncle Tom, and Others: Character Studies Among the Old Slaves of the South, Fifty Years Later*, the book presented elderly ex-slaves as people living out of time, relics of bygone days trapped in a world that no longer existed except in the tableaux Matthews created. In one study, Matthews presented a freedwoman named Murriah Flood as the antithesis of "Old Mary," the nurse who had abandoned Grace Elmore just after the Civil War. In the photograph taken by Matthews, Flood wears a nineteenth-century-style bodice, apron, and head wrap, just as she might have in the old days before the war. According to the caption that accompanied the photograph, she worked as a nurse for her former mistress's great-grandchildren. Matthews devoted much of the chapter on the Faunsdale Plantation in Alabama, where Flood lived and worked both in slavery and in freedom, to the gracious behavior of the "saintly mistress" who provided the enslaved laborers with religious instruction. Matthews provides little personal information about Flood or Faunsdale's other surviving former slaves, except that she left the place shortly after the war, but after "an unhappy experience," she soon returned. The reader is left to conclude that Flood's decision to return to Faunsdale and spend her life caring for her former mistress's family was so much better than whatever she had done while she was away that it required no further explanation.[14]

In addition to written texts like Matthews's, white Americans staged Lost Cause publicity stunts in the early twentieth century to keep the mythology alive, and elderly ex-slaves played an important role in such performances. "Old Slave Day" festivals pretended to honor "loyal" ex-slaves in southern communities who had stayed with their white families. These celebrations offered white attendees an opportunity to indulge in a generous helping of nostalgia along with their barbeque. In Southern Pines, North Carolina, a small town about one hundred miles from Nash County where Priscilla and Lewis grew up, Old Slave Day coincided with the annual Spring Blossom Festival. At the end of the week's festivities, the town councilmen and festival organizers feted an estimated one hundred elderly men and women who had once belonged to the local slaveholding families. As the *New York Times* reported in 1935, "At noon the old slaves were seated on benches forming a circle on the lawns of the village park, where visitors had the opportunity of talking with them while a picnic lunch was being served."[15]

Photograph of Murriah Flood, a formerly enslaved woman at Fausdale Plantation in Alabama. Taken in 1915, the photograph presents Flood as the ideal loyal ex-slave who chose to stay with her former mistress's family after emancipation.
COURTESY NEW YORK PUBLIC LIBRARY

Following the luncheon, a crowd of as many as 7,000 visitors enjoyed a Black choir singing "Negro spirituals" and a sermon from a local Black minister who was an ex-slave himself. Later in the afternoon, a troupe of Black youth performed the "buck and wing," a style of tap dancing made famous by white minstrel shows as well as Black dancers like Bill "Bojangles" Robinson. The day concluded with a "free-for-all" boxing match that involved at least ten boxers and a concert from the Fort Bragg marching band.[16]

The elderly people and other members of the Black community who attended these events had many reasons for doing so, not least of which was the fact that in the Jim Crow South, you risked the ire

According to local whites, Old Slave Day was the best day of these formerly enslaved people's post-emancipation lives. A field worker for the FWP snapped this photograph at the 1937 event in Southern Pines, North Carolina.
COURTESY LIBRARY OF CONGRESS

of local whites if you refused. It was often easier to play along in order to get along. And perhaps some enjoyed being celebrated, even if it was all for show. The care and concern whites showed them was fleeting; tomorrow most would go back to their hardscrabble lives, but at least they would go home that night with a full stomach.

· —— ·

ANDREW BOONE was hungry. Tomatoes, sliced and warmed in a dry, hot pan to give them a little flavor—that's all he had to eat the day the FWP field-worker came to visit him in the old tobacco barn he called home in rural Wake County, North Carolina. He had no grease to cook them in. He rarely had any meat from which to collect any. The day before he ate some bread, but that was all gone. He had cooked up the tomatoes on an open fire under a lean-to he had constructed next to the barn, which really wasn't much of a barn anymore. They hadn't hung tobacco in it for years. Boone had been a farmhand all his life, working first for his old master just after freedom and then for his master's children until they all died. Then he found work wherever he could. But he was ninety now and no longer able to perform the exhausting manual labor that was required of farmhands. His last employer let him live in the old barn when he was no longer able to work.[17]

Without any means of support, Boone had reached one of his lowest moments when the fieldworker arrived. "I set down by the road thinking about how to turn and what to do to get a meal, when you come along," Boone told the interviewer. Taking pity on the old man, the white interviewer gave him some money. Boone thanked him saying, "I guess God made you give it to me."[18]

Other fieldworkers found their interview subjects in similar states of hunger and poverty. When the interviewer arrived at Gable Locklier's place near Marion, South Carolina, on a Wednesday afternoon, his last full meal had been on the previous Sunday. Ninety-year-old Mintie Wood, who was blind and earned a few cents by salvaging old rags and bottles from her neighbors in St. Louis, admitted to eating only twice a day. After her noontime meal, she sated her hunger by drinking water throughout the rest of the day and night. Julia Brown was in the middle of telling the story of how she met her second husband when she cut the interview short. "Lord, honey, I got such a pain in my stomach I don't believe I can go on. It's a gnawing kind of pain. Just keeps me weak all over."[19]

The interviewer promised to return in a few days to finish the interview. But she felt so sorry for Brown that she stopped at a small store in town and bought the woman some groceries. The store owner knew Brown, whom she referred to as "Aunt Sally," and shared that she, too, also gave the old woman and her elderly son food.

When the interviewer returned with the food, Julia Brown was overcome with joy. She eagerly tore open the bags and began to eat. As Brown cradled the eggs contained in her package, she promised the interviewer that she would make them last by cooking only one at a time.[20]

In the immediate aftermath of the Civil War, food was so scarce in many locations that freedpeople, now forced to "root, hog, or die," had no choice but to take whatever they could find, wherever they could find it. White southerners used their hunger against them, arresting freedpeople for stealing meager quantities of food: fifteen ears of corn, nine pounds of meat, an orange. The records of the Freedmen's Bureau record countless such incidents, documenting the efforts to re-enslave emancipated people with long prison sentences for the crime of being hungry. Isaac Lloyd, convicted of stealing two pigs near Brazos, Texas, pleaded with the court to have mercy on him because he "could not get enough to eat." So did Chester Scott, who also stole a hog and was sentenced to two years in prison. Scott admitted that the hog belonged to the man he was working for at the time, but he "did not get enough to eat." Danile Loflay stole a bushel and a half of corn, which he took to his children because they "were starving." Like Scott, Loflay was sentenced to two years in jail.[21]

Contrary to the Lost Cause narrative emerging at the time, white southerners did not spare old people in their scheme to instill order on what they believed was the topsy-turvy world of emancipation. The Freedmen's Bureau agent in Dallas, Texas, was particularly disturbed by the case of John Montgomery, "a lame old man crippled in both feet" who was accused of stealing seven pounds of pigs' feet. But the agent ultimately sided with the white man who brought spurious charges against Montgomery for the sake of preserving law and order. Montgomery admitted to taking the pieces left over from a hog slaughter but claimed he had permission from the plantation cook and had done so on several prior occasions. However, when the landowner found out, he accused Montgomery of stealing. The landowner persuaded the cook to deny that she had given the old man permission, and while the agent believed Montgomery's version of events, he lamented that it was an "extremely hard case." Like Lloyd, Scott, and Loflay, the old man was sentenced to prison, a tough but necessary outcome in the bureau's eyes. Freedpeople were dishonest and disinclined to work, according to white logic. If steep penalties for theft were not enforced, even for the aged and disabled like Montgomery, there would be no end to the disorder of post-emancipation society.[22]

The long emancipation consisted of cycles of national economic collapse, crop failures, and crushing debt peonage that made food security an elusive prize for many rural Blacks in the postbellum South. The Great Depression brought about another period defined by food scarcity. One study conducted in the early 1930s suggested that Black farm families spent at least half their money on food, mainly the "Three M's": meal, meat, and molasses. Forced to buy on credit from plantation stores, Black tenants were charged ten percent or more in interest on every purchase. Once inside, they found only a limited range of staples, including salt pork, meal, flour, and sugar. A wider selection of higher-quality meat, produce, and other goods was available only to cash buyers. The South's one-crop system discouraged planting food for home consumption. Tenants planted cotton up to their doorsteps, and if they managed to raise a vegetable patch somewhere out of sight, the landowner might charge them a portion of their cotton crop if he found out. Black farm families were less likely to have a milk cow or chickens than white farm families, meaning they did not have regular access to milk or eggs. Not surprisingly, many Black southerners were malnourished. One nutritional study conducted in 1928 found that more than half the Black people living in the Mississippi Delta were deficient in protein, iron, and calcium.[23]

Most rural Black southerners "did not have that far to fall when the Great Depression arrived," but the economic downturn of the 1930s worsened their already precarious economic conditions. Overall, Black unemployment rose to nearly fifty percent while it peaked at thirty-seven percent for white Americans. The price of cotton plummeted to six cents a bushel by 1933, driving the one-quarter of Black farmers who owned their land to the brink of collapse along with the rest of their sharecropping neighbors. Because of their advanced age, the charter generation was particularly vulnerable. While a few received some form of poor relief from their state—Julia Brown mentioned that she received seventy-five cents a week from the Georgia Department of Public Welfare—most had not seen any money from the 1935 Social Security Act, the federal benefits system that allowed monthly cash payments for people over the age of sixty-five. Many of the interview subjects had heard of these new government pensions but had little detailed information about how to get them. As representatives of the federal government, the FWP fieldworkers found themselves fielding questions about the pensions and fielding requests for assistance in applying for them.[24]

Robert Falls did not understand the system's residency requirements. He had moved to Tennessee three years earlier from North Carolina and had been told he had to wait another year to qualify for a pension from Tennessee. He hoped the interviewer could help him. Maybe she could write a letter or help him fill out forms, something that neither he nor his daughter with whom he lived was capable of doing.[25]

Elias Dawkins also wanted to know more about government pensions. He had only heard rumors about them, but he hoped the FWP worker could tell him more. He needed it desperately. "I is too shame to beg," Dawkins said. It was then that Dawkins admitted to eating a cow "chip" for nourishment when he had nothing else.[26]

These dire conditions sometimes led interviewees to compare their current living situation with how they had lived under slavery and during the immediate post-emancipation period. While some acknowledged that things were far worse back then, others recalled that they had better food and more of it when they were enslaved. Although some scholars have been quick to dismiss these favorable memories of slave rations as a form of nostalgia or misremembering, historian Stephanie Shaw urges readers to take the narrators at their word. Individuals' memories of good or plentiful food do not negate the stories of strict rationing and starvation told by other enslaved people. Circumstances varied; prime hands sometimes received more food, as did a cook's family members. "But more to the point," Shaw concludes, "while the stark deprivation that freedpeople experienced during the Great Depression might have made their memories of food during slavery more vivid, it did not have to make those memories incorrect."[27]

It also doesn't mean that the Lost Cause narrative of slaveholder paternalism was true, or that formerly enslaved people bought into it. When interviewers asked them if they preferred slavery to freedom (a favorite question among white interviewers brought up to revere the Lost Cause), elderly freedpeople answered carefully. Few dared to be confrontational with a white interviewer, but most found ways to make their views on the subject clear.[28]

"It's all hard, slavery and freedom, when you can't eat," Andrew Boone said from his seat in front of his dilapidated tobacco barn.[29]

. —— .

PRISCILLA JOYNER ENJOYED a level of economic security that others in the charter generation did not. As she pointed out to Thelma Dunston, she owned her own home, thanks to years of hard work and a little good fortune. She had children to rely on. Her daughter Liza lived nearby and could help out whenever her mother needed her. The Joyners' eldest, Frank, lived in New York and worked as a porter at a garage. He may have sent some money home if Priscilla was in need, but his ability to help out financially was limited. Frank had a large family to support. In 1930, he lived in a Bronx apartment with four grown children and two grandchildren. The Great Depression took its toll on urban Black laborers just as it did their rural southern kin. Frank's financial situation probably seemed uncertain throughout the 1930s.[30]

Family support could be a blessing for the elderly, but it could also cause tension. While some of the charter generation like Andrew Boone lived alone and worried about how to get by, others resented having to live with younger family members who did not appreciate their experiences or wisdom. "I don't know nothing about these fast present-day ways of living," admitted eighty-year-old Easter Huff at her home in Athens, Georgia. Huff believed younger folks lacked discipline and worried about the behavior he'd witnessed. "This young race lives so fast," he lamented, "they needs to know what a hard time us had."[31]

Huff loved "to talk 'bout the old times," but younger folks did not want to hear about slavery and how bad things used to be for their grandparents and great-grandparents. Those stories seemed so far removed from the reality of life in the twentieth century, a world with automobiles and telephones and ready-made clothes. Yes, times were still hard, and if you thought about it even a little bit, it was hard to avoid the conclusion that the grandson of an enslaved person living in 1930s Georgia had a lot more in common with his grandparents than he might care to admit. But they did not need to have it pointed out to them. It was too demoralizing.[32]

"My folks don't want me to talk about slavery," Sarah Debro told her interviewer. She thought she knew why. "They's shame [we] ever was slaves."[33]

As mentioned earlier, Sarah Debro's narrative was a coming-of-age story about being taken to live in the main house with her mistress in order to be the woman's "pet." In the house, young Sarah learned to love the relatively easy life she had compared to field hands, whom her mistress taught her to look down upon. She had clean dresses and good food. She slept on a soft pallet next to her mistress's bed. When freedom came, Sarah did not want to go back to her own mother to live in the quarters, and she cried at night in the cramped, cold, uncomfortable living conditions she now had. She said her mistress was always good to her, and that she loved her.[34]

If this was the same story Sarah Debro told her children and grandchildren, one imagines how it might have worn thin over the years.

What felt like reminiscing to her may have seemed like complaining to her relations. They interpreted her memories of how good she had it as a young enslaved servant as a judgment on *their* living conditions, which may not have been that far removed from what Debro had experienced after the war. Maybe they felt the old woman still carried the sense of superiority that her mistress drilled into her as a child. And Debro may have interpreted their irritation as shame. But it was also possible that a younger generation of Black southerners might find Debro's claims of love and devotion toward her enslaver shameful indeed.

Whichever was the case, Debro felt alienated from those who had not experienced slavery firsthand. Priscilla also feared that the past would drive a wedge between her and her children. Her life story, much like Debro's, was complicated, and the interviewers' questions scratched at old wounds that had never quite healed over. While Priscilla seemed content to let bygones be bygones when it came to Ann Eliza's will and the Joyner brothers' likely theft of her inheritance, the injustice ate at Frank. His incessant search for the letter from Jolly Joyner disturbed his mother, who wished he could just forget about it and enjoy his infrequent visits home. Her daughter, Liza, was named after Ann Eliza, but she refused to go by her full name.[35]

The FWP interviewers conjured up painful memories for some and, as Priscilla had feared when Lewis and Dunston arrived at her home, threatened to upend whatever hard-won peace they had established. But as painful as reliving the past could be, some elderly freedpeople were ready to talk. Will Sheets could no longer get around because he had lost his feet to "blood poisoning." He could not travel out to see people, and he missed the social connections he had before he became disabled. "I get powerful lonesome sometimes," he admitted. He enjoyed regaling his interviewer with old stories about his childhood. He remembered his parents, getting to eat sorghum candy at Christmastime as a child, and later, at his wedding. His bride wore a plain calico dress, but she looked beautiful to him.[36]

Gabe Hines. Courtesy Library of Congress

Gabe Hines also faced old age alone and disabled. Ever since a stroke left him "bandy in the knees," he could walk only with the help of two mismatched canes, one about six inches longer than the other. Hines's body may have been feeble, but his memory was sharp. He told the fieldworker a detailed story about how, during Reconstruction, he and his wife Anna had been tricked into leaving their home in Barbour County, Alabama, and going to Columbus, Georgia, to farm for a planter who wouldn't pay them. The landowner had promised them a nice cabin to live in, but it would hardly pass for a stable. Gabe and Anna spent the better part of a year there before they returned to Alabama. Gabe still lived in the house where he and Anna spent the rest of their lives, but it didn't feel like home since she had died. He grieved not only her but also the unhappy year they had spent in Columbus. Time was precious, and it pained him to think about any of it, especially his time with Anna, having been wasted. Everyone else he knew was gone, too. Gabe Hines had little to look forward to, except reuniting with his departed family and friends in the next life. "Maybe when I get to where Anna is, it will be old times all over again," he said.[37]

The charter generation longed for certain aspects of the past: the family members who had gone, their youth, and better health. But their nostalgia was not the same as Edward Pollard's and those white southerners who organized festivals that purported to honor elderly ex-slaves. They rejected those bad-faith attempts to implicate them in the various Lost Cause myth-making schemes that preoccupied much of American culture in the early decades of the twentieth century. For a brief moment, during some of the leanest days of the Great Depression, the voices of the elderly freedpeople became a vital component in a large-scale, federally sponsored public history project—the first and only one of its kind in the United States. The FWP provided them with an opportunity to author their own histories rather than remain passive characters in other people's stories. Like other forms of autobiography, these oral life narratives mark freedpeople's desire to be understood, and to understand for themselves slavery's impact on their lives and their long struggles to make meaningful lives in its shadow.[38]

.———.

PRISCILLA WASN'T WELL when Thelma Dunston first visited her in the late 1930s. She was slowing down, which was to be expected with anyone about to turn eighty. Her feet and legs swelled terribly sometimes, which was why she was wearing a pair of Lewis's old work boots that day. With the laces taken out, she could just get them on her feet. The edema signaled a more serious decline—heart or kidney disease were the most likely culprits. Like Lewis, who had suffered for years from kidney disease, Priscilla was experiencing a similar slow, agonizing decline. When her legs swelled, she would have had a hard time walking. Her feet would have felt numb and heavy, and sometimes the skin on her feet and ankles, stretched tight by the swelling, might have wept fluid.[39]

But as troubling as the pain and discomfort she felt in her body, Priscilla was also disheartened by the reality that the house and garden were becoming too much for her. She could no longer keep up with the orders for bouquets and corsages from the "biggest white ladies in town." It pained her to have to turn down those orders, not only because she hated to disappoint anyone but also because she needed the money. It was her only source of regular income. The sense of frailty that was slowly but steadily invading her body and mind—and along with it the knowledge that she could no longer rely upon her own strength and determination to see her through another chapter in life—compounded and perhaps even outweighed her pecuniary vulnerability.[40]

Liza came by every day or two to help out. Other than that, she was alone. She told Dunston that she had a young boy staying with her for a while, but it didn't work out. "He was an orphan," she explained, "and I was keeping so's to put him through school. But he was no count."

One day when Priscilla wasn't home, he searched the house and found a ten-dollar gold piece she had put away. When Priscilla noticed it was missing, she asked him about it, and he told a story about a thief who had come in the house and robbed her. Eventually he confessed to taking the coin. This kind of behavior Priscilla could not forgive.

Although she felt she had no choice but to send him away, Priscilla clearly missed having someone in the house. Her children had scattered. Liza was the only one with whom she had regular contact. Two of her boys, Frank and Harry, were in New York, having joined the Great Migration of southern Blacks to northern cities beginning around the time of the First World War. Priscilla also told Dunston that Hyman and his sister, Jencie, were "up North somewhere." But Hyman and his family lived just three houses up the street from his mother. Jencie had died of TB along with her brother, David, and Priscilla, the youngest sibling, during those terrible years of sickness between 1912 and 1920. But the elder Priscilla believed her youngest daughter was living in Rocky Mount.[41]

How can we explain Priscilla's obvious confusion over the location of some of her children? It could be that she was showing signs of dementia. Old age often scrambles memories. Ill health and exhaustion could have compromised her mental clarity. The trauma of having lost three of her children at such young ages and in close succession to TB may have taken its toll as she grew older. If she did suffer from dementia, it did not affect the veracity of her life narrative. Aside from some confusion around the date she and Lewis moved to Suffolk—she said it was "during the Spanish War," but according to the census the move occurred a decade prior to that—the details she dictated to Thelma Dunston are correct.[42]

As for Hyman, maybe she hadn't seen much of him recently. She told Dunston it had been ten years since she had seen any of her sons, but it's hard to imagine she wouldn't have laid eyes on Hyman coming in and out of the neighborhood. But perhaps that's all there had been, a momentary sighting. Had there been a family quarrel that drove a wedge between Hyman and his mother? Did Hyman drift away after Lewis's death in 1926, leaving Liza to take care of their mother? Whatever the reason, her children's absence from her home pained Priscilla and caused her to think about spending her final days alone. "I guess I'd just as soon live the short time I got left alone. It can't be long," she told Dunston.[43]

Priscilla Joyner would live for several more years. *The Negro in Virginia*, the book Dunston and Roscoe Lewis were working on, the one they used to coax her story with, was published in 1940. If Priscilla knew of its existence, or if she had seen what her contribution had been reduced to in the end, we do not know. It's unlikely she knew of controversies surrounding the book's publication or the struggles Lewis had with his white supervisor and her heavy editorial hand. Priscilla's story contradicted the Lost Cause narrative that Lewis's supervisor wanted the book to tell about slavery and the people who endured its crushing weight. So did the stories many other freedpeople recounted to Lewis and the other Black fieldworkers employed to collect their narratives. If not for their efforts, however imperfect they might have been, Priscilla's story, and the stories of hundreds more formerly enslaved Virginians, would have been lost or severely distorted by white efforts to flatten their varied and sometimes troubling emancipation stories.

NINE

THE BOOK

. —— .

A S DIRECTOR OF THE Virginia Writers' Project (VWP), the state-level subsidiary of the FWP, Eudora Woolfolk Ramsay Richardson exerted considerable editorial control over the collection and transcription of the charter generation interviews that Roscoe Lewis and his staff collected, as well as the writing of *The Negro in Virginia*. Richardson was a well-known figure in Richmond society. The daughter of a popular Southern Baptist minister and college president and the wife of a prominent Virginia attorney, Richardson moved in all the right circles and knew all the right people. It's little wonder she landed the coveted position at the VWP.

Richardson's position was not merely a reflection of the powerful men in her life, however. In fact, anyone who insinuated that she had not earned her reputation as a diligent, capable, and talented organizer of people and projects would have experienced Richardson's withering glare if not the prick of her sharp wit. The former suffragist, who had traveled throughout the state on behalf of women's right to vote, was not afraid to voice her opinions. A satirist and the author of several books, including a biography of Confederate vice president Alexander

Hamilton Stephens, she bristled at the criticism that women could not write history. As the editor in charge of a small army of fieldworkers and juggling a host of overlapping projects ranging from architectural surveys and the production of a state guidebook to the cataloging of county historical records to oral history interviews, Richardson certainly knew how to multitask and, when she needed to, exert her authority over those she supervised.[1]

Richardson was a "new southern woman." Born to wealth and privilege, she nonetheless eschewed the helplessness and delicacy that characterized white women of her class. She undoubtedly considered herself a lady while rejecting many of the trappings of femininity. She did not keep her opinions to herself. She married and had children but continued to pursue interests outside the home. She believed women were just as capable as men and ought to have the same opportunities in education, work, and politics. She considered herself politically progressive.[2]

Eudora Ramsay Richardson.
COURTESY UNIVERSITY OF VIRGINIA SPECIAL
COLLECTIONS

Except when it came to matters of race and historical memory. Her dedication to the ideas of southern nobility and white paternalism, and her nostalgia for an idyllic past filled with kind masters and loyal slaves, proved her to be as old-fashioned as any of her more traditional contemporaries who rejected her liberal politics. With them she found common cause in the Lost Cause.

This made her a particularly troublesome supervisor for Lewis and his team of Black fieldworkers. When it came to the ex-slave narratives, Richardson saw herself as a gatekeeper whose duty it was to ensure a truthful rendering of slavery in the Old Dominion. To say that she did not fully appreciate Lewis's goal of writing American history from the Black perspective would be an understatement. She doubted that Lewis was capable of producing what she considered to be accurate history, not because he was trained as a chemist but because he was Black and lacked the requisite objectivity needed to conduct the project successfully. As she explained to Henry Alsberg, the FWP's founding director in Washington, she thought Lewis was too close to his subjects and too willing to believe whatever they told him.

"The ex-slaves who are quoted have told interesting stories," she wrote, referencing an early draft of the book, "yet stories that must be taken with the well-known grain of salt that Mr. Lewis is not administering."[3]

Richardson read the interview transcripts with much skepticism. Not only did she doubt that some of the people Lewis interviewed had ever been slaves—they couldn't be *that* old—the ones who were couldn't possibly remember that far back. She found the detailed recollections of one eighty-year-old man, who provided the precise dimensions of the house he had lived in as a slave, preposterous.[4]

More galling to Richardson was the fact that Lewis took seriously his subjects' memories of punishments they had received. She balked at any suggestion that slave owners did not treat their human property well. "A good Negro was valuable property that an owner would not neglect. A fine horse or a good hunting dog is kept fit. Surely an expensive slave . . . would be kept fit," Richardson insisted when a formerly enslaved person recalled being fed meager rations of cornbread and often going hungry.[5]

No interview incensed Richardson more than the one Lewis's fieldworkers conducted with Henrietta King, a woman living in Portsmouth whose deformed face told the story of her enslavement. King told Lewis's fieldworker that when she was a young girl her mistress crushed her face under her rocking chair as punishment for taking a piece of candy the woman had intentionally left out where she would find it. No doctor was called to set King's broken jaw and cheekbone, and she bore the deformity for the rest of her life. As King described it, her face looked like it had melted on one side. Little children thought it was a scary "false face" and ran from her. She couldn't eat solid food because her jaw did not function properly.[6]

When Richardson read King's account, she concluded that it was a "gross exaggeration" and immediately struck it from the draft of *The Negro in Virginia*. When Lewis insisted that it was true and reported her unjustified edit to John D. Newsome, Alsberg's successor in Washington, Richardson set out to prove him wrong. She drove from Richmond to Portsmouth and asked for "the old woman who had been severely beaten by her mistress." To her surprise, everyone knew who she meant and quickly pointed her in the right direction. Still, Richardson expected to find someone with little if any physical marks left from a childhood beating. But when King appeared before her, Richardson was chastened. She admitted as much in a letter to Newsome. "She looks exactly as Mr. Lewis describes her and told me, almost word for word the story Mr. Lewis relates," she wrote. She promptly added Henrietta King's narrative back into the manuscript.[7]

Richardson did not give Priscilla Joyner's narrative such a generous reading. As editor of *The Negro in Virginia*, she did more than simply remove the unsavory story of Ann Eliza's possible interracial relationship from Priscilla's lengthy narrative. In fact, she appears to have made up a quotation out of whole cloth. In a chapter entitled "The Great House," which Richardson edited to demonstrate the trusting relationships between Virginia slave owners and their bondspeople, Priscilla is purported to have said:

> My old mistress was the best woman in the world. She may
> have owned slaves, but she never sold any. She brought me

up just like one of her own children until I was twelve years old. Then she paid for me to go to a colored school with my own people.[8]

The words attributed to Priscilla Joyner do not appear in Dunston's draft of the interview transcript. However, they appear in all three drafts of the full book manuscript. This fact suggests that either Lewis altered Priscilla's testimony when he added it to the manuscript in anticipation of Richardson's criticism, or that Richardson ventriloquized an alternative version of Joyner's life story in an earlier draft of the chapter that has not survived. But Lewis was determined to present the ex-slave testimony accurately through the rest of the manuscript. His repeated confrontations with Richardson over his reliance on this evidence make it unlikely that he voluntarily changed Priscilla's narrative. It is also possible that Dunston may have removed this portion of Priscilla's testimony when she transcribed her notes, but no other version of the interview has been found. Moreover, given the ambivalence with which Priscilla spoke of her relationship to Ann Eliza, it seems out of character for her to heap praise on the woman who was responsible for her lonely, unhappy childhood.[9]

Richardson's attitude toward Lewis, his fieldworkers, and what she referred to as the "Negro book" points to her as the source of the change. Upon receiving the full draft of the manuscript, Richardson took up her red pen and set out to rework the manuscript. She cut nearly twelve percent of the manuscript, including passages related to "left-handed marriages," or interracial sexual relationships, between slaveholders and their slaves. She also added passages that helped rehabilitate the image of slavery in Virginia as a benign and paternalistic institution.[10]

Years later, when a researcher asked about her editorial process, she recounted how she took it upon herself to correct the "bias" she found in Lewis's draft. "I just went away, took all the material with me, went down to a cottage, shut the door, and stayed down there two weeks without even a telephone," she explained. After a slight pause, she added, "And rewrote the material."[11]

Perhaps Richardson was inspired to enhance Priscilla's story by something Priscilla herself had said in her interview when she questioned the true nature of her relationship to Ann Eliza. "You understand, of course, that I'm only telling you what was told me," she informed Thelma Dunston that day as the two women talked in Priscilla's front yard. "I don't really know who my parents were. But Miss Ann Liza claimed me and made me call her 'mother.'"[12]

Priscilla's doubts, unresolved from a lifetime of secrets and denial, also served a larger purpose. Richardson felt the need to eliminate the scandalous implications of Ann Eliza's possible choice to take a Black lover from the book. It was easier for Richardson and the white readership she envisioned reading the book to imagine a kindly mistress taking in a young, enslaved girl and caring for her as one of her own. That kind of *Gone with the Wind* nostalgia captivated white Americans in the 1930s and 1940s, even those educated readers who might buy a book featuring Black historical actors. Critics applauded *The Negro in Virginia* for documenting "the American Negro's history" while at the same time conforming to narrative conventions that made white readers comfortable. Reviewers held it up as a model of historical research and writing. One publication proclaimed that the book was "so brilliantly edited that it reads as though it might be the individual work of a singularly competent historian." No doubt Richardson was pleased.[13]

But *The Negro in Virginia*, like the ex-slave interviews on which it was based, was not the product of one individual, no matter how determined Richardson was to be its sole author. Roscoe Lewis and Thelma Dunston were coauthors. So were the elderly ex-slaves, including Priscilla Joyner, who seized the opportunity presented by the FWP to author their own life stories and rewrite American history.

. —— .

WHEN HENRY ALSBERG wasn't fielding complaints about the incompetence of Black fieldworkers from Eudora Ramsay Richardson, he was fielding complaints from Sterling Brown, head of the Office of Negro Studies (part of the FWP), about the incompetence and racism of white writers and supervisors like Richardson. A realist poet and a leader of the Harlem Renaissance, Brown spearheaded the inclusion of ex-slaves in the FWP's larger project of collecting first-person narratives from everyday Americans.

Initially, the architects of this first-person narratives project did not imagine that ex-slaves should be included. William T. Couch, the white director of the University of North Carolina Press and adviser on the Southern Life Histories Project, questioned the value of what ex-slaves might bring to the effort to document the lives of working southerners. In a memorandum circulated to fieldworkers in the South, he warned them that elderly ex-slaves were typically too mired in the past to be of use in a project that aimed to "throw light on the present." He advised interviewers to try to keep any ex-slaves they might interview on track by steering them away from memories about slavery or anything other than "their present mode of living." But he doubted that any amount of steering or coaxing would produce much usable material. Instead, he encouraged writers to focus on "exceptional Negroes" who had "achieved positions of importance in their communities." He believed separate biographies of such extraordinary individuals could find an audience, presumably among mostly white readers. This advice directly contradicted Couch's general directive to capture the experiences of representative people rather than the exceptional or unique.[14]

Brown disagreed. He believed that southern Blacks, especially the members of the charter generation, were guardians of American folk culture. He had spent years traveling throughout the South, talking with rural Black folks, listening to the way they spoke, noting the variations in cadence, and collecting idioms and patterns of their unique vernacular expression. Brown understood that without their voices, any project that aimed to document the everyday lives of people in the United States would be incomplete.

Fortunately, Alsberg and other FWP leaders, particularly the folk-lorists who treasured the kind of folktales that elderly Black south-erners often told, rejected Couch's contention that formerly enslaved people had little to offer. An outspoken advocate of Black inclusion in New Deal cultural projects, Alsberg handpicked Brown to supervise Negro Studies and edit manuscripts produced on behalf of the FWP that related to African American life. Once installed at the FWP, Brown faced numerous challenges, including the staffing of projects throughout the United States. Many state units, especially in the Jim Crow South, were not eager to hire Black fieldworkers. Even in north-ern states, administrators sometimes claimed that no "competent" Black workers were available for projects. Granted, states like Vermont had small Black populations, but Brown, along with Alsberg, pushed those administrators to look harder. Brown also intervened in situa-tions where a state's few Black workers were ostracized or mistreated. In Oklahoma, Brown pushed back when white fieldworkers refused to share the building's only water fountain with their one Black col-league. He refused to ask Alsberg for money to install a second foun-tain, and eventually, the state authorities acquiesced to his demands that everyone drink from the same one.[15]

But Brown's most frustrating battle came in the form of the manu-scripts he received from white writers opining about Black history and life. After reading multiple drafts of essays about southern towns sub-mitted for inclusion in the State Guide series and marking up each draft line by line and delivering clear but constructive criticism to the individual writers (many of whom complained to their supervisors about what they felt was Brown's heavy hand), little changed. It wasn't so much that the writing failed technically, although a lot of it was terribly sentimental, dripping with overused clichés and hyperbolic flourishes, amateurish conventions for which Brown had little patience.

Brown's primary concern had to do with the ideological scaffolding on which the white southern writers employed by the FWP built their essays. After reading yet another draft of the essay submitted for Beaufort, South Carolina, Brown expressed his

Sterling Brown. COURTESY SCURLOCK STUDIO RECORDS, ARCHIVES CENTER, NATIONAL MUSEUM OF AMERICAN HISTORY, SMITHSONIAN INSTITUTION

frustrations in a letter to Alsberg, in which he criticized the writer's negative portrayal of Black schools during Reconstruction: "The essay is improved, but the Old South lingers on. There is nowhere an ungrudging admission that the schools have influenced the community, that the experiment of the government has at all succeeded."[16]

Brown reported to Alsberg that a sociologist friend of his—a white southerner no less—had visited Beaufort earlier in the year and assured Brown that "the picture of backwardness and unhurried contentment [painted by the South Carolina state guide] is by no means the only, nor the chief impression."[17]

Brown also possessed firsthand experience of the region under question. He had visited coastal Georgia himself a decade earlier while collecting material that would filter into the poems in his acclaimed collection *Southern Road*. The two regions were "similar geographically, historically, and racially." Brown concluded that Beaufort was unlikely to be the Black cultural backwater the FWP writer portrayed it to be.[18]

Brown's exasperated letter, one of many he wrote to Alsberg, highlights the important cultural work that he hoped the WPA and the various projects sheltered under its umbrella, especially the FWP and the Office of Negro Studies, might perform in 1930s America. In particular, Brown hoped that the State Guide series as well as the Slave Narratives project might offer corrective historical narratives to the well-worn Lost Cause tradition that dominated southern history and literature by the 1880s. By giving voice to African Americans as both writers of these new histories and as historical actors playing key roles in the dramas of emancipation and Reconstruction, Brown believed American history could be rewritten.

But his vision of a "cultural emancipation" directed by Black writers and collaborators, most notably the elderly ex-slaves interviewed by the FWP, faced considerable challenges. These cultural arts projects were constantly under threat from Congress, which sought repeatedly to cut funds to projects they suspected of harboring Communist sympathizers. Suspicious of "cultural elites," Republicans and southern Democrats hostile to the New Deal used time-honored attacks against intellectuals and artists to undercut President Roosevelt's authority and the WPA's longevity. The addition of "Negro Studies" in 1936 further rankled conservative politicians and alienated the WPA and the projects under its umbrella like the FWP from a large portion of the Washington establishment, ultimately leading to its defunding in the early 1940s.[19]

In addition to this perpetual external threat, the projects Brown sought to protect were under siege from the inside, as his letter to Alsberg makes clear. Staffed mostly by unemployed white workers, the State Guide series and ex-slave interviews reflected the racial worldviews of those workers. Few of the white interviewers who traveled around the South in search of elderly ex-slaves had any training with interviewing techniques. They routinely ignored directives from Brown regarding what kinds of questions to ask and how to transcribe the responses. Typically, they were someone's nephew or son-in-law; connections rather than ability often dictated who hopped on the federal payroll. Some of them fancied themselves budding novelists preparing to take the reins of the southern literary world from writers like Margaret Mitchell. They portrayed ex-slaves as quaint and exotic, remnants of a forgotten time when everyone knew their place. They rendered Black speech in such heavy dialect that the transcripts read like an Uncle Remus tale.

Many just found the work dull, and while they were thankful to have a job in the midst of the Great Depression, it was just that—a job. For the FWP's greater cultural mission of preserving the stories of everyday Americans, they could not have cared less. As for Brown's mission of rewriting southern history from the perspective of formerly enslaved people, well, that was hardly their concern either.

Brown probably would have preferred to deal with those disinterested journeymen rather than self-satisfied editors like Eudora Richardson or interviewers with literary pretensions like Gertha Couric. A fieldworker who interviewed ex-slaves in southeastern Alabama, Couric exhibited a penchant for "local color" and embellished her transcripts accordingly. She began her introduction of freedwoman Hannah Irwin as follows:

> "Yas'm, I'll be pleased to tell you 'bout whut I remembers aroun' de time of de War."

> Aunt Hannah sat stolidly in a chair that virtually groaned under her weight; and gave utterance to this sentiment through a large thick mouth, while her gold ear rings shook

with ever turn of her head, and her dim eyes glowed with memory's fires.[20]

Gertha Couric's transcript of her interview with Irwin is one of the best examples of the condescending and demeaning way that many white fieldworkers portrayed their subjects. Relying on phonetic spellings to convey a contrived sense of Black speech, Couric's transcription mimicked other white writers who parodied Black southern speech in an attempt to render their characters as nonthreatening, comical, and backward. Couric also focused on the outlandish or exotic she saw in Irwin's physical appearance—her size, her "thick mouth," her large gold earrings. In her attempt to set the scene of her meeting with Irwin and the other formerly enslaved people she interviewed, it is apparent that Couric relished the task before her and imagined she was giving their life some literary and historical importance.[21]

The way Couric rendered Irwin's speech particularly irked Brown. Brown wanted fieldworkers to focus their attentions on the expressiveness of Black southern speech, "the turns of phrase that have flavor and vividness" that he conveyed so evocatively in *Southern Road*. In a later essay reflecting on his lifelong fascination with Black speech, Brown summarized what he hoped to capture in the ex-slave interviews. "I love Negro folk speech, and I think it is rich and wonderful. It is not dis and dat and split verb. But it is 'Been down so long that down don't worry me . . . ,'" he wrote in 1973.[22]

To avoid the minstrelizing effect of dialect writing, Brown directed fieldworkers to avoid the worst conventions of the genre, such as:

Ah for I
Poe for po' (poor)
Hit for it
Tuh for to
Wuz for was

Baid for bed

Ouh for our [23]

Couric obviously ignored these instructions, as did countless other white fieldworkers.

Brown was concerned not only with making sure that Black voices were included in the projects he directed but also with how those Black voices would be used to represent the larger program of cultural renewal that drove the FWP. Hoping that the best ex-slave interviews would be published in a single narrative volume, Brown thought it necessary for the testimonies to be written in a single voice, not only for clarity's sake but also to convey a unified persona of the "ex-slave." Brown envisioned the "ex-slave" as an oppositional voice well positioned to answer previously unasked questions such as: *What did the ex-slaves expect from freedom?*[24]

By eliciting responses to such open-ended questions about desire and expectation, Brown hoped to move beyond the quaint and eccentric, which guided fieldworkers like Couric as well as folklorists who were interested primarily in collecting tales of superstitions, conjuring, and folk remedies. Brown openly confronted the representational politics of the archive he was creating, revealing how the project was not simply a repository of ex-slave voices but rather an active creation of those voices to speak to the full historical experience of Black Americans.

But white fieldworkers, even those with the best of intentions and who followed Brown's instructions to the letter, might have trouble eliciting candid responses from elderly Black subjects. Racial etiquette in the Jim Crow South demanded deference to whites of any age, and elderly interviewees born into slavery were often wary of speaking openly and honestly about their experiences to anyone who might take offense at what they had to say. A white fieldworker from Mississippi reported that Liza McGhee was "hesitant about talking freely as she feared the white people were planning to enslave her again." McGhee expressed her desire to talk to the worker but admitted she was worried that someone else might read what she had to say and re-enslave her.

"I remember some things about old slave days," she said, "but I don't want to say nothing that will get me in bondage again. I am too old now to be a slave. I couldn't stand it."[25]

Mississippi officials never forwarded McGhee's narrative to the FWP in Washington to be cataloged and stored in the Library of Congress. In the 1970s, researchers uncovered her testimony along with many other less-than-rosy memories of slavery hidden away in the Mississippi state archives.[26]

Other evidence demonstrates that ex-slaves were inclined to alter their testimony depending on who was interviewing them. In Charleston, Susan Hamlin's two interviews by fieldworkers of different races provide an informative case study in the power of racial etiquette to shape ex-slave testimony. With the Black interviewer, Hamlin spoke openly about the suffering she and others had endured as slaves, which worried the project's white supervisor. That supervisor, like Eudora Ramsay Richardson, doubted the veracity of Hamlin's narrative, so she dispatched a white fieldworker to conduct a second interview. Indeed, the two transcripts differed considerably. When reinterviewed by the white fieldworker, Hamlin evaded questions about how her master had treated her. And when the interviewer pressed her with leading questions that telegraphed the desired answer, Hamlin testified to her master's generosity and indulgence. For the white supervisor, this was proof that Black fieldworkers were incompetent interviewers, and more importantly, that ex-slaves were liars.[27]

· —— ·

JUST AS EUDORA RAMSAY RICHARDSON curated the interviews Roscoe Lewis and his fieldworkers collected, Sterling Brown also curated the testimonies, albeit for a contrary purpose. While

Richardson worked to justify the racial status quo and demonstrate the benevolence of white Virginians and their slaveholding ancestors, Brown aimed to put an end to the Old South mythology that lingered in the manuscripts he read. The racial composition of the FWP made Brown's work difficult. White fieldworkers, steeped in the literature of the Lost Cause and practitioners of the dialect writing that minstrelized Black speech, made Brown's curation of the interviews difficult. Racial etiquette in the 1930s compounded the problem by making ex-slaves hesitant to reveal their true feelings and recollections to people they didn't trust and a process they didn't fully comprehend.

This might lead one to assume that interviews conducted by Black fieldworkers were more likely to elicit "authentic" memories than those conducted by white interviewers. However, problems of class, power, individual personality, and the emotional difficulty of recounting some of the more traumatic experiences remained potent forces in shaping the outcome of interviews, even those between people of the same race.

"I don't like to think about them times, much less talk about 'em," said Beverly Jones to Lee White—one of Roscoe Lewis's team of Black fieldworkers—who arrived at Jones's home near Gloucester Courthouse, Virginia.

Jones's reluctance stemmed in part from the painful memories of the "patterollers" (slave patrollers) and the slave sales that claimed several of his relations. But he was quick to point out to Lee that his master was a "purty good old codger" who never hired an overseer and gave his slaves plenty to eat. This led Jones to conclude "slavery was a good thing for the niggers, some of 'em anyway."[28]

Similarly, Elizabeth Sparks was reluctant to tell Claude Anderson, a young Black man working for Lewis and the VWP sent to interview her, about her experiences as a slave. ". . . I kin tell yer, but I ain't," she declared. "S'all past now, so I say let 'er rest; 's too awful to tell anyway." After some prodding, Sparks relented, agreeing to tell Anderson "some to put in yer book" but refusing to tell him "the worse."[29]

What Sparks shared with Anderson was bad enough—memories of beatings done with brooms and leather straps, of open wounds doused in brine, of her aunt Caroline made to stand to knit late into the night after she became sleepy and fell asleep in her chair. Yet Sparks insisted that she held back the worst because she wanted to spare Anderson the knowledge of "all those mean white folks."[30]

Not only did Black interviewers like White and Anderson transcribe their interviews using some of the same conventions of dialect writing that white interviewers used ("git" for get, "yer" for your, etc.), their class status set them apart from their subjects, many of whom were illiterate and impoverished. There's no evidence that Roscoe Lewis was rude to Priscilla Joyner, but he introduced himself as a professor, and his assistant, Dunston, was a schoolteacher. They were smartly dressed, which stood in stark contrast to Priscilla, whom Dunston described as wearing an old but clean "housedress" paired with men's shoes "stringless and run over at the heels." An accurate depiction of what she was wearing, but Dunston went further than this, describing the rest of Priscilla's appearance in an unflattering manner. Her body was "flabby and shapeless," and she had "cluster of inch-long strands [of hair] protruding from her chin." An amateurish attempt to provide the kind of "color" that Eudora Ramsay Richardson wanted, such a raw description of Priscilla's appearance undoubtedly would have embarrassed the woman whose self-consciousness was readily apparent to Dunston, who sent Lewis on an "errand" so that the older woman would open up to her.[31]

Certainly no one could accuse Zora Neale Hurston of being amateurish or insensitive in her approach to ethnography or writing, but even she experienced some difficulty when gaining the trust of her intended subjects. When she visited a lumber camp in Loughman, Florida, Hurston expressed frustration that while the community seemed interested in her and often came by her digs to see what she was up to, they were evasive when she asked them about anything of substance. "This worried me," she wrote to a friend, "because I saw at once that this group of several hundred Negroes from all over the South was a rich field for folk-lore, but here I was figuratively starving to death in midst of plenty."

Her new car and city clothes attracted their attention as well as their suspicion. Someone eventually told her that the people thought she must be a revenue officer, and since some of them sold homemade liquor and had spent time in jail, they did not trust her. To gain their trust, she cooked up a story about being a bootlegger on the run, which explained her shiny car and fancy clothes, and soon enough, they warmed to her and all her questions.[32]

As Hurston's example demonstrates, a shared racial identification did not guarantee that even the most capable interviewers would be able to establish a productive rapport with their subjects. Southern Blacks, as Hurston herself acknowledged, could be cagey even on the most seemingly innocent topics. And while they might be more dissembling with a white interviewer, they could also be evasive with Black ones, albeit for different reasons. In the Jim Crow South, their safety often depended on being able to read subtle nonverbal cues and linguistic signals. Elderly freedpeople maintained vivid memories of the delicate cat-and-mouse games they had to play with their owners and overseers in order to survive. Even so long after freedom, they continued to exhibit caution when talking to strangers. Self-protection was second nature.[33]

But not all interviewees held back their true feelings, even from white interviewers. Betty Krump, who lived in Helena, Arkansas, told Irene Robertson, a white interviewer, exactly how she felt about being freed. In her interview, Krump is openly antagonistic and mocks Robertson's assumption that the invading Union Army mistreated her. "I jus' love the Yankees for freeing us," Krump plainly told her. "They run white folks outer their houses and put colored folks in 'em."[34]

When Robertson asked if she loved her master and mistress, Krump informed her of who she truly loved. "I'm so glad the Yankees come," she said. "They so pretty. I love 'em."[35]

Robertson pressed Krump on why she loved the people who destroyed the plantation on which she lived, leaving her and the other slaves destitute. This line of questioning must have annoyed Krump, who then ramped up her antagonism toward Robertson by pointing out what she saw as the woman's performance of civility and enlightenment, the very qualities she insisted the Yankees did not possess:

> "I can tell 'em [Yankees] by the way they talk and acts. You
> ain't none," Krump informed Robertson. "You don't talk
> like 'em. You don't act like 'em. I watched you yesterday. You
> don't walk like em. You act like the rest of these southern
> women to me."[36]

Betty Krump was having none of Robertson's attempts to endear herself to her subject, or lull Krump into making Robertson her confidant, to pretend, if only for a few minutes, that they were friends.

Even so, Krump goes on to tell a very detailed account of the Union troops' arrival on the plantation, and how her mother and other enslaved people there reacted to them—all despite the tense interview dynamics between Krump and Robertson. We should also give Robertson some credit for preserving the conversation. She continued it despite Krump's open hostility. She also did not editorialize about Krump's attitude or dismiss it, and most importantly, she didn't edit it out.

· —— ·

FOUR YEARS AFTER efforts to collect the life histories of ex-slaves began, *The Negro in Virginia* was published in 1940 to considerable acclaim. It became a Book of the Month Club selection in June of that year, and critics praised the book's scholarly accomplishments as well as its readability. W. E. B. Du Bois lauded Roscoe Lewis, "a natural scientist . . . unhampered by some of the narrower conventions of historical research." In particular, Du Bois appreciated that Lewis avoided weighing the book down with too many footnotes, and applauded the chemist for providing a wide-ranging scope that stretched from the colony's founding to the present day. However, Du Bois underestimated the input of Eudora Ramsay Richardson, the editor he referred to only as "the white woman who was state supervisor" of the VWP. Du Bois was impressed with Richardson's statement that through her work on the project she had "come to understand the viewpoint of Negro leaders in Virginia." In his mind, this was a startling admission for any white person to make. But had Du Bois known of Richardson's efforts to undermine Lewis or her role in rewriting much of the final manuscript, his appraisal of the book might have been different.[37]

In fact, it was Richardson's influence that led some reviewers to heap praise on the volume. White reviewers generally liked the tone, which they found objective and lacking both the accusatory quality (toward whites) and the overly laudatory perspective (toward Black Virginians) they had expected from a book ostensibly written by Black writers. One hailed it "a grand book," one that was "free from both bitterness and prejudice and equally free of sentimentality and pretentiousness."[38]

Historian Herbert Aptheker, a white scholar who was an expert on American slavery and a close friend of Du Bois, was more critical of this kind of enforced objectivity. He concluded the book was "a good piece of work . . . marred occasionally by factual errors and a tendency towards 'diplomatic' writing." But Aptheker found the inclusion of the ex-slave voices the book's signal feature. "The verbatim statements are the most beautiful as well as the most precious portions of the work," he wrote in the journal *Negro History*.[39]

Of course, not all of the statements were verbatim. Like Du Bois,

Aptheker was unaware of the internal struggles at the VWP between Richardson and Lewis.

Sterling Brown hoped to produce at least five more volumes focused on Black life. In 1939, with World War II looming over the horizon, Congress eliminated funding for the FWP. Although projects underway would continue until 1943 with state support, no new publications of the kind Brown envisioned materialized. Du Bois believed that the politicians who thought such efforts were a waste of taxpayer dollars "ought to be made to read this book." *The Negro in Virginia* would be the only book of its kind to emerge from the FWP, and its mixed legacy as both a triumph of Black history and a monument to the Old South made it representative of the larger struggle to represent the experiences of the charter generation.[40]

EPILOGUE

Priscilla's Garden

PRISCILLA JOYNER died on January 13, 1944, just six days shy of her eighty-sixth birthday. Her only surviving daughter, Liza, gave the attending physician the information he needed to fill out her death certificate. Female, colored, widowed. Birthplace: Nash County, North Carolina. Usual occupation: housework. The doctor spelled Priscilla's mother's name like it sounded, *Anliza*. And in the space for her father's name, he simply wrote "unknown."[1]

Crocker Funeral Home would see to her funeral, just as they had for her husband and children who preceded her in death. It was no small affair. The choir of St. Paul Baptist Church joined two soloists, three pastors, and several other speakers who remembered Priscilla Joyner, including twenty-two grandchildren, twenty-five great-grandchildren, and one great-great-grandchild. Relatives from North Carolina traveled to Suffolk to say goodbye along with Liza, Frank, and Harry, her surviving children. Priscilla was then buried in Oaklawn Cemetery beside Lewis, David, Mamie, Jencie, Priscilla, and Hyman, who died in 1942.[2]

A death certificate and obituary can tell us only so much. The identity markers these documents convey—*female, colored, widowed*, as stated on her death certificate, or "Wife of Lewis Joyner," the headline of her obituary—fail to convey many of the key facets of her life and personality. We do not know precisely how she was eulogized at her funeral, what stories the mourners told about her as they shared a post-funeral meal in the church fellowship hall or back at Liza's house. Did they speak of her tireless devotion to her family, friends, and neighbors? Did they shake their heads at her many sorrows, all those children lost to TB, and her endurance in spite of it all? Did they whisper about her early years, her white mother, the way her half-brothers cheated her out of her inheritance?

In my search to better understand the importance of Priscilla Joyner's life and what her legacy may have been for those who knew her, I found one tiny shard of insight. It is a 1962 announcement celebrating the flower show winners at the 52nd Annual Tidewater Fair. That fall, eighteen years after her death, the Priscilla Joyner Garden Club of Suffolk placed third.[3]

It may not seem like much, but for me that notice brought Priscilla's story full circle. The first time I "met" her, when I read Dunston's interview, she was in her garden. The garden was obviously a place of refuge for her, and she used its blossoms as a buffer to soften the difficult memories that Dunston and Lewis's visit stirred up. She was proud of what she had accomplished and the fact that others took pleasure in the beauty she had created. It took skill and knowledge, which she may have acquired as a young girl from the notable gardeners of Freedom Hill, a town that would become famous for its flowers. The people there, Priscilla's people, planted the seeds of freedom and coaxed beauty from the unforgiving earth that L. L. Dancy begrudgingly gave them, earth that had soaked up the sweat and blood of generations of their people.

The constant planting, dividing, weeding, transplanting, pruning back, praying for rain, lugging buckets of water when there was none—it was all so much hard work. It was also a supreme act of faith. Put in the seedlings, pack the soil with crushed eggshells and leftover coffee grounds, and hope. This was how those who knew Priscilla Joyner remembered her. They honored her memory by giving their garden club her name, a tribute to her patience and persever-ance, and also her artistry. In the same way, Black poet and novelist Alice Walker reflected on her own mother who, like Priscilla, was a renowned gardener. The flowers were so numerous and beautiful around Walker's childhood home in Georgia that strangers would often get out of their cars "and ask to stand or walk among my moth-er's art." Walker recalled watching her mother in the garden and how the overworked, exhausted woman—who spent her days working in the fields alongside her husband, and her evenings cooking, canning, and sewing—looked as she tended to her prized flowers:

> I notice that it is only when my mother is working in her
> flowers that she radiant. . . . She is involved in work her soul
> must have. Ordering the universe in the image of her per-
> sonal conception of Beauty.[4]

Black women like Priscilla Joyner and Alice Walker's mother, along with countless others who created life and beauty with the "only mate-rials [they] could afford"—salvaged rags and scraps of fabrics, dirt, and seeds—made more than just food and clothing and bed coverings. They wove together generations of families with threads of love; they grew a culture of caretaking and artistry that has sustained a people for centuries.[5]

Priscilla's story would continue to fascinate Roscoe Lewis, who published an article about her life in 1959. It was part of a larger book project he was working on entitled "O Freedom," which he envisioned as a corrective to other studies, including *The Negro in Virginia*, which focused on "the bizarre and sometimes fantastic episodes of the slave period with scant attention paid to the lives of slaves themselves." The article replicated much of the interview material contained in Lewis's files, with some additions that may or may not have been Priscilla's own words. For instance, when Lewis recounted his first visit to Priscilla and her efforts to deflect his questions by showing him her garden, he added a quotation that does not appear in the original transcription.[6]

"This is my pride," Priscilla says to him in the essay. "I practically live out here in my flowers. I declare, I hardly take the time to fix me a bite to eat."[7]

The essay also adds details about how Priscilla's half-siblings tormented her when they were small, including how her younger brother, Jolly, would sing, "Prissy's Black, Prissy's Black," when their mother was not around.

"And whenever we'd wash for meals, they'd always whisper to me to scrub real hard and try to wash the dirt off my face," Lewis quotes Priscilla as telling him.[8]

Perhaps Lewis was working from a different set of notes that did not survive.

More troubling is the way Lewis wrote Thelma Dunston completely out of the story. It's clear from the original transcription that Lewis was not the one conducting the interview; Dunston relays how she sent him and the schoolteacher who brought them on an "errand" in the hope that Priscilla might open up to her. However, in Lewis's essay, he portrayed himself as the lone interviewer and claimed much of Dunston's writing as his own.

What we are left with are accounts of Priscilla's interview that may not reflect her actual testimony. Dunston's transcript varies to some degree from Lewis's published essay, and both of those present a wildly different portrait of a life than the unverified snippet that Eudora Ramsay Richardson included in *The Negro in Virginia*. And what is true for Priscilla Joyner's narrative is also true for a vast majority of the FWP ex-slave narratives. Although there are a few scratchy audio recordings of interviews in existence, there are no other sources that reproduce the interviews verbatim. We only have the edited interview transcripts to rely on.[9]

Despite these limitations, which are present to a degree in *every* primary source we use to reconstruct past lives, these narratives remain a valuable resource for delving into the inner lives of the charter generation of freedom. They are some of the only firsthand accounts of the Civil War and emancipation from men and women who otherwise left little in the way of historical records. Many of them, unlike Priscilla Joyner, were illiterate. Oral histories, where they exist, give us the opportunity to hear the voices of people who otherwise would be lost to history. Even when those memories may be faulty, exaggerated, or embellished, first-person testimony contains what historian Christopher Browning refers to as "the essence of an ineffable experience." Browning, an expert on the testimony of Holocaust survivors, encourages us to focus less on mistakes or inaccuracies within these narratives, and instead pay attention to the fragments of thoughts, feelings, and images that structure all human memory.[10]

Sterling Brown envisioned these ex-slave narratives as a radical component of the New Deal's larger project of cultural renewal. Unfortunately, his hope that American democracy might in some way be regenerated through the life stories of freedom's charter generation remained largely unfulfilled during his lifetime. While the New Dealers' appropriation of other Civil War–era icons, most notably Abraham Lincoln, "inspired a significant number of Americans to think about race and interracial compassion in fundamentally new ways," popular representations of enslaved people in films like *Gone with the Wind* (1939) are testament to the enduring strength of the Lost Cause worldview throughout much of the twentieth century.[11]

Brown's vision for a single narrative of ex-slave testimony never fully materialized. Neither did the project Lewis planned. After enrolling at American University in Washington, DC, to pursue a doctorate in social sciences and public policy, Lewis worked on the manuscript off and on for years, but he died in 1961 before he could complete either his degree or the book. Folklorist B. A. Botkin featured the interviews in *Lay My Burden Down*, published in 1945, but according to one reviewer the book "labor[ed] to become something more than a collection of anecdotes." The sheer volume of material might be to blame, the reviewer admitted, but it also had to do with the content itself and the representational issues Sterling Brown anticipated. According to one review, the narratives "present[ed] a tradition of slavery which at the same time parallels and contrasts strikingly with the halcyon recollections of the white South." This might prove confusing for some who expected "history" to be clear-cut and unequivocal. Others only looked for confirmation of what they already believed to be true. Critical readers might recognize the contrasts and appreciate the potential nuance, but for those less skeptical or skillful, the Old South lingered on.[12]

In the end, Roscoe Lewis was right about one thing. The tendency to use these interviews to construct a composite autobiography of the charter generation, including Brown's vision of a "unified voice" emanating from the ex-slave narratives, has become one of the biggest obstacles to using these rich and varied sources. If we expect unanimity among the narrators, then we set ourselves up for disappointment and ultimately failure. There simply is no single perspective contained within the interviews. Many of the narrators' life stories echo one another in significant ways. Some of their experiences may be seen as representative of broader trends. But no single life story can be used to stand in for all the others.

I chose to focus on Priscilla Joyner's narrative because of its many exceptional qualities as much as the ways it dovetails with other interviews. Her story allowed me to do the opposite of what Sterling Brown imagined: convey the texture of individual experience and the power of a single life to amplify the contours of history. We can learn much from Priscilla about the long emancipation as it unfolded across the seven decades between the Civil War and the Great Depression. But her story also allows us a rare glimpse into the hopes, desires, and losses of a woman born neither slave nor free. Priscilla Joyner's long emancipation may have never felt truly complete to her. Slavery has enjoyed a long afterlife in the United States, and the charter generation was particularly vulnerable to its emotional and physical legacies. We do know that Priscilla found her place, her sense of belonging, in the community of freedpeople first at Freedom Hill and later among the striving Black town of Suffolk. But her path to those places of sanctuary was hers and hers alone.

And so it was for the other members of the charter generation. Their stories are not valuable solely because they represent some greater historical truth. Their stories are valuable because they were *theirs*, and because they chose to tell them, imperfectly, to an unlikely army of public historians thrown together in the midst of a global economic crisis by a government that had shown very little concern for the fate of ex-slaves since Reconstruction. Talking with the FWP fieldworkers may have provided these elderly people an opportunity to process the traumatic events of their lives and possibly move beyond them. The process of storytelling can be therapeutic, and we can hope that the narrators found some solace in the process. But even if they did not, these emancipation stories provide a much-needed counter-balance to the numbers and statistics upon which scholars often rely in order to discern and categorize patterns in the aggregate whole of a population. If we read them carefully and listen, we can detect what it felt like to be free: the sweet joy of peach juice rolling off a chin; holding a beloved's hand as they vowed that only in death would they part; feet hitting the stony ground as they walked. The emotions, the sensory descriptions, and the narrative complexity of the FWP testimonies make them invaluable. As scholar Saidiya Hartman asks, "Is narration its own gift and its own end, that is, all that is realizable when overcoming the past and redeeming the dead are not?"[13]

Between 1861 and 1865, four and a half million individuals began to walk across a line that we now recognize as separating the world of slavery from the world of not slavery. Each one of them had an emancipation story. Some of them are excerpted in these pages. Many more are in the archives of the FWP. More still were lost to war and time. For all those stories, the ones that remain accessible to us, as well as those that do not, may this book be your invitation to imagine what other stories might be told.

ACKNOWLEDGMENTS

I COULD NOT have written this book without the financial, intellectual, and emotional support of many institutions and individuals. Research and writing take time. Although more and more sources are digitized every day, historical research still requires travel to consult manuscript sources that aren't available online. The University at Buffalo was instrumental in providing me with both research funds and time away from teaching to complete the book. The UB Humanities Institute Faculty Fellowship funded a full semester leave, and the History Department and the College of Arts and Sciences provided crucial research money to support work in the National Archives in Washington, DC, and archives in North Carolina and Virginia. A Sydney and Francis Lewis Fellowship from the Virginia Museum of History enabled me to spend two glorious weeks in Richmond. Finally, a Public Scholar Award from the National Endowment for the Humanities gave me a year to finish up the research and draft the manuscript.

Numerous archivists and librarians helped me track down leads and crucial materials. Donzella Maupin and Andreese Scott at the Hampton University Archives have provided invaluable assistance both in person and from afar. Pam Edmondson at the Edgecombe County Memorial Library helped locate rare photographs of Princeville, and Chandrea Burch at the North Carolina State Historic Preservation Office tracked down the originals and assisted me with obtaining the reproduction rights. Anne Causey at the University of Virginia Special Collections scoured boxes of materials to find the photograph of Eudora Ramsay Richardson I needed as well as scan a copy of the original *Negro in Virginia* manuscript for me during the Covid-19 lockdown. Kay Peterson at the National Museum of American History assisted me in obtaining a photograph of Sterling Brown, and numerous other staff at the Southern Historical Collection at UNC-Chapel Hill, the North Carolina Department of Archives and History, and the Virginia Museum of History have generously and cheerfully aided in my quest. While in Richmond, I was lucky to meet Peyton Brown, a native of Nash County, who put me in touch with her father, Joe. Joe invited me to a meeting of the Nash County Civil War Roundtable when I was in Rocky Mount, where I met a distant cousin of Lafayette Dancy.

I have also benefited from the intellectual and emotional support of countless friends and colleagues. Among them, Jason Young provided encouragement when this book was just some loose thoughts in my head. At the Tyler Symposium in 2016, Hannah Rosen and her colleagues at William & Mary gave me the opportunity to talk about the project as it was beginning to take shape. Since my graduate school days, Steven Hahn has been a steadfast supporter, and his comments on the book proposal, as well as his invitation to present a chapter at NYU's Global Nineteenth Century Workshop, helped me clarify ideas and argumentation. I am also grateful to Peter Carmichael for making me a part of the Gettysburg College's summer Civil War Institute, where I spoke about the FWP ex-slave narratives to a large crowd of Civil War enthusiasts. Special thanks also to Paul Quigley and the lovely folks at Virginia Tech for allowing me to be a part of the Legacies of Reconstruction lecture series. Although we don't always agree on the successes and limitations of Reconstruction, Manisha Sinha graciously invited me to a lively conference on the Greater Reconstruction at UConn in 2019, and the comments and suggestions I received were immensely helpful. Kidada Williams read the entire manuscript and her insights into the history of slavery, memory, and trauma were invaluable. Megan Kate Nelson and Tammy Ingram read several chapter drafts, and their friendship and unwavering support got me across the finish line. I'm very lucky to be able to call upon one or all "the Steves"—Steven Hahn, Stephen Berry, and Stephen Kantrowiz—all of whom provided encouragement, letters of recommendation, and good advice, as always.

Many friends and colleagues in Buffalo also provided valuable assistance and encouragement. Dr. Gregg Cherr took time from his more important work to help me decipher death certificates and understand various medical conditions listed therein. Claire Schen, Tamara Thornton, and Gail Radford were reliable sources of support, gossip, and wine. My dear friend Theresa McCarthy always found time for lunch and moral support all while setting up a whole new academic department singlehandedly. And although they've moved on from UB, my other "Buffalo Gals"—Theresa Runstedtler, Cindy Wu, and LaKisha Simmons—remain steadfast friends and confidants.

My agent, Lisa Adams, has been a tremendous source of support throughout the long creative process. She worked with me for nearly ten months to shape the book proposal and get it into the right editorial hands. Those hands belonged to Amy Cherry who, along with the amazing production team at Norton, have helped to create a book that I am tremendously proud of.

Finally, I can never fully express how much love and appreciation I have for Darrell Stevens and our daughter, Amelia. Amelia's long-awaited arrival provided a non-negotiable deadline for completing the manuscript, and her presence in my life has made everything sweeter. It is to her that this book is dedicated.

NOTES

PROLOGUE: The Interview

1. My description of the interview scene in Priscilla's yard is gleaned from a description of the meeting contained in the interview transcript published in Charles L. Perdue Jr., Thomas E. Barden, and Robert K. Phillips, eds., *Weevils in the Wheat: Interviews with Virginia Ex-Slaves* (Charlottesville: University of Virginia Press, 1976), 171–78. (Hereafter abbreviated as *Weevils*.) I have also relied on photographs reprinted in *Weevils* (p. 172) and contained in the Roscoe Lewis Papers at Hampton University.

2. Lewis's assistant remains unnamed in the interview records. However, based upon other interviews she conducted, and the style of narration and "scene setting" she used at the beginning of her transcripts, I am fairly certain the interview was conducted by Thelma Dunston. For a list of interviewers who worked under Lewis's supervision, see *Weevils*, Appendices 4 and 5, 356–66.

3. *Weevils*, 173. The interview transcript reproduced in *Weevils* spells Priscilla's surname with an "i" (Joiner), but the name is typically spelled with a "y" (Joyner) in the census and other historical records. Therefore, I will use that spelling throughout the book.

4. Priscilla discussed her fatigue and failing health in her interview on p. 177 of *Weevils*.

5. *Weevils*, 177.

6. Alice Walker's insights into gardening as a form of artistic expression for Black women who otherwise were denied opportunities for creativity has enabled me to view Priscilla's flower garden as a refuge from the ugliness of the world. See Walker, "In Search of Our Mother's Gardens," in *In Search of Our Mother's Gardens: Womanist Prose* (New York: Harcourt, Brace, Jovanovich, 1983), 231–43.

7. For a list of interview questions Dunston drew from, see *Weevils*, Appendix 6, 367–76.

8. *Weevils*, 178.

9. Priscilla discussed the letter and Frank's determination to find it in *Weevils*, 178.

10. *Weevils*, 173.

11. *Weevils*, 174.

12. Laurel Thatcher Ulrich, *Well-Behaved Women Seldom Make History* (New York: Vintage, 2008).

13. Ira Berlin coined the term "charter generation" to describe the first people to become enslaved in the Atlantic world before slavery and racial caste became solidified in North America. Theirs was a period of transition, and the charter generation,

many of whom were born free, lived as cultural brokers in a world that was increasingly unfree, a "society with slaves" but not yet fully subsumed by the demands of a slave society. Just as there was a charter generation of slavery, I argue that there was also a charter generation of freedom who experienced life on both sides of emancipation. See Berlin, *Many Thousands Gone: The First Two Centuries of Slavery in North America* (Cambridge: Harvard University Press, 2009).

14. On the long emancipation, see Ira Berlin, *The Long Emancipation: The Demise of Slavery in the United States* (Cambridge: Harvard University Press, 2015). See also Carole Emberton, "Unwriting the Freedom Narrative," *Journal of Southern History* 82, no. 2 (May 2016): 377–94. Jacqueline Dowd Hall began charting the historical connections between the 1860s and the 1960s, and many others have taken up her work since. See Hall, "The Long Civil Rights Movement and the Political Uses of the Past," *Journal of American History* 91, no. 4 (2005): 1233–63. On the long history of the Black struggle for voting rights, see Carol Anderson, *One Person, No Vote: How Voter Suppression Is Destroying Our Democracy* (New York: Bloomsbury, 2018). On the rise of mass incarceration, see in particular Douglas Blackmon, *Slavery By Another Name: The Reenslavement of Black Americans from the Civil War to World War II* (New York: Anchor Books, 2009); Michelle Alexander, *The New Jim Crow: Mass Incarceration in the Age of Colorblindness* (New York: New Press, 2010); Heather Ann Thompson, "Why Mass Incarceration Matters: Rethinking Crisis, Decline, and Transformation in Postwar American History," *Journal of American History* 97, no. 3 (December 2010): 703–34; Khalil Gibran Muhammad, *The Condemnation of Blackness: Race, Crime, and the Making of Modern Urban America* (Cambridge: Harvard University Press, 2010); and Talitha LaFlouria, *Chained in Silence: Black Women and Convict Labor in the New South* (Chapel Hill: University of North Carolina Press, 2015).

15. On the history of emotions, see Jan Plamper, *The History of Emotions: An Introduction* (Oxford, UK: Oxford University Press, 2015). On the emotions of slavery and enslaved people, see Heather Andrea Williams, *Help Me to Find My People: The African American Search for Family Lost in Slavery* (Chapel Hill: University of North Carolina Press, 2012), and Tiya Miles, *All That She Carried: The Journey of Ashley's Sack, a Black Family Keepsake* (New York: Random House, 2021).

16. William Stott, *Documentary Expression and Thirties America* (Chicago: University of Chicago Press, 1973), 204. See also Ann Banks, *First Person America* (New York: W. W. Norton, 1991). Smaller projects dedicated to documenting the firsthand experiences of formerly enslaved people preceded the FWP. Those included Black sociologist Charles Johnson's project at Fisk University and John B. Cade's at Southern University. Both projects ran from 1929 to 1930. A student of Johnson's, Ophelia Settle Egypt, conducted approximately one hundred interviews of ex-slaves living in Tennessee for the Fisk project. They were published as *The Unwritten History of Slavery: Autobiographical Accounts of Negro Ex-Slaves* (Washington, DC: Microcard Editions, 1968 [1945]). Egypt's papers at Howard University document her decades-long efforts to publish a history of slavery based on these interviews. Both Johnson and Cade were motivated to record ex-slave testimony to counter the work of white historian U. B. Phillips, who argued that slavery was a beneficial system for the enslaved and that most were happy to be enslaved in *American Negro Slavery: A Survey of the Supply, Employment, and Control of Negro Labor, as Determined by the Plantation Regime*

(New York: D. Appleton, 1918). Johnson used the interviews in his rebuttal to Phillips, *Shadow of the Plantation* (Chicago: University of Chicago Press, 1934). Cade published "Out of the Mouth of Ex-Slaves," *Journal of Negro History* 20, no. 3 (July 1935): 294–337.

17. Botkin quoted in Lawrence R. Rodgers and Jerrold Hirsch, eds., *America's Folklorist: B. A. Botkin and American Culture* (Norman: University of Oklahoma Press, 2010), 10. "Questionnaire for Ex-Slaves," *Weevils*, Appendix 6, 365–76.

18. Virginia Writers' Project, *The Negro in Virginia* (Winston-Salem: John F. Blair, 1994), 50.

19. For instance, in his study of antebellum slave markets, Walter Johnson wrote that he avoided using the FWP narratives because he believed the "rhetorical situation" produced by white interviewers in the 1930s irreparably tainted the testimony. See Johnson, *Soul by Soul: Life Inside the Antebellum Slave Market* (Cambridge: Harvard University Press, 1999), 226. Sharon Ann Musher also warns about the pitfalls of using the interviews in "The Other Slave Narratives: The Works Progress Administration Interviews," *The Oxford Handbook of African American Slave Narratives* (New York: Oxford University Press, 2014), 101–38. For more on the long debate about the narratives' representativeness and usefulness, see among others, C. Vann Woodward, "History from Slave Sources," *American Historical Review* 79, no. 2 (April 1974): 470–81; John Blassingame, "Using the Testimony of Ex-Slaves: Approaches and Problems," *Journal of Southern History* 41, no. 4 (November 1975): 473–92; Norman Yetman, "Ex-Slave Interviews and the Historiography of Slavery," *American Quarterly* 36, no. 2 (Summer 1984): 181–210. See also Paul D. Escott, *Slavery Remembered: A Record of Twentieth-Century Slave Narratives* (Chapel Hill: University of North Carolina Press, 2000).

20. Charles Edgar Wideman reveals how the narrators sometimes embedded "hidden transcripts" within the interviews that white interviewers did not pick up on. See Wideman's essay, "Charles Chesnutt and the WPA Narratives: The Oral and Literature Roots of Afro-American Literature," in Henry Louis Gates Jr., ed., *The Slave's Narrative* (New York: Oxford University Press, 1985), 59–78. Sophie White finds similar subtexts in her close reading of enslaved people's judicial testimony in colonial America and argues that despite the constraints of that particular archive, enslaved people found ways to speak about their experiences and perspectives. See White, *Voices of the Enslaved: Love, Labor, and Longing in French Louisiana* (Chapel Hill: University of North Carolina Press, 2019).

21. More recently, historians have embraced the interviews despite their problems. See Celia E. Naylor, *African Cherokees in Indian Territory: From Chattel to Citizens* (Chapel Hill: University of North Carolina Press, 2008); Daina Ramey Berry, *The Price for Their Pound of Flesh: The Value of the Enslaved, from Womb to Grave, in the Building of a Nation* (Boston: Beacon Press, 2017); Stephanie Jones-Rogers, *They Were Her Property: White Women Slaveholders in the Antebellum South* (New Haven: Yale University Press, 2019); Edward Baptist, *The Half Has Never Been Told: Slavery and the Making of American Capitalism* (New York: Basic Books, 2014), as well as his essay "Stol' and Fetched Here: Enslaved Migration, Ex-Slave Narratives, and Vernacular History," in Edward Baptist and Stephanie Camp, eds., *New Studies in the History of American Slavery* (Athens: University of Georgia Press, 2006), 243–74; and Marie Jenkins Schwartz, who argues that the interviews have been overly scrutinized by historians in "The WPA Narratives as Historical Sources," in *The Oxford Handbook of the African*

American Slave Narrative, 89–100. LaKisha Michelle Simmons uses the narratives to delve into the painful experiences of infant and child mortality among Black mothers in "Black Feminist Theories of Motherhood and Generation: Histories of Black Infant and Child Loss in the United States," *Signs: A Journal of Women in Culture and Society* 46, no. 2 (Winter 2021): 311–35. See also Saidiya Hartman, *Scenes of Subjection: Terror, Slavery, and Self-Making in Nineteenth-Century America* (New York: Oxford University Press, 1997), 11. In an essay discussing the film *Twelve Years a Slave*, historian Annette Gordon-Reed writes about "history's cruel irony, that the individuals who bore the brunt of the system—the enslaved—lived under a shroud of enforced anonymity" because they were largely illiterate and few documentary records of their lives remain. See Reed, "Slavery's Shadow," *The New Yorker*, October 23, 2013.

22. Paula Fass, "Cultural History/Social History: Some Reflections on a Continuing Dialogue," *Journal of Social History* 37 (Autumn 2003): 45.

23. Scholars of enslaved people have embraced the speculative as a way to write a history of the enslaved without re-creating the erasures and violence of the archives. In particular, Marisa Fuentes cautions against calls to find more and more sources since we will only come up with other fragmented sources that privilege power and erase the powerless. See Fuentes, *Dispossessed Lives: Enslaved Women, Violence and the Archive* (Philadelphia: University of Pennsylvania Press, 2016), 6. Saidiya Hartman has long advocated for a creative reading and writing of history. She describes her latest work as a book that "elaborates, augments, transposes, and breaks open archival documents so they might yield a richer picture of the social upheaval that transformed Black social life in the twentieth century." See Hartman, *Wayward Lives, Beautiful Experiments: Intimate Histories and Social Upheavals* (New York: W. W. Norton, 2019), xiv. I have also been inspired by Annette Gordon-Reed's efforts to re-create the lives of Sally Hemings and her family. In her introduction to *The Hemingses of Monticello*, she reminds us of the importance of the writer's own intuition and experience in the writing of history. She writes, "[W]e should not be afraid to call upon what we know in general about mothers, fathers, families, male-female relationships, power relationships, the contours of life in small closely knit communities, as we try to see [our subjects] in the context of their own time and place." See Gordon-Reed, *The Hemingses of Monticello: An American Family* (New York: W. W. Norton, 2009), 32.

24. Koritha Mitchell discusses the preoccupation with protest in her study of Black people's alternative ways of creating belonging. See Mitchell, *From Slave Cabins to the White House: Homemade Citizenship in African American Culture* (Urbana: University of Illinois Press, 2021), 3. Hurston quoted in Robert Hemenway, "Folklore Field Notes from Zora Neale Hurston," *Black Scholar* 7, no. 7 (April 1976): 41.

1. 2/F/M

1. U.S. Dept. of Interior (Census Office), "Instructions to U.S. Marshals" (Washington, DC: Geo. W. Bowman, 1860), 3.

2. Virginia enumerator quoted in Mary Penner, "Project: Census," *Ancestry* (March/April 2010): 46.

3. Frederick Law Olmsted, *A Journey in the Seaboard Slave States* (New York: Dix & Edwards, 1856), 320–21.

4. Entry for Jno. W. Bryant, Dwelling No. 723, Mannings, Nash Co., North Caro-

lina; Entry for Rix Joyner, Dwelling No. 1388, Dortches, Nash County, North Carolina, both in *1860 U.S. Federal Census*, Ancestry.com.

5. *Weevils*, 174.

2. Child of No One

1. *Weevils*, 174.

2. Henry Bibb, *Narrative of the Life and Adventures of Henry Bibb, the American Slave,
Written by Himself* (New York: Author, 1849), 14. "Documenting the American South."
http://docsouth.unc.edu/neh/bibb/bibb.html. Interview with Patsy Mitchner, "Born
in Slavery: Slave Narratives from the Federal Writers' Project, 1936–1938," Library of
Congress, https://www.loc.gov/resource/mesn.111/?sp=252. Hereafter cited as "Born in
Slavery."

3. *Weevils*, 174.

4. Mary Chesnut, *A Diary from Dixie* (New York: D. Appleton, 1905), 21–22.

5. On antebellum sexual relations between white women and Black men, see Martha Hodes, *White Women, Black Men: Illicit Sex in the 19th-Century South* (New Haven:
Yale University Press, 1997).

6. Act XII, *Laws of Virginia*, December 1662 (Hening, *Statutes at Large*, 2: 170).
On the myth of the Black rapist and lynching, see Crystal Feimster, *Southern Horrors:
Women and the Politics of Rape and Lynching* (Cambridge: Harvard University Press,
2011), and Diane Miller Sommerville, *Rape and Race in the Nineteenth Century South*
(Chapel Hill: University of North Carolina Press, 2004).

7. Ira Berlin, *Slaves Without Masters: The Free Negro in the Antebellum South* (New
York: New Press, 1974).

8. 1850 U.S. Census, Nash County, North Carolina, "Wright Batchelor," Ancestry.
com.

9. 1850 U.S. Census, Nash County, North Carolina, "Wright Batchelor," Ancestry.
com.

10. 1850 U.S. Census, Nash County, North Carolina, "Jonathan Joyner," Ancestry.
com.

11. On slavery and social capital, see Robert Putnam, *Bowling Alone: The Collapse and
Revival of American Community* (New York: Simon & Schuster, 2000), 294.

12. On the sexual exploitation of slaves, see Jennifer Morgan, *Laboring Women:
Reproduction and Gender in New World Slavery* (Philadelphia: University of Pennsyl-
vania Press, 2004); Thomas Foster, "The Sexual Abuse of Black Men Under American
Slavery," *Journal of the History of Sexuality* 20, no. 3 (September 2011): 445–64; Gregory
D. Smithers, *Slave Breeding: Sex, Violence, and Memory in African American History*
(Gainesville: University of Florida Press, 2012).

13. For more on the emotional bonds of enslaved families and plantation communities, see among others, Herbert Gutman, *The Black Family in Slavery and Freedom,
1750–1925* (New York: Vintage, 1975); Brenda Stevenson, *Life in Black and White: Family
and Community in the Slave South* (New York: Oxford University Press, 1997); and more
recently, Williams, *Help Me to Find My People*; and Tera Hunter, *Bound in Wedlock:
Slave and Free Black Families in the Nineteenth Century* (Cambridge: Harvard University Press, 2017).

14. Stephanie Jones-Rogers discusses the tension women's slaveholding often caused

in their marriages. See *They Were Her Property*, esp. Ch. 2, "Missus Done Her Own Bossing," 57–61. 1860 U.S. Census, Slave Schedules, Nash County, North Carolina, "Dortches," Ancestry.com.

15. *Weevils*, 174. 1860 U.S. Census, Slave Schedules, Nash County, North Carolina, "Dortches," Ancestry.com.

16. For more on how slaveholding parents sought to protect their daughters' interests, see Jones-Rogers, *They Were Her Property*, 19.

17. 1860 U.S. Census, Slave Schedules, Nash County, North Carolina, "Dortches," Ancestry.com; Berlin, *Slaves Without Masters*. See also John Hope Franklin, *The Free Negro in North Carolina, 1790–1860* (Chapel Hill: University of North Carolina Press, 2000 [1943]), and more recently, Warren Eugene Milteer Jr., *North Carolina's Free People of Color, 1715–1885* (Baton Rouge: Louisiana State University Press, 2020).

18. *State v. Griffin Stewart*, Nash County, SSCMR #4749, North Carolina Department of Archives and History, Raleigh, North Carolina (hereafter cited as NCDAH); *State v. Alfred Hooper and Elizabeth Suttles*, N.C. 201 (1844); and *State v. Joel Fore and Susan Chesnut*, 23 N.C. 378 (1841); Martha Hodes also discusses these cases in *White Women, Black Men*, 49–50. Laura Edwards argues that antebellum state laws were enforced—or not enforced—locally, and any understanding of early American law must take into account this larger legal order. See Edwards, *The People and Their Peace: Legal Culture and the Transformation of Inequality in the Post-Revolutionary South* (Chapel Hill: University of North Carolina Press, 2009).

19. David Dodge, "The Free Negroes of North Carolina," *Atlantic Monthly* (January 1886): 29.

20. Hodes, *White Women, Black Men*, 3.

21. As Ted Maris-Wolf points out, although laws requiring bastard children to be apprenticed were not always enforced at the local level, they nonetheless incited great fear among mothers of illegitimate children. See Maris-Wolf, *Family Bonds: Free Blacks and Re-Enslavement in Antebellum Virginia* (Chapel Hill: University of North Carolina Press, 2015).

22. *Midgett v. McBryde* (1855).

23. *Midgett v. McBryde* (1855).

24. Franklin, *The Free Negro in North Carolina*, 122–31.

25. Karen Zipf notes that the few cases of apprentices suing masters involves cases where the apprentices were removed from the county where they were bound out, a direct violation of state law aimed to protect free Black children from being taken somewhere else and kept as a slave or actually sold into slavery. See Zipf, *Labor of Innocents: Forced Apprenticeship in North Carolina, 1715–1919* (Baton Rouge: Louisiana State University Press, 2005), 16–18.

26. Sommerville, *Rape and Race*; Hodes, *White Women, Black Men*.

27. *Weevils*, 174.

28. *Weevils*, 174–75.

29. Benjamin Sherwood to "B.S. Hedrick and Family," copy of speech delivered in Iowa, April 7, 1860, David M. Rubenstein Rare Book & Manuscript Library, Duke University; also quoted in Hodes, *White Women, Black Men*, 50–51.

30. Harriet Jacobs, *Incidents in the Life of a Slave Girl, Written by Herself* (New York: Penguin, 2000 [1861]), 58.

31. Pauli Murray, *Proud Shoes: The Story of an American Family* (Boston: Beacon Press, 1999), 45–48.

32. Interview with Sarah Debro, "Born in Slavery: Slave Narratives from the Federal Writers' Project, 1936–1938," Library of Congress. Accessed July 1, 2021. https://www.loc.gov/collections/slave-narratives-from-the-federal-writers-project-1936-to-1938/about-this-collection/ (hereafter cited as "Born in Slavery"). This online database contains the interview transcripts printed in the multivolume set edited by George Rawick, *The American Slave: A Composite Autobiography* (Westport, CT: Greenwood Press, 1972–1979).

33. Interview with Sarah Debro, "Born in Slavery." Karen Sanchez-Eppler suggests how enslaved children were particularly vulnerable to the paternalistic ethos of slaveholders in her essay "'Remember, Dear, when the Yankees came through here, I was only ten years old.'": Valuing the Enslaved Child of the WPA Slave Narratives," in Anna Mae Duane, ed., *Child Slavery Before and After Emancipation: An Argument for Child-Centered Slavery Studies* (Cambridge: Cambridge University Press, 2017), 32–33. See also Wilma King, *Stolen Childhood: Slave Youth in Nineteenth-Century America*, 2nd ed. (Bloomington: Indiana University Press, 2011).

34. *Weevils*, 174.

3. The Ebb and Flow of Freedom

1. *Weevils*, 174.

2. *Weevils*, 175.

3. *The Statutes at Large of the Confederate States of America, Passed at the Second Session of the First Congress, 1862*, "Documenting the American South." Accessed July 1, 2021. https://docsouth.unc.edu/imls/csstat62/csstat62.html; "Rix Joyner Compiled Military Service Record," Fold3.com.

4. Quoted in David S. Heidler and Jeanne T. Heidler, eds., *Encyclopedia of the American Civil War*, vol. 1 (Santa Barbara: ABC-CLIO, 2000), 327–28.

5. David Stick, *The Outer Banks of North Carolina, 1584–1958* (Chapel Hill: University of North Carolina Press, 1990); Bruce Catton, *Mr. Lincoln's Army* (New York: Anchor, 1990 [1951]), 262; James McPherson, *Battle Cry of Freedom* (New York: Oxford University Press, 1988), 372–73.

6. *National Anti-Slavery Standard*, quoted in Patricia Click, *Time Full of Trial: The Roanoke Freedmen's Colony, 1862–1867* (Chapel Hill: University of North Carolina Press, 2001), 24.

7. On the importance of watermen and waterways, see David Celceski, *The Waterman's Song: Slavery and Freedom in Maritime North Carolina* (Chapel Hill: University of North Carolina Press, 2012); Jacobs, *Incidents in the Life of a Slave Girl*, 126–27.

8. On the importance of movement to the collapse of American slavery, see Yael Sternhell, *Routes of War: The World of Movement in the Confederate South* (Cambridge: Harvard University Press, 2012).

9. Vincent Colyer, *Brief Report of the Services Rendered by the Freed People to the United States Army in North Carolina* (New York: V. Colyer, 1864), Eastern Carolina University Digital Collections. Accessed February 26, 2021. https://digital.lib.ecu.edu/13431.

10. Click, *Time Full of Trial*, 10–11. For a wider look at wartime emancipation and the Civil War's refugee crisis, see Amy Murrell Taylor, *Embattled Freedom: Journeys*

Through the Civil War's Slave Refugee Camps (Chapel Hill: University of North Carolina Press, 2018).

11. Catherine Edmondston, *Journal of a Secesh Lady: The Diary of Catherine Ann Devereux Edmondston, 1860–1866* (Raleigh: North Carolina Division of Archives, 1979), 670.

12. Interview with Clara Jones, "Born in Slavery."

13. Thomas Kingsbury, "The Number of Troops Furnished by North Carolina," *Our Living and Our Dead*, vol. 2 (Raleigh, NC: 1875), 431–34; Thomas Livermore, *Numbers and Losses in the Civil War in America* (Boston: 1901); Hacker, "A Census-Based Account of the Civil War Dead," *Civil War History* 57, no. 4 (2011): 307–48.

14. John G. Barrett, *The Civil War in North Carolina* (Chapel Hill: University of North Carolina Press, 1995), 165–66. See also Barton A. Myers, *Rebels Against the Confederacy: North Carolina's Unionists* (Cambridge: Cambridge University Press, 2014).

15. Interview with William Sykes, "Born in Slavery." On white refugees, see Sternhell, *Routes of War*; David Silkenat, *Driven from Home: North Carolina's Civil War Refugee Crisis* (Athens: University of Georgia Press, 2018); and Thavolia Glymph, *The Women's Fight: The Civil War's Battles for Home, Freedom, and Nation* (Chapel Hill: University of North Carolina Press, 2020), 25–32.

16. Sykes, "Born in Slavery."

17. Interview with Jane Lee, "Born in Slavery."

18. Interview with Jeff Bailey, "Born in Slavery."

19. On the ages of enslaved people, see Marie Jenkins Schwartz, *Born in Bondage: Growing Up Enslaved in the Antebellum South* (Cambridge: Harvard University Press, 2001), and Sanchez-Eppler, "'Remember, Dear,'" 29.

20. Interview with Cheney Cross, "Born in Slavery."

21. Interview with Nancy Washington, "Born in Slavery."

22. Interview with Alice Green and Hannah Brooks Wright, both in "Born in Slavery."

23. Interview with Frank Larkin, "Born in Slavery."

24. Interview with James Bolton, "Born in Slavery."

25. Interview with Margaret Hughes, Eliza Evans, and Mary Jane Hardridge, all in "Born in Slavery."

26. Interview with Mittie Freeman, "Born in Slavery."

27. On the Lieber Code, see John Fabian Witt, *Lincoln's Code: The Laws of War in American History* (New York: Free Press, 2012).

28. Interview with Sam Word, "Born in Slavery."

29. Interview with Lizzie McCloud, "Born in Slavery."

30. Interview with Lizzie McCloud, "Born in Slavery."

31. *New York Times*, May 17, 1865.

32. Interview with Lizzie McCloud, "Born in Slavery."

33. P. Gabrielle Foreman, "Manifest in Signs: Reading the Undertell in Incidents in the Life of a Slave Girl," in Deborah M. Garfield and Rafia Zafar, eds., *Harriet Jacobs and Incidents in the Life of a Slave Girl: New Critical Essays* (Cambridge: Cambridge University Press, 1996), 100–130. See also Darlene Clark Hine, "Rape and the Inner Lives of Black Women in the Middle West," *Signs* 14, no. 4 (Summer 1989): 912–20.

34. Interview with Lizzie McCloud, "Born in Slavery."

35. On General Order No. 28, see Alecia P. Long, "(Mis)Remembering General Order No. 28: Benjamin Butler, the Woman Order, and Historical Memory," in Lee-Ann Whites and Alecia P. Long, eds., *Occupied Women: Gender Military Occupation and the American Civil War* (Baton Rouge: Louisiana State University Press, 2009), 17–32. See also Lisa Tendrich Frank, "Bedrooms as Battlefields: The Role of Gender Politics in Sherman's March," also in *Occupied Women*, 33–48; Crystal Feimster, "General Benjamin Butler and the Threat of Sexual Violence during the American Civil War," *Daedalus* (Spring 2009): 126–34; and Crystal Feimster, "'How Are the Daughters of Eve Punished?' Rape During the American Civil War," in Elizabeth Anne Payne, ed., *Writing Women's History* (Oxford: Mississippi University Press, 2011), 64–78.

36. Feimster, "'How Are the Daughters of Eve Punished?'" 73.

37. Interview with Hannah Austin, "Born in Slavery."

38. On Sherman's March, see Anne Sarah Rubin, *Through the Heart of Dixie: Sherman's March and American Memory* (Chapel Hill: University of North Carolina Press, 2014), especially Ch. 1, "Stories of the Great March," which documents the troop movements and reactions of civilians.

39. *Weevils*, 175.

40. Conversation with Emmanuel Dabney, NPS Ranger, Petersburg Battlefield, June 20, 2017; Earl J. Hess, *In the Trenches at Petersburg: Field Fortifications and Confederate Defeat* (Chapel Hill: University of North Carolina Press, 2011), 215–28.

41. Civil War Richmond, http://www.mdgorman.com/Hospitals/hospitals.htm; Rebecca Barbour Calcutt, *Richmond's Wartime Hospitals* (New Orleans: Pelican Publishing, 2005).

42. Interview with Patsy Moore, "Born in Slavery."

43. Interview with Patsy Moore, "Born in Slavery."

44. Interview with Patsy Moore, "Born in Slavery."

45. Stanley French, "The Cemetery as Cultural Institution: The Establishment of Mount Auburn and the 'Rural Cemetery' Movement," *American Quarterly* 26, no. 1 (March 1974): 37–59; Keith Eggener, *Cemeteries* (New York: W. W. Norton, 2010); Ladies Hollywood Memorial Association Register, Virginia Museum of History and Culture, Richmond, Virginia; Chris L. Ferguson, *Southerners at Rest: Confederate Dead at Hollywood Cemetery* (Winchester, VA: Angle Valley Press, 2008), 150.

46. On the Lost Cause, the Ladies Hollywood Memorial Association, and the United Daughters of the Confederacy, see among others, Gaines M. Foster, *Ghosts of the Confederacy: Defeat, the Lost Cause, and the Emergence of the New South, 1865–1913* (New York: Oxford University Press, 1987); Karen Cox, *Dixie's Daughters: The United Daughters of the Confederacy and the Preservation of Confederate Culture* (Tallahassee: University of Florida Press, 2003); and Carolina Janney, *Burying the Dead but Not the Past: Ladies' Memorial Associations and the Lost Cause* (Chapel Hill: University of North Carolina Press, 2008).

47. *Weevils*, 175.

48. *Weevils*, 175.

49. *Weevils*, 175.

4. The Pursuit of Happiness

1. Thirty-Ninth Congress, Civil Rights Act of 1866 (Washington, DC: U.S. Government Printing Office, 1866); *Dred Scott v. Sandford* (1857). On the revolutionary

nature of the Civil Rights Act and the Fourteenth Amendment, see Martha Jones, *Birthright Citizens: A History of Race and Rights in Antebellum America* (Cambridge: Cambridge University Press, 2018); Eric Foner, *Reconstruction: America's Unfinished Revolution, 1863–1877* (New York: Harper & Row, 1988); and more recently, Eric Foner, *The Second Founding: How the Civil War and Reconstruction Remade the Constitution* (New York: W. W. Norton, 2019).

2. Prince Murell et al., Petition, December 17, 1865. Records of the Assistant Commissioner of the State of Alabama (Tuscaloosa), Bureau of Refugees, Freedmen, and Abandoned Lands (BRFAL), Record Group 105, National Archives Records Administration (NARA), Microfilm pub. 809, reel 6 (hereafter cited as RG 105).

3. On Jefferson's use of the phrase, see Pauline Maier, *American Scripture: Making the Declaration of Independence* (New York: Vintage, 1988); Arthur M. Schlesinger, "The Lost Meaning of the 'Pursuit of Happiness,'" *William and Mary Quarterly* 21, no. 3 (July 1964): 326–27.

4. Harriet Martineau, "Scenes in America," *Metropolitan Magazine* (February 1838): 92. On the Enlightenment and the transformation of sentiment, see Darrin McMahon, *Happiness: A History* (New York: Grove Press, 2006).

5. "First Debate: Ottawa, Illinois," National Park Service. Accessed February 15, 2021. https://www.nps.gov/liho/learn/historyculture/debate1.htm.

6. *Weevils*, 175–76.

7. Interview with Dora Franks, "Born in Slavery."

8. Interview with Dora Franks, "Born in Slavery."

9. Interview with Mose Davis, "Born in Slavery."

10. Interview with Mary Lindsey, "Born in Slavery."

11. Interview with Mary Lindsey, "Born in Slavery."

12. Interview with Robert Glenn, "Born in Slavery."

13. Interview with Robert Glenn, "Born in Slavery."

14. Interview with Robert Falls, "Born in Slavery."

15. Interview with Robert Glenn, "Born in Slavery."

16. J. T. Trowbridge, *The South: A Tour of Its Battlefields and Ruined Cities* (Hartford, CT: L. Stebbens, 1866).

17. Trowbridge, *The South*, 232.

18. Trowbridge, *The South*, 231.

19. Trowbridge, *The South*, 232.

20. Trowbridge, *The South*, 232.

21. Helen Paris Wiley, "From Slave to Sharecropper: Changes in Labor Organization in Nash and Edgecombe Counties, North Carolina 1865–1900," master's thesis (Durham: Duke University, 1981), 16. For more on postwar labor relations throughout the region, see Steven Hahn et al., eds., *Freedom: A Documentary History of Emancipation, Series 3: Land and Labor, 1865* (Chapel Hill: University of North Carolina Press, 2017); Julie Saville, *The Work of Reconstruction: From Slave to Wage Laborer in South Carolina, 1860–1870* (Cambridge: Cambridge University Press, 1996); Leslie Schwalm, *A Hard Fight for We: Women's Transition from Slavery to Freedom in South Carolina* (Urbana: University of Illinois Press, 1997); Tera Hunter, *To 'Joy My Freedom: Southern Black Women's Lives and Labors After the Civil War* (Cambridge: Harvard University Press, 1997); Nancy Bercaw, *Gendered Freedoms: Race, Rights, and the Politics of the Household in*

the Delta, 1861–1875 (Tallahassee: University of Florida Press, 2003); Thavolia Glymph, *Out of the House of Bondage: The Transformation of the Plantation Household* (Cambridge: Cambridge University Press, 2008).

22. Ted Ownby, *American Dreams in Mississippi: Consumers, Poverty, and Culture, 1830–1998* (Chapel Hill: University of North Carolina Press, 2002), 59.

23. Interview with Prince Johnson, "Born in Slavery." On enslaved people's property ownership practices, see also Dylan Penningroth, *Claims of Kinfolk: African American Property and Community in the Nineteenth-Century South* (Chapel Hill: University of North Carolina Press, 2003).

24. Charles Nordhoff, *The Cotton States in the Spring and Summer of 1875* (New York: D. Appleton, 1876), 72.

25. "Record of Outrages Reported in the Subdistrict of Wilmington from Dec. 28, 1866 to Jan. 13, 1867," Records of the Assistant Commissioner for North Carolina, RG 105, microfilm pub. m843, reel 33.

26. "Record of Outrages."

27. "Record of Outrages."

28. "Chairman of the Orangeburg, South Carolina, Commission on Contracts to the Freedmen's Bureau Commissioner; Enclosing a Speech to the Freedpeople; and the Commissioner's Reply, June 12, 1865," Freedmen and Southern Society Project. Accessed on February 16, 2021. http://www.freedmen.umd.edu/Soule.htm.

29. Contract between David Barlow and eight freedpeople cited in Wiley, *From Slave to Sharecropper*, 17. Georgia woman quoted in Grady McWhiney, *Reconstruction and the Freedman* (Chicago: Rand McNally, 1963), 31.

30. McWhiney, *Reconstruction and the Freedman*, 31.

31. White League Platform, quoted in Glenn M. Linden, *Voices from the Reconstruction Years, 1865–1877* (San Diego: Harcourt Brace/Cengage, 1998), 205. Italics mine.

32. On the violence of the so-called Redemption Movement, including the White League, see Carole Emberton, *Beyond Redemption: Race, Violence, and the American South After the Civil War* (Chicago: University of Chicago Press, 2013).

33. Thomas Jefferson, *Notes on the State of Virginia* (Philadelphia: Prichard and Hall, 1788), 148.

34. Jefferson, *Notes on the State of Virginia*.

35. Diane Miller Sommerville discusses white perceptions of enslaved people's emotions in *Aberration of Mind: Suicide and Suffering in the Civil War Era South* (Chapel Hill: University of North Carolina Press, 2018), 138. Interview with Caroline Hunter in *Weevils*, 150.

36. Interview with Ed McCrorey, "Born in Slavery." For another version of this story, see Julia Larkin, "Born in Slavery."

37. Interview with Ed McCrorey and Julia Larkin, "Born in Slavery."

38. Interview with Ed McCrorey and Julia Larkin, "Born in Slavery."

39. Robert Manson Myers, ed., *The Children of Pride*, vol. 3 (New York: Popular Library, 1972), 1408.

40. Myers, ed., *The Children of Pride*, 1274.

41. Sommerville, *Aberration of Mind*, 146–47. On the role of science and social science in creating a narrative of Black criminality, see Muhammad, *Condemnation of Blackness*.

42. Interviews with W. L. Bost and Susan High, "Born in Slavery."

5. Freedom Hill

1. 1870 U.S. Census, Cokey Township, Edgecombe County, North Carolina, "Jim Price," Ancestry.com. Marriage license for Ida Joyner, North Carolina Marriage Records, 1724–2011, Ancesty.com. I discovered Ida's existence accidentally when her 1948 death certificate appeared as a "hint" for Ann Eliza. The document lists "Anliza Joyner" as her mother. North Carolina, Death Certificates, 1909–1975, "Ida Joyner," Ancestry.com.

2. 1870 U.S. Census, Edgecombe County, North Carolina, Chesterfield District, "Harriett Dancy," Ancestry.com.

3. "Yankees Occupied Town After War," undated Tarboro *Southerner* clipping, Princeville file, Edgecombe County Municipal Library. See also Joe A. Mobley, "In the Shadow of White Society: Princeville, a Black Town in North Carolina, 1865–1915," *North Carolina Historical Review* 63, no. 3 (July 1986): 340–84.

4. 1880 U.S. Census, "Liberty Hill," Edgecombe County, North Carolina. Ancestry.com. The settlement was designated "Liberty Hill" on the census but is most often referred to as Freedom Hill in historical sources.

5. Horace James, "Annual Report of the Superintendent of Negro Affairs in North Carolina," 8. Library of Congress. Accessed July 1, 2021. https://www.loc.gov/item/60055003/.

6. Amy Murrell Taylor charts the dangerous effects of military removal policies in *Embattled Freedom*, 83–100.

7. James, "Annual Report," 9.

8. On violence and disease within "contraband" or refugee camps, see Taylor, *Embattled Freedom*, and Jim Downs, *Sick from Freedom: African-American Illness and Suffering During the Civil War and Reconstruction* (New York: Oxford University Press, 2012). Taylor notes how military officials and relief workers often tried to dictate the style of planned settlements like the one at New Bern with "idealized visions for how the landscape of freedom should look" (p. 72). The Federal Emergency Management Agency (FEMA) ordered the architectural survey after floods resulting from Hurricane Floyd in 1999 nearly submerged Princeville. See "Historic Architectural Survey of Princeville, North Carolina" (Gaithersburg, MD: URS Group, 2000) in clipping file, Edgecombe County Memorial Library, Tarboro, North Carolina.

9. Melissa McDonald, "Cotton Press, Tarboro, Edgecombe County, North Carolina," Architectural Data Form, 1983. Library of Congress. Accessed on February 18, 2021. https://cdn.loc.gov/master/pnp/habshaer/nc/nc0000/nc0025/data/nc0025data.pdf.

10. Ibram X. Kendi, "Introduction," in Ibram X. Kendi and Keisha Blain, eds., *Four Hundred Souls: A Community History of African America, 1619–2019* (New York: Penguin Random House, 2021), xvi.

11. *Tarboro Southerner* (1901) quoted in Mobley, "In the Shadow of White Society," 363.

12. Tyler Kendall, "'The People What Makes the Town': Semiotics of Home and Town Spaces in Princeville, North Carolina," *North Carolina Folklore Journal* 54, no. 1 (Spring-Summer 2007): 42.

13. U.S. IRS Tax Assessment Lists, 1862–1918, "L.L. Dancy," Ancestry.com. On Dancy and Lloyd's ceding of land to the local freedpeople, see Mobley, "In the Shadow of White Society," 341.

14. "Jonathan Norfleet to Capt. Thomas Richards, Jan. 13, 1866," BRFAL, Records of the Field Offices for North Carolina, RG 105, microfilm 1909, reel 55. The Rocky Mount office appeared to be particularly sensitive to freedpeople's desires to reconstitute family relations. In the case of Sallie Orrfield, the superintendent in Raleigh asked the Rocky Mount field agent to intervene on Orrfield's behalf when a white farmer attempted to kidnap her sons and apprentice them. See H. C. Vogell to Gardiner Merriam, March 13, 1866, on the same reel.

15. "Apprentice bond and affidavit for Harriett Dancy, Dec. 28, 1868," Apprentice Bonds and Records, Edgecombe County Records, NCDAH.

16. "Record of Outrages, June 1866–Jan. 1867," BRFAL, Records of the Assistant Commissioner for North Carolina, microfilm 843, reel 33.

17. 1860 U.S. Census, Slave Schedules, Edgecombe County, North Carolina, "L.L. Dancy," Ancestry.com.

18. Peter Wood, "Slave Labor Camps in Early America: Overcoming Denial and Discovering the Gulag," in Carla Gardina Pestana and Sharon V. Salinger, eds., *Inequality in Early America* (Hanover, NH: University Press of New England, 1999), 222–38. See also Baptist, *The Half Has Never Been Told*.

19. Edisto Island Petition, "Freedmen and Southern Society Project," University of Maryland. Accessed January 18, 2016. http://www.freedmen.umd.edu/Edisto%20 petitions.htm.

20. Julie Saville, *The Work of Reconstruction: From Slave to Wage Laborer in South Carolina, 1860–1870* (Cambridge: Cambridge University Press, 1994), 18.

21. Edisto Island Petition.

22. Saville, *Work of Reconstruction*, 18. See also Sydney Nathans, *A Mind to Stay: White Plantation, Black Homeland* (Cambridge: Harvard University Press, 2017).

23. Interview with Warren McKinney, "Born in Slavery."

24. Interview with Warren McKinney, "Born in Slavery."

25. Carol Stack, *Call to Home: African Americans Reclaim the Rural South* (New York: Basic Books, 1996), 44, 18.

26. Penningroth, *Claims of Kinfolk*, 171.

27. Elizabeth Hyde Botume, *First Days Amongst the Contrabands* (Boston: Lee and Shepard Publishers, 1893), 125–26.

28. Mary Ames, *From a New England Woman's Diary in Dixie in 1865*, 38, Documenting the American South. Accessed February 18, 2021. https://docsouth.unc.edu/ church/ames/ames.html.

29. On the importance of clothing in slavery, see Miles, *All That She Carried*, 127–63.

30. On public education in North Carolina, see Ronald E. Butchart, *Northern Schools, Southern Blacks, and Reconstruction: Freedmen's Education, 1862–1875* (Santa Barbara: Greenwood Press, 1980); Michael Goldhaber, "A Mission Unfulfilled: Freedmen's Education in North Carolina, 1865–1870," *Journal of Negro History* 77, no. 4 (1992): 199–210; James D. Anderson, *The Education of Blacks in the South, 1860–1935* (Chapel Hill: University of North Carolina Press, 2010); and Hilary Green, *Educational Reconstruction: African-American Schools in the Urban South, 1865–1890* (New York: Oxford University Press, 2016).

31. On northern aid societies and freedmen's education, see Joe M. Richardson, *Christian Reconstruction: The American Missionary Association and Southern Blacks,*

1861–1890 (Tuscaloosa: University of Alabama Press, 2009); Jacqueline Jones, *Soldiers of Light and Love: Northern Teachers and Georgia Blacks, 1865–1873* (Athens: University of Georgia Press, 1992); Anderson, *Education of Blacks in the South*; Butchart, *Northern Schools, Southern Blacks, and Reconstruction*; Granville County incident reported in Goldhaber, "A Mission Unfulfilled," 205.

32. "Jas. Jackson to F.A. Fiske, April 6, 1868," Records of the Field Offices for the State of North Carolina, RG 105, microfilm pub. 1909, reel 55.

33. For example, see F.A. Fiske to Geo. W. Bradshaw, June 28, 1866; Fiske to N. Chandler, July 6, 1866; Fiske to Henry Striker, July 6, 1866; Fiske to Rev. E.P. Smith, Jan. 25, 1867; F.A. Fiske to Lt. J.A. Allison, June 20, 1867; Fiske to Miss K.A. Means, May 22, 1868, all in RG 105, Records of the Superintendent of Education for the State of North Carolina, m844, reels 1 & 2.

34. F.A. Fiske to Rev. E.P. Smith, Jan. 25, 1867, RG 105, Records of the Superintendent of Education for the State of North Carolina, m844, reel 1.

35. "F.A. Fiske to Annie Spellman, June 6, 1868," Records of the Superintendent of Education for the State of North Carolina, RG 105, microfilm 844, reel 2.

36. William F. Dougherty, "Remarks, April 1, 1868," American Missionary Association Archives, North Carolina, reel 153 (hereafter cited as AMA).

37. Frederick Douglass, *Narrative of the Life of Frederick Douglass* (Boston: Anti-Slavery Office, 1845), 36; "Monthly Report of Jackson Freedman School for December 1869," AMA Manuscripts, North Carolina, reel 3.

38. *Weevils*, 176.

39. *The Lincoln Primer, or First Reader* (Boston: American Tract Society, 1864), preface.

40. William Stone, *Bitter Freedom: William Stone's Record of Service in the Freedmen's Bureau* (Columbia: University of South Carolina Press, 2008), 40.

41. *Weevils*, 176. Italics mine.

6. Roots of Love

1. *Weevils*, 176.

2. *Weevils*, 176.

3. *Weevils*, 176.

4. "Jordan Joyner" in 1790, 1820, 1830, 1840, 1850, and 1860 U.S. Census; Civil War Soldiers Records and Profiles; and North Carolina Land Grant Files, 1693–1960, all on Ancestry.com.

5. "Louisa Lucas," North Carolina Death Certificates, 1909–1975, Ancestry.com.

6. Fisk University Social Science Institute, *Unwritten History of Slavery: Autobiographical Accounts of Negro Ex-Slaves* (Washington, DC: Microcard Editions, 1968 [1945]), 87.

7. Fisk University Social Science Institute, *Unwritten History of Slavery*, 39.

8. Fisk University Social Science Institute, *Unwritten History of Slavery*, 39.

9. Interview with Alexander Robertson, "Born in Slavery."

10. *Weevils*, 174.

11. Libra R. Hilde, *Slavery, Fatherhood, and Paternal Duty in African American Communities over the Long Nineteenth Century* (Chapel Hill: University of North Carolina Press, 2020), 165.

12. Author bell hooks explores how slavery shaped Black love in *Salvation: Black People and Love* (New York: William Morrow, 2001).

13. Philip S. Foner and George E. Walker, eds., *Proceedings of the Black National and State Conventions, 1865–1900* (Philadelphia: Temple University Press, 1980), 180.

14. Sandy Dwayne Martin, *For God and Race: The Religious and Political Leadership of AMEZ Bishop James Walker Hood* (Columbia: University of South Carolina Press, 1999), 180.

15. On the history of enslaved marriages, see Hunter, *Bound in Wedlock*.

16. Hunter, *Bound in Wedlock*. See also Amy Dru Stanley, "Instead of Waiting for the Thirteenth Amendment: The War Power, Slave Marriage, and Inviolate Human Rights," *American Historical Review* 115, no. 3 (June 2010): 732–65.

17. Hunter, *Bound in Wedlock*, 238.

18. Stephanie Coontz, *Marriage, a History: From Obedience to Intimacy, Or How Love Conquered Marriage* (New York: Viking, 2005), 9.

19. Interview with J. F. Boone, "Born in Slavery." See also Gregory D. Smithers, *Slave Breeding: Sex, Violence, and Memory in African American History* (Tallahassee: University of Florida Press, 2012).

20. On the role of enslaved marriage in the cultural evolution of ideas of marriage in the United States, see Tess Chakkalahal, *Novel Bondage: Slavery, Marriage, and Freedom in Nineteenth-Century America* (Urbana: University of Illinois Press, 2011).

21. Jacobs, *Incidents in the Life of a Slave Girl*, 41.

22. Jacobs, *Incidents in the Life of a Slave Girl*, 44. On the importance of marriage as a form of slave resistance, see Emily West, *Chains of Love: Slave Couples in Antebellum South Carolina* (Champaign: University of Illinois Press, 2004).

23. Interview with Sena Moore, "Born in Slavery."

24. Interview with Sena Moore, "Born in Slavery."

25. Elizabeth J. Lewandowski, *The Complete Costume Dictionary* (Lanham, MD: Scarecrow Press, 2011), 22; Georgina O'Hara Callan, *The Encyclopaedia of Fashion* (New York: Henry Abrams, 1986); 30, 257; "Terminology: What Is a Balmoral Petticoat?" The Dreamstress, Leimomi Oakes, November 28, 2012, http://thedreamstress.com/2012/11/terminology-what-is-a-balmoral-petticoat/.

26. Tera Hunter discusses "taking up" as a form of enslaved intimacy. See *Bound in Wedlock*, 31–32.

27. Interview with Sena Moore, "Born in Slavery."

28. Edgecombe County, Records of Cohabitation. NCDAH, Raleigh.

29. Laura Edwards discusses Dink Watkins in *Gendered Strife and Confusion: The Political Culture of Reconstruction* (Urbana: University of Illinois Press, 1997), 57–58.

30. Charity McAllister, "Born in Slavery."

31. RG 105, m1909, reel 55.

32. Interview with Tanner Spikes, "Born in Slavery."

33. Interview with Tina Johnson, "Born in Slavery."

34. On the politics of respectability within the Black community, see Evelyn Brooks Higginbotham, *Righteous Discontent: The Women's Movement in the Black Baptist Church, 1880–1920* (Cambridge: Harvard University Press, 1994); Hine, "Rape and the Inner Lives of Black Women." See also LaKisha Michelle Simmons, *Crescent City Girls: The Lives of Young Black Women in Segregated New Orleans* (Chapel Hill: University of

North Carolina Press, 2015), and Nazera Sadiq Wright, *Black Girlhood in the Nineteenth Century* (Urbana: University of Illinois Press, 2016).

35. Interview with Martha Colquitt, "Born in Slavery."

36. Interview with Martha Colquitt, "Born in Slavery." On enslaved people's weddings, see Hunter, *Bound in Wedlock*, 45–50.

37. Interview with Georgia Johnson, "Born in Slavery."

38. Martha Colquitt, "Born in Slavery."

39. Simon May, *Love, a History* (New Haven: Yale University Press, 2013), 6.

40. May, *Love, a History.*

41. Interview with Cora Weathers, "Born in Slavery."

7. The House on Second Avenue

1. Tenth Census of the United States (1880), entries for "Lewis Joyner" and "Reuben Joyner," Stony Creek, Nash County, North Carolina, Ancestry.com.

2. Roger Ransom and Richard Sutch, *One Kind of Freedom: The Economic Consequences of Emancipation* (New York: Cambridge University Press, 2001); Edward Royce, *The Origins of Southern Sharecropping* (Philadelphia: Temple University Press, 2010); Gerald Jaynes, *Branches Without Roots: Genesis of the Black Working Class in the South* (New York: Oxford University Press, 1986); Saville, *The Work of Reconstruction.*

3. On white landowners' frustrations with cotton production as it evolved in the late nineteenth and early twentieth centuries, see Pete Daniel, *Breaking the Land: The Transformation of Cotton, Tobacco, and Rice Cultures Since 1880* (Urbana: University of Illinois Press, 1986).

4. Theodore Rosengarten, *All God's Dangers: The Life of Nate Shaw* (Chicago: University of Chicago Press, 1975), 121.

5. Rosengarten, *All God's Dangers.*

6. On white women's allegations of rape, see Crystal Feimster, *Southern Horrors.* See also James Goodman, *Stories of Scottsboro* (New York: Vintage, 1995).

7. *Boston Globe*, May 9, 1887.

8. *Carolina Watchman* (Salisbury, NC), May 19, 1887.

9. On early Black migration out of the South, see Nell Irvin Painter, *Exodusters: Black Migration to Kansas After Reconstruction* (New York: W. W. Norton, 1992), and Steven Hahn, *A Nation Under Our Feet: Black Political Struggles in the Rural South from Slavery to the Great Migration* (Cambridge: Belknap Press, 2003).

10. G. F. Pyle, "The Diffusion of Cholera in the United States in the Nineteenth Century," *Geographical Analysis* 1, no. 1 (January 1969); Charles E. Rosenberg, *The Cholera Years: The United States in 1832, 1849, and 1866* (Chicago: University of Chicago Press, 1987).

11. *Weevils*, 176.

12. 1900 United States Census, Nansemond County, Holy Neck, Virginia, "Lewis Joyner," Ancestry.com. On the history of Holy Neck, see "Blacks in Nansemond County," Box 5, Wilbur Earnest MacClenny Papers, Special Collections, University of Virginia, Charlottesville, Virginia.

13. For an estimate of wages for Black laborers, including draymen, in this period, see Lorenzo J. Greene and Carter G. Woodson, *The Negro Wage Earner* (New York: Van Rees Press, 1930), 111. On the importance of the lumber industry for Black south-

erners, see William Powell Jones, *The Tribe of Black Ulysses: African American Lumber Workers in the Jim Crow South* (Urbana: University of Illinois Press, 2005).

14. *American Lumberman*, January 10, 1920, 80; *Lumber*, October 11, 1920, 30; "Lewis Joyner," Suffolk City Directory, 1912, 1920, 1925, all on Ancestry.com. On the popularity of the driving occupations among freedmen, see Earnestine Lovell Jenkins, *Race, Representation & Photography in 19th-Century Memphis* (New York: Routledge, 2016), 95. On Norfolk draymen, see Earl Lewis, *In Their Own Interests: Race, Class, and Power in Twentieth-Century Norfolk, Virginia* (Berkeley: University of California Press, 1993), 14.

15. 1910 United States Census, Nansemond County, Holy Neck, Virginia, Ancestry.com. See also Annette Montgomery, *Suffolk* (Mount Pleasant, SC: Arcadia Publishing), 81.

16. Glass quoted in Lewis, *In Their Own Interests*, 21.

17. On the effects of disenfranchisement measures on Black voting in Norfolk, see Lewis, *In Their Own Interests*, 21–22. According to *Measuring Worth*, a project dedicated to establishing historical economic values, $1.50 in 1910 would amount to as much as $42.00 today. "How Much Is a Dollar from the Past Worth Today?" *Measuring Worth*. Accessed March 14, 2021. https://www.measuringworth.com/dollarvaluetoday/?amount=50&from=1910.

18. 1910 Census; Montgomery, *Suffolk*.

19. The calculation of the possible current value of the Joyner home is from *Measuring Worth* at measuringworth.com. On the importance of land and property ownership, see Nathans, *Mind to Stay*; Kendra Taira Fields, *Growing Up in the Country: Family, Race, and Nation after the Civil War* (New Haven: Yale University Press, 2018); Nathan Connolly, *A World More Concrete: Real Estate and the Remaking of Jim Crow South Florida* (Chicago: University of Chicago Press, 2013); and Sara Broom, *The Yellow House: A Memoir* (New York: Grove Atlantic, 2019).

20. Virginia Savage McAlester, *A Field Guide to American Houses* (New York: Alfred A. Knopf, 2015), 142–43. According to the address listed on Priscilla's interview transcript, the Joyners lived at 819 Second Avenue, which is now a vacant grass lot. The house used for comparison sits at 827 Second Avenue and is listed as being built in 1900. Listing information and photographs are available on Zillow.com, https://www.zillow.com/homedetails/827-2nd-Ave-Suffolk-VA-23434/79302729_zpid/, accessed July 1, 2021.

21. John W. De Forest, *A Union Officer in the Reconstruction*, ed. David Potter (Baton Rouge: Louisiana State University Press, 1997), 94.

22. Mitchell, *From Slave Cabins to the White House*, 10. On "welfare queens," see Julilly Kohler-Hausmann, "'The Crime of Survival': Fraud Prosecutions, Community Surveillance, and the Original 'Welfare Queen,'" *Journal of Social History* 41, no. 2 (Winter 2007): 329–54.

23. Lewis, *In Their Own Interests*, 90.

24. White quoted in Jennifer Ritterhouse, *Growing Up Jim Crow: How Black and White Southern Children Learned Race* (Chapel Hill: University of North Carolina Press, 2006), 109. See also Leon Litwack, *Trouble in Mind: Black Southerners in the Age of Jim Crow* (New York: Penguin, 1999).

25. Richard Wright, *Black Boy: A Record of Childhood and Youth* (New York: Harper Perennial, 1993 [1945]), 87.

26. Fitzhugh Brundage, *The Southern Past: A Clash of Race and Memory* (Cambridge: Harvard University Press, 2008), 155. On Black history textbooks, see Jeffrey Aaron Snyder, *Making Black History: The Color Line, Culture, and Race in the Age of Jim Crow* (Athens: University of Georgia Press, 2018), 55–61.

27. In her study of Black Atlanta, Tera Hunter lists a number of middle-class social clubs, including the Douglass Literary Club and the Smart Set Social Club. Hunter also discusses the emergence of commercial leisure activities such as barrooms and dance clubs that catered to both middle- and working-class Blacks. See Hunter, *To 'Joy My Freedom*, 148, 151–67.

28. Silas Xavier Floyd, *Floyd's Flowers: or, Duty and Beauty for Colored Children, Being One Hundred Short Stories Gleaned from the Storehouse of Human Knowledge and Experience* (Atlanta: Hertel, Jenkins & Co., 1905), 46–49. For more on Black girlhood in the early twentieth century, see Marcia Chatelain, *South Side Girls: Growing Up in the Great Migration* (Durham: Duke University Press, 2015), and LaKisha Michelle Simmons, *Crescent City Girls: The Lives of Young Black Women in Segregated New Orleans* (Chapel Hill: University of North Carolina Press, 2015).

29. *Weevils*, 177. Lakisha Simmons writes about intergenerational grief and the "long history of loss in Black women's lives," including the historically high rates of infant mortality, in "Black Feminist Theories of Motherhood and Generation," 312, 314–15.

30. Information on David Joyner's illness taken from his death certificate dated June 15, 1912, Virginia Death Records, 1912–2014, Ancestry.com. For a general description of common symptoms, see Samuel Kelton Roberts Jr., *Infectious Fear: Politics, Disease, and the Health Effects of Segregation* (Chapel Hill: University of North Carolina Press, 2009), 1–3.

31. Roberts, *Infectious Fear*, 4.

32. Death certificate for David Joyner, Virginia Death Records, 1912–2014; 1910 United States Census, Suffolk, Suffolk City, "L.W. White," both on Ancestry.com.

33. Hunter, *To 'Joy My Freedom*, 187–18.

34. Thomas Dormandy, *The White Death: A History of Tuberculosis* (New York: New York University Press, 2000).

35. John Herbert Claiborne, "The Negro—His Environments as a Slave—His Environments as a Freedman," *Transactions of the Tri-State Medical Association of the Carolinas and Virginia* (Richmond: Williams Printing Co., 1900), 96.

36. Claiborne, "The Negro," 97.

37. "Communities Must Join in Fight," *Richmond Times Dispatch*, May 16, 1916.

38. Joseph J. France, "Study and Prevention of Tuberculosis Among Colored People of Virginia," *Southern Workman* 34 (1905): 494–98; W. E. B. Du Bois, "The Health and Physique of the Negro American," *American Journal of Public Health* 93, no. 2 (1906): 272–76.

39. France, "Study and Prevention of Tuberculosis." On the sanatorium movement, see Helen Bynum, *Spitting Blood: The History of Tuberculosis* (New York: Oxford University Press, 2012), 128–59; Sheila M. Rothman, *Living in the Shadow of Death: Tuberculosis and the Social Experience of Illness in American History* (Baltimore: Johns Hopkins University Press, 1995), 194–246.

40. On primary versus secondary infection, see Roberts, *Infectious Fear*; John B. Huber, "Acute Pulmonary Tuberculosis: Part I," *American Journal of Nursing* 16, no. 1 (1915): 25–30.

41. Death certificates for Mamie Randall, Jencie Wright, and Priscilla Joyner, Virginia Death Records, 1912–2014, Ancestry.com; death certificate for Elizabeth Bullock, North Carolina Death Certificates, 1909–1976, Ancestry.com.

42. Montgomery, *Suffolk*, 74; Crocker Funeral Home, Inc. Accessed July 1, 2021. https://www.crockerfuneralhome.com/history. On the history of African American funerary practices and "homegoings," see Suzanne E. Smith, *To Serve the Living: Funeral Directors and the African American Way of Death* (Cambridge: Harvard University Press, 2010), and Karla F. C. Holloway, *Passed On: African American Mourning Stories, a Memorial* (Durham: Duke University Press, 2002).

43. Montgomery, *Suffolk*, 74.

44. Quoted in Neil R. McMillen, *Dark Journey: Black Mississippians in the Age of Jim Crow* (Urbana: University of Illinois Press, 1990), 92.

45. Smith, *To Serve the Living*, 43.

46. Holloway, *Passed On*, 3. On Du Bois's views on burial societies and burial insurance, see Smith, *To Serve the Living*, 41–42.

47. Hortense Powdermaker, *After Freedom: A Cultural Study of the Deep South* (New York: Viking, 1939), 122.

48. Quoted in Smith, *To Serve the Living*, 43.

49. Interview with Georgina Cassibry, "Born in Slavery."

50. Death certificate for "Anneliza Joyner," North Carolina Death Certificates, 1909–1976, Ancestry.com. On life expectancy in the United States, see "Mapping History: Life Expectancy 1850–2000," https://mappinghistory.uoregon.edu/english/US/US39-01.html, accessed June 3, 2020.

51. *Weevils*, 177–78.

52. *Weevils*, 177–78.

53. *Weevils*, 177–78.

54. *Weevils*, 177–78.

55. *Weevils*, 177–78.

56. *Weevils*, 177.

8. No Country for Old Age

1. On the history of aging in the United States, see among others David Hackett Fischer, *Growing Old in America* (New York: Oxford University Press, 1977); W. Andrew Achenbaum, "The Obsolescence of Old Age in America," *Journal of Social History* 8 (Fall 1974): 48–62; W. Andrew Achenbaum and Peter Stearns, "Old Age and Modernization," *Gerontologist* 18 (June 1978): 307–12; Carol Haber, *Beyond Sixty-Five: The Dilemma of Old Age in America's Past* (Cambridge: Cambridge University Press, 1983); and Thomas R. Cole, *The Journey of Life: A Cultural History of Aging in America* (Cambridge: Cambridge University Press, 1993).

2. Corinne T. Field and Nicholas L. Syrett, "Age and the Construction of Gendered Race and Citizenship in the United States," *American Historical Review* 125, no. 2 (April 2020): 438.

3. Field and Syrett, "Age and the Construction of Gendered Race," 440–42.

4. Death certificate for Lewis Joyner. Virginia, U.S. Death Records, 1912–2014. Ancestry.com.

5. *Weevils*, 178.

6. Edward Pollard, *Black Diamonds Gathered in the Darkey Homes of the South* (New York: Pudney & Russell, 1859), 22. On Pollard's time in California, see Jack P. Maddex, *The Reconstruction of Edward A. Pollard: A Rebel's Conversion to Postbellum Unionism* (Chapel Hill: University of North Carolina Press, 1974).

7. Pollard, *Black Diamonds*, 21; Edward Pollard, *The Lost Cause: A New Southern History of the War of the Confederates* (New York: E. B. Treat & Co., 1866).

8. On aging and slavery, see Leslie Pollard, "Aging and Slavery: A Gerontological Perspective," *Journal of Negro History* 66, no. 3 (Autumn 1981): 228–34; Stacy K. Close, *Elderly Slaves of the Plantation South* (New York: Routledge, 1997); Berry, *The Price for Their Pound of Flesh*; and Jenifer L. Barclay, *The Mark of Slavery: Disability, Race, and Gender in Antebellum America* (Urbana: University of Illinois Press, 2021).

9. Arney Robinson Childs, ed., *The Private Journal of Henry William Ravenel, 1859–1887* (Columbia: University of South Carolina Press, 1947), 240.

10. Trowbridge, *The South*, 155–56.

11. Marli F. Weiner, ed., *Heritage of Woe: The Civil War Diary of Grace Brown Elmore, 1861–1868* (Athens: University of Georgia Press, 1997), 122.

12. "Uncle Ned," *America Singing: Nineteenth Century Song Sheets*, Library of Congress. Accessed Jun 15, 2020. https://www.loc.gov/collections/nineteenth-century -song-sheets/?q=uncle+ned&st=slideshow#slide-1; Joel Chandler Harris, *The Complete Tales of Uncle Remus* (New York: Houghton Mifflin, 2002); Jason Sperb, *Disney's Most Notorious Film: Race, Convergence, and the Hidden Histories of Song of the South* (Austin: University of Texas Press, 2012).

13. Essie Collins Matthews, *Aunt Phebe, Uncle Tom and Others: Character Studies Among the Old Slaves of the South, Fifty Years After* (Columbus, OH: Champlin Press, 1915), 56.

14. Matthews, *Aunt Phebe*, 90.

15. On white celebrations of the "Old Negro," including "Old Slave Days," see Litwack, *Trouble in Mind*, 179–216. See also Catherine Stewart, *Long Past Slavery: Representing Race in the Federal Writers' Project* (Chapel Hill: University of North Carolina Press, 2016), 30–32; "An 'Old Slave Day' at Southern Pines," *New York Times*, April 12, 1935, L28.

16. "An 'Old Slave Day' at Southern Pines."

17. Interview with Andrew Boone, "Born in Slavery."

18. Interview with Andrew Boone, "Born in Slavery."

19. Interview with Gable Locklier; interview with Mintie Gilbert Wood; interview with Elias Dawkins; interview with Julia Brown, all in "Born in Slavery."

20. Interview with Julia Brown, "Born in Slavery."

21. List of Freedwomen and Men Confined in Texas State Penitentiary at Huntsville, Walker Co. Records of the Assistant Commissioner for the State of Texas, "Miscellaneous Records Relating to Murders and Other Criminal Offenses Committed in Texas, 1865–1868," RG 105, m821, reel 32.

22. List of Freedwomen and Men Confined in Texas State Penitentiary.

23. Arthur Raper, *Preface to Peasantry: A Tale of Two Black Belt Counties* (Columbia: University of South Carolina Press, 1936), 42, 52; Powdermaker, *After Freedom*, 79; Charles Johnson, *Shadow of the Plantation* (Chicago: University of Chicago Press, 1934), 100–102. On plantation stores, see Ownby, *American Dreams in Mississippi*, 61–81;

Dorothy Dickins, *A Nutrition Investigation of Negro Tenants in the Yazoo Mississippi Delta* (Starkville: Mississippi State University, 1928).

24. Cheryl Lynn Greenberg, *To Ask for an Equal Chance: African Americans in the Great Depression* (New York: Rowman & Littlefield, 2010), 1; interview with Julia Brown, "Born in Slavery."

25. Interview with Robert Falls, "Born in Slavery."

26. Interview with Elias Dawkins, "Born in Slavery."

27. Stephanie Shaw, "Using the WPA Ex-Slave Narratives to Study the Impact of the Great Depression," *Journal of Southern History* 69, no. 3 (August 2003): 633. Walter Johnson also notes the prevalence of food memories in the narratives in *River of Dark Dreams: Slavery and Empire in the Cotton Kingdom* (Cambridge: Harvard University Press, 2013), 178–79.

28. Shaw, "Using the WPA Ex-Slave Narratives," 634–35.

29. Interview with Andrew Boone, "Born in Slavery."

30. 1930 United States Census, New York, Bronx, District 0347, "Frank Joyner," Ancestry.com.

31. Interview with Easter Huff, "Born in Slavery,"

32. Interview with Easter Huff, "Born in Slavery."

33. Interview with Sarah Debro, "Born in Slavery."

34. Interview with Sarah Debro, "Born in Slavery."

35. *Weevils*, 178.

36. *Weevils*, 178.

37. Interview with Gabe Hines, "Born in Slavery."

38. Although they focus on written texts, Sidonie Smith and Julia Watson's analysis of autobiography is instructive for understanding what was at stake for individuals who gave their life narratives to the FWP. See Smith and Watson, *Reading Autobiography: A Guide for Interpreting Life Narratives*, 2nd ed. (Minneapolis: University of Minnesota Press, 2010). See also Eve Troutt Powell, *Tell This in My Memory: Stories of Enslavement from Egypt, Sudan, and the Ottoman Empire* (Palo Alto: Stanford University Press, 2012).

39. "Lewis Joyner" and "Priscilla Joyner," Virginia Death Records, 1912–2014, Ancestry.com.

40. *Weevils*, 177.

41. *Weevils*, 177.

42. *Weevils*, 176.

43. *Weevils*, 177.

9. The Book

1. Andrea Ledesma, "Eudora Ramsay Richardson (1891–1973)," Alexander Street, Part III: Mainstream Suffragists – National American Woman Suffrage Association. Accessed July 1, 2021. https://documents.alexanderstreet.com/d/1010113862.

2. On southern women and politics, see Anne Firor Scott, *The Southern Lady: From Pedestal to Politics, 1830–1930* (Charlottesville: University of Virginia Press, 1995).

3. Richardson quoted in *Weevils*, xxii.

4. *Weevils*, xxii.

5. Richardson quoted in *Weevils*, xxii.

6. Interview with Henrietta King, *Weevils*, 190–92.

7. Richardson to Newsome, February 18, 1940, Works Progress Administration Central Files: Virginia (Box 2706), NARA, College Park, Maryland (hereafter cited as RG 69).

8. Virginia Writers' Project, *The Negro in Virginia*, 50.

9. "Priscilla Joiner" in Roscoe Lewis Collection, Hampton University.

10. "Draft of the Negro in Virginia," 25–27. Manuscripts of *The Virginia Guide* and *The Negro in Virginia*, University of Virginia Special Collections, Charlottesville, Virginia. See also the foreword to *The Negro in Virginia*, xiii.

11. Richardson quoted in *The Negro in Virginia*, xii.

12. *Weevils*, 174.

13. Book of the Month Club advertisement, June 1940; *American Mercury*, September 1940, both quoted in *The Negro in Virginia*, xiv–xv.

14. William T. Couch, "Answers to Frequent Queries on Life Histories," n.d., and "Memorandum Concerning Proposed Plans for Work of the Federal Writers' Project in the South," both in WPA Files, Alabama Department of Archives and History, Montgomery, Alabama.

15. Lauren Sklaroff, *Black Culture and the New Deal: The Quest for Civil Rights in the Roosevelt Era* (Chapel Hill: University of North Carolina Press, 2009), 89–95.

16. Sterling Brown to Henry Alsberg, August 11, 1937. RG 69 (Box 2705).

17. Sterling Brown to Henry Alsberg.

18. Sterling Brown to Henry Alsberg.

19. Sklaroff, *Black Culture and the New Deal*, 2. See also Monty Noam Penkower, *The Federal Writers' Project: A Study in Government Patronage of the Arts* (Urbana: University of Illinois Press, 1977); Jerre Mangione, *The Dream and the Deal: The Federal Writers' Project, 1935–1943* (Syracuse: Syracuse University Press, 1996); Jerrold Hirsh, *Portrait of America: A Cultural History of the Federal Writers' Project* (Chapel Hill: University of North Carolina Press, 2003); and Stewart, *Long Past Slavery*.

20. Interview with Hannah Irwin, "Born in Slavery." I discuss this interview in more detail in "The Freedwoman's Tale: Reconstruction Remembered in the Federal Writers' Project Ex-Slave Narratives," in Carole Emberton and Bruce Baker, eds., *Remembering Reconstruction: Struggles Over the Meaning of America's Most Turbulent Era* (Baton Rouge: Louisiana State University Press, 2017), 109–36.

21. Scholars have long discussed the problematic way that white fieldworkers like Couric conducted and transcribed their interviews with elderly ex-slaves. See C. Vann Woodward, "History from Slave Sources," *American Historical Review* 79 (1974): 470–81; John Blassingame, "Using the Testimony of Ex-Slaves: Approaches and Problems," *Journal of Southern History* 41, no. 4 (November 1975): 473–92; Norman Yetman, "Ex-Slave Interviews and the Historiography of Slavery," *American Quarterly* 36, no. 2 (Summer 1984): 181–210; Donna Spindel, "Assessing Memory: Twentieth-Century Slave Narratives Reconsidered," *Journal of Interdisciplinary History* 27 (1996): 247–61; and Sharon Ann Musher, "The Other Slave Narratives: The Works Progress Administration Interviews," in *The Oxford Handbook of African American Slave Narratives*, ed. John Ernest (New York: Oxford University Press, 2014), 101–38; Stewart, *Long Past Slavery*, 77–86, 208–9.

22. Sterling Brown, "Notes by an editor on dialect usage in accounts by interviews with ex-slaves (To be used in conjunction with Supplementary Instructions 9E)," June

20, 1937, RG 69; Sterling Brown, *A Son's Return: Selected Essays of Sterling A. Brown*, ed. Mark Sanders (Boston: Northeastern University Press, 1996), 16–17.

23. Brown, "Notes by an editor."

24. Henry Alsberg to State Directors of the Federal Writers' Project, "Suggestions to Interviewers," in George Rawick, *From Sunup to Sundown: The Making of the Black Community*, vol. 1 (Greenwood, CT: Greenwood Press, 1971), 174. See also Sharon Ann Musher, "Contesting 'The Way the Almighty Wants It': Crafting Memories of Ex-slaves in the Slave Narrative Collection," *American Quarterly* 53, no. 1 (2001): 10; and Todd Carmody, "Sterling Brown and the Dialect of New Deal Optimism," *Callaloo* 33, no. 3 (2010): 820–40.

25. Interview with Liza McGhee, Mississippi Slave Narratives from the WPA Records, MSGen Web Slavey Narrative Project, http://msgw.org/slaves/mcghee -xslave.htm.

26. Neil R. McMillen, "WPA Slave Narratives," *Mississippi History Now*. Accessed July 21, 2020. http://mshistorynow.mdah.ms.gov/articles/64/wpa-slave-narratives.

27. Stewart, *Long Past Slavery*, 138–39.

28. *Weevils*, 181.

29. *Weevils*, 273.

30. *Weevils*, 274.

31. *Weevils*, 173.

32. Valerie Boyd, *Wrapped in Rainbows: The Life of Zora Neale Hurston* (New York: Scribner, 2003), 163–64.

33. On the pitfalls of intra-racial oral history, see Adrienne Petty, "Family Ties, Color Lines, and Fault Lines: Oral Histories of Land Ownership and Dispossession," *Reviews in American History* 47, no. 3 (September 2019): 436–44.

34. Interview with Betty Krump, "Born in Slavery."

35. Interview with Betty Krump, "Born in Slavery."

36. Interview with Betty Krump, "Born in Slavery."

37. W. E. B. Du Bois, "The Virginia Negro," *Phylon* 2, no. 2 (1941): 191–92.

38. Jonathan Daniels, "The Negro in Virginia," *Saturday Review* (September 7, 1941): 15.

39. Herbert Aptheker, "The Negro in Virginia," *Negro History* (September 10, 1940): 22.

40. Du Bois, "The Virginia Negro," 192.

EPILOGUE: Priscilla's Garden

1. Death certificate for Priscilla Joyner, Virginia Death Records, 1912–2014. Ancestry.com.

2. "Wife of Lewis Joyner," *New Journal and Guide*, March 4, 1944.

3. *Virginian Pilot*, October 17, 1962.

4. Walker, "In Search of Our Mother's Gardens," 241.

5. Walker, "In Search of Our Mother's Gardens," 239. On the enduring power of Black women's creativity as both a tool of survival and an expression of love, see Miles, *All That She Carried*.

6. Roscoe Lewis, "The Life of Priscilla Joyner," *Phylon* 20, no. 1 (1959): 71–81; "Appli-

cation for Grant in Aid of Research," February 14, 1952, Roscoe E. Lewis Papers, Hampton University Archives.

7. Lewis, "The Life of Priscilla Joyner," 71.

8. Lewis, "The Life of Priscilla Joyner," 75.

9. "Voices Remembering Slavery: Freed People Tell Their Stories," Library of Congress, https://www.loc.gov/collections/voices-remembering-slavery/about-this -collection/.

10. Christopher R. Browning, *Collected Memories: Holocaust History and Post-War Testimony* (Madison: University of Wisconsin Press, 2003), 38. Michael Gomez makes a similar case for the ex-slave narratives in *Exchanging Our Country Marks: The Transformation of African Identities in the Colonial and Antebellum South* (Chapel Hill: University of North Carolina Press, 1998), 199. See also Emberton, "The Freedwoman's Tale," 109–38.

11. Nina Silber, "Abraham Lincoln and the Political Culture of the New Deal," *Journal of the Civil War Era* 5, no. 3 (2015): 365.

12. "Roscoe Lewis to Edwin Embree, April 1, 1942," Roscoe Lewis Papers; "HI Professor, Author is Dead," *Daily Press*, September 15, 1961, clipping in Roscoe Lewis Papers; Olive Westbrooke, "*Lay My Burden Down: A Folk History of Slavery*. B. A. Botkin," *American Journal of Sociology* 52, no. 1 (1946): 70.

13. On the power of storytelling to shape the storyteller's relationship to the past, see Miles, *All That She Carried*, 231–35; Saidiya Hartman, "Venus in Two Acts," *Small Axe* 12, no. 2 (2008): 1–14; 3.

INDEX